THE
LONGEVITY
ECONOMY

JOSEPH F. COUGHLIN

THE

UNLOCKING *the* WORLD'S FASTEST-GROWING,

LONGEVITY

MOST MISUNDERSTOOD MARKET

ECONOMY

PUBLICAFFAIRS

PublicAffairs
Hachette Book Group
1290 Avenue of the Americas, New York, NY 10104
www.publicaffairsbooks.com
@Public_Affairs

Printed in the United States of America

First Edition: November 2017

Published by PublicAffairs, an imprint of Perseus Books, LLC, a subsidiary of Hachette Book Group, Inc.

The publisher is not responsible for websites (or their content) that are not owned by the publisher.

Library of Congress Cataloging in Publication Control Number: 2017042065

ISBNs: 978-1-61039-663-9 (HC), 978-1-61039-665-3 (EB)

LSC-C

10   9   8   7   6   5   4   3   2   1

For Emily, Mary, and Catherine

A NOTE ON COLLABORATION

IN THE WORLD of research publications, it's a poorly kept secret that the names following that of the first author are often responsible for the bulk of the hard work. The same is very much true in the case of this book. *The Longevity Economy*, frankly put, could never have been written without the help of my collaborator and friend, the science writer Luke Yoquinto. There is scarcely a sentence between the covers of this book that has not benefited from his research and reportage, his storytelling skill and keen editorial eye. He conducted several of this book's interviews and helped me over the course of many months turn my disorganized thoughts into a form that, I hope you will agree, is at least marginally coherent. Some sections ahead, meanwhile, evolved out of ideas Luke and I first put forward in such publications as *The Washington Post* and *Slate*. For his hard work and prodigious talent, not to mention his ability to keep me on task, I owe him my profound thanks.

CONTENTS

INTRODUCTION:
THE LONGEVITY PARADOX

ACH OF US will grow old—if we're lucky. The same can be said for nations: luck, in the form of prosperity, gives rise to older populations as surely as a good growing season leads to an ample harvest. Today, most countries around the world are about to haul in the biggest longevity crop of all time: the fruit of all the affluence, education, and technological progress that burgeoned in the second half of the 20th century.

The effect will be enormous. The aging of populations represents the most profound change that is *guaranteed* to come to high-income countries everywhere and most low- and middle-income ones as well. There may be other big shifts headed our way—related to climate change, say, or global geopolitics, or technological advancement—but their particulars are still up in the air. We can only speculate about how London will cope with sea-level rise, or Tokyo with self-driving cars. But we know exactly how global aging will unfold. We know when and where it will happen and to what degree. We know which subpopulations are likely to live long lives, and shorter lives, and how prepared they are for their future.

Because population aging will manifest in such dramatic-yet-predictable ways, when companies make long-term plans for the future, there should be nothing higher on their priorities list than preparing for an older world. It's worth planning for the unexpected, after all, but only after you prepare for the guaranteed.

With few exceptions, however, companies—and nonprofits and governments—are not getting ready. The reason why is a mystery. In fact, from my perspective as the founder of the Massachusetts Institute of Technology (MIT) AgeLab, a research organization devoted to studying the intersection of aging and business, it's *the* mystery.

Happily, I'm here to report, there is an answer. It's so simple that it almost defies belief: *old age is made up.*

That doesn't mean I think arthritis is imaginary or that we can will ourselves to live forever. Rather, the meaning of "old"—whether you're talking about the life stage, the "senior" population, or even your conception of self—is what academics would call "socially constructed" and everyone else might call a mass delusion or a story that no one realizes is fictional. Certain bits of our current idea of old age are grounded in biology. But most of it was invented by human beings for short-term, human purposes over the past century and a half. Today, we're stuck with a notion of oldness that is so utterly at odds with reality that it has become dangerous. It constrains what we can do as we age, which is deeply troubling, considering that the future of our older world will naturally hinge on the actions of the older people in it. It also distracts companies from serving the true needs of aging consumers, an already staggeringly powerful group that is growing larger, wealthier, and more demanding with every passing day.

The Setup

The world is growing older for three reasons, the most obvious of which is the fact that people are simply living longer. The story of the United States resembles that of most high-income nations: the majority of American babies born in 1900 could not expect to see their 50th birthday; as of 2015, life expectancy in the United States had reached 79 years. Even larger gains have unfolded in Western Europe, East Asia, and elsewhere. Of major economies, Japan leads the world with a life expectancy of 84 years; it's followed closely by Spain, Switzerland,

Italy, and Singapore. Nipping at their heels are most other western and southern European countries as well as standouts elsewhere in the world such as South Korea, Chile, Australia, New Zealand, Canada, and Israel.

If I were teaching this information to my graduate students, some wisenheimer in the back of the room would have chimed in by now: "What about childhood mortality?" It's true: the biggest component of the post-1900 life expectancy bump is due to the fact that far more of us survive childhood than we did over a century ago, particularly the gauntlet of diseases that threaten kids from birth to age five. However, it would be woefully incorrect to say that *all* of our life expectancy gains are due to diminished child mortality. For one thing, we've also cut back on deaths for people in their twenties, thirties, forties, and fifties. A 30-year-old American man in 1900, for instance, was six times more likely to die within a year than a 30-year-old man is today, and a 30-year-old woman was *12-and-a-half times* more likely to die within a year. As a result of things like public health measures, indoor plumbing, a lack of world wars (knock wood), modern medicine, antibiotics, safer workplaces, and—a big one—safer childbirth, far more of us are reaching 65 than ever before.

And the gains don't stop there, because those who make it to 65 now get to stick around for longer. In 1900, a 65-year-old woman in the United States could expect to live to 78; 76 for men. Today these figures have reached 85.5 and 82.9, respectively. That is to say, over a century's worth of scientific and economic progress has bought those of us who make it to 65 an extra seven years. And that's just the United States—in Japan, the average 65-year-old woman can expect to reach age 89. That's right: it's now utterly unremarkable for Japanese women to live well into their 90s—and Spanish, French, Italian, and Korean women are right behind them.

But longer lives only account for part of why the world is growing older. A bigger factor, especially in lower-income countries, is the fact that birth rates around the world plummeted in the second half of the

20th century, a trend that in many cases has only picked up speed following the turn of the new millennium. As of 2015, fertility rates in every world region except Africa are near or below what's considered the "replacement rate," which in most high-income countries hovers around 2.1 children per woman. (Slightly more than two children per woman are needed to keep a population stable, because not every one of those children will survive to childbearing age.)

There are two sides to the fertility coin. Heads is the tale of the incredible, shrinking, high-income nations. Once again, Japan is the standout example: it has a one-word immigration policy ("No!") and a very low fertility rate—1.46 children per woman, as of 2015. As a result of both, its population is shrinking more rapidly than any country outside Eastern Europe, a low-fertility region that is also losing large chunks of its population to emigration. Many countries other than Japan, such as Germany, Italy, Singapore, and South Korea, have similarly low or even lower fertility rates—much of southern and western Europe has been subreplacement for decades—but the shrinking effect in these countries is somewhat counterbalanced by an influx of immigrants. Still, Germany and Italy are projected to shrink by 2050, and so would be the United States, with its fertility rate of 1.9, if not for its twin bulwarks of immigration and the relatively large families that first-generation immigrants tend to have. (In fact, barring long-term changes in immigration policy, the slow-but-steady growth the United States is projected to experience by 2050 is unique. Of the handful of countries led by India and Nigeria that are expected to contribute to the bulk of the world's population growth by 2050, the United States is the only high-income nation.)

The flip side of the fertility coin can be seen in lower-income nations where the birth rate, though still above replacement, has plummeted to where it is from great heights. India is a good example: in 1960, the average woman gave birth to 5.9 children; as of 2014, that number stands at 2.4, a precipitous drop. Similar stories have played out in Brazil, Chile, South Africa, Thailand, Indonesia, Turkey, Mexico, the Philippines, and elsewhere. In each case, the result is a society with a high-and-climbing proportion of older people. According to the United Nations, two-thirds of the world's older adults live in developing countries, and that's where the greatest part of the world's old-age growth is currently coming from.

Finally, a third factor is contributing to global aging: the baby boomers. Many countries involved in World War II experienced a massive, postwar fertility bump, and, with some variation (Japan's boom was limited mainly to the second half of the 1940s, for instance, while Germany's was delayed by about a decade and followed by a baby bust), those babies are now becoming grandparents and even great-grandparents.

Thanks to both increased longevity and the baby boom, we now live in a world chock full of older people, with, as of 2015, 617 million people aged 65-plus, a population roughly double that of the United States, the world's third-largest country. That number will increase to one billion by 2030 and continue to grow through the first half of the 21st century, reaching an estimated 1.6 billion by 2050. During that time, low fertility will do its work: the world's youth population will remain flat, and its working-age population will grow only modestly. As a result, by 2050, the worldwide proportion of the 65-plus will have doubled from today's 8.5 percent to 16.7 percent—nearly the age breakdown of 2015 Florida.

And if we're looking at a world of Floridas, many high-income countries have already left the Sunshine State far behind. Japan, as usual, leads the pack. More than one in four Japanese people is 65 or older, while Germany, Greece, Italy, Portugal, Sweden, and other European countries have crossed the 20-percent mark. The number for the United States, 15 percent, is being held down for the time being by immigration and relatively high birthrates. By 2030, however, the United States will have joined the 20-percenters—welcome to the Sunshine States of America—and many countries already in that group will have crossed the 25-percent mark. Japan will be out ahead of the herd with an astounding third of its population aged 65 and up, a soci-ety the likes of which the world has never seen.

As other countries follow suit, one thing that probably won't hap-pen (barring extreme events) will be a reversal of the trend. When a country's birth rates drop, they don't tend to rocket back up. When life expectancy extends, it doesn't retract much, except in times of calam-ity. And right when attrition is claiming the bulk of the baby boom generation, its children will begin to claim their AARP memberships. In short, when nations turn grey, they stay that way indefinitely.

Here's the point for the business world. First, the emerging pop-ulation of older adults isn't just big. It's so enormous, it's as though a new *continent* were rising out of the sea, filled with more than a bil-lion air-breathing consumers just begging for products that fulfill their demands. In fact, as outlandish as that image is, it's not even adequate to illustrate how important global aging will be. Societies won't just be older; they will function differently. Not just in the obvious ways, either. Eldercare responsibilities, healthcare spending, and pension lia-bilities will naturally ramp up. However, we'll also see changes as wide ranging as new labor markets; amplified demand for products* that seemingly have nothing to do with age, such as smart-home technolo-gies; new forces affecting family composition and rituals; and far more. There will be new political agendas and fracture points. Jury pools may even skew older and interpret laws differently.

Most important, consumer demands will change right at the moment that spending by older adults (and *on* older adults) skyrock-ets. In Japan, the country that most closely resembles the future demo-graphics of high-income nations, bellwethers of change are everywhere

---

* As you read on, the word "product" will come up frequently. I subscribe to the broadest possible definition of the term: not just goods that companies produce, but also services, combinations of the two, and more. The lessons ahead apply to the design and marketing of physical goods, financial products, online services, nonprofit and volunteer services—you name it. Even, in some cases, the "product" of govern-ment: policy.

you look. Take karaoke, one of the nation's great pastimes. During daylight hours, the Shidax Corporation, which runs the largest chain of karaoke establishments in Japan, now converts many of its karaoke rooms into classrooms where people, primarily women in their fifties, sixties, and seventies, can choose from more than 50 courses on subjects ranging from dance to languages to traditional flower arrangement. Meanwhile, starting as early as 2007, the country's largest chain of eyewear shops, Paris Miki, began selling more reading glasses than all other types of eyewear. Perhaps most telling, in 2011, Unicharm, the country's largest provider of sanitary products, reported selling more adult diapers than baby diapers. By 2026, the same will have taken place in the United States.

Although the Japanese consumer economy has already changed in fundamental ways, the aging of Japan is still far from its peak. Countries elsewhere in the world are just getting started, and older demographic groups are already dominant spenders. Older adults in the high-income world spend an average of $39,000 per year, while those aged 30 to 44, squeezed by student debt and residual effects of the Great Recession, spend only $29,500. In the United States, which has the highest head count of older adults among all wealthy countries, spending by people aged 50 and over came to $5.6 trillion in 2015, while those under 50 accounted for $4.9 trillion. The spending of the 50-plus, combined with downstream effects, accounted for nearly $8 trillion dollars' worth of economic activity—nearly half of that year's gross domestic product (GDP). That number is large enough to boggle the mind, but here's what it represents: the outsize power wielded by the single most important consumer group in any one nation. What this number doesn't account for, however—despite being larger than the GDP of every country except the United States, China, and the European Union—is the sheer magnitude of what's to come. In fact, for companies that figure out how to provide value to an aging world, $8 trillion is a conservative—even worst-case—estimate of the size of the overall prize.

First, as Japan has seen, aging leads to shifts in spending patterns that might once have been considered immovable. Even if the raw total economic activity of the world's older adults stayed inexplicably level for the next 35 years, changes in the *way* that money is spent would spell opportunity for companies considering jumping into the longevity economy as well as a threat to entrenched interests.

But spending in the longevity economy will not stay flat. The sheer rate of growth of the older population in the majority of countries guarantees that future spending on a global scale will dwarf current levels. Restricting its estimate to those aged 60 and up, market research firm Euromonitor predicts that by 2020, worldwide older-adult spending will reach $15 trillion—and that's still well before global aging will fully hit its stride. By 2030, the Boston Consulting Group estimates that the 55-plus population will have been responsible for 50 percent of the US consumer spending growth since 2008, 67 percent of that of Japan, and 86 percent of that of Germany. It's no exaggeration to say that the world's most advanced economies will soon revolve around the needs, wants, and whims of grandparents.

Future extrapolations of current spending patterns are valuable up to a point, but one thing they can't do is determine how much older adults *could* spend, in theory, if they wanted or needed to. This is where the real opportunity lies. In the United States alone, 50-plus consumers control 83 percent of household wealth. Between 2007 and 2061, they will hand down an eye-popping $53 trillion to their heirs (with some going to estate taxes, charity, and estate clearing costs). All told, it will be the largest wealth transfer in history—assuming the would-be benefactors don't spend it first, which is a big assumption. Researchers have determined that American baby boomers, more than any preceding generation, do not consider it important to leave money to their heirs. In many cases, it's not a matter of choice: many will outlive their savings. The fact that there is still an incomprehensible sum slated to be handed down to the next generation, however, despite the fact that most older adults would rather not leave a bequest, is telling.

It suggests that future spending in the longevity economy could easily be far greater than projected, should companies come up with products inspiring enough to be worth the expense.

The Breakdown

What's most remarkable is that none of this should be remarkable. These statistics and projections are the kinds of things any subscriber to *The Economist* or *Businessweek* or the *Wall Street Journal* can't help tripping over on occasion. I have read these sorts of articles—and written them, and been quoted in them—for nearly a quarter century. As of 2017, the leading edge of the baby boom generation is well into its retirement years, something companies were first told would happen decades ago. And yet, the Economist Intelligence Unit has determined that just 31 percent of companies take global aging into account in their marketing and sales plans, while the Boston Consulting Group has determined that less than 15 percent of companies have established any sort of business strategy focused on older adults. Age 49 still serves as a de facto cut-off that many marketers don't bother to cross, and less than 10 percent of marketing dollars are aimed specifically at the 50-plus. Even as late as the mid-2010s, despite a small uptick in cross-generational casting in commercials, advertisers spend 500 percent more on millennials than on all other age groups combined.

It should come as no surprise, then, that older adults find their relationship with consumer-facing businesses lacking. More than half of the 30,000 respondents in a 60-country survey told Nielsen that they "do not see advertising that reflects older consumers." Of the rare campaigns that do feature older adults—mostly emanating from the pharmaceutical and retirement industries—older viewers find their contemporaries' portrayal unappealing and overly stereotypical. In one 2014 survey of 400 people aged 70 and older, less than 20 percent said that they liked advertising that seemed aimed at them, and less than half thought that older adults in commercials were presented as "people to be respected."

The failure to connect with older adults extends well beyond advertising. Half of respondents to the international Nielsen poll said that it was hard to find product labels that could be read easily, for instance, and 43 percent reported difficulties finding easy-to-open packaging—factors that are both more than capable of nudging a customer toward a competitor. Statistics like these are known; what's harder to quantify is how many older people suffer in silence due to design that assumes a younger user. In the pages ahead, I describe an age-simulating suit, invented by my team at the AgeLab, that helps younger designers empathize with older bodies. It's necessary in no small part because older consumers won't just tell you what's bothering them. In many cases, they assume that discomfort is normal—until they encounter a product or environment that disproves that notion. Failure to connect with older consumers doesn't stop at their physiology, however. Many products also utterly miss the mark by violating their desires and self-image. But the most devastating business mistake of all is the one that's impossible to measure: the failure to innovate. How many would-be, life-improving products have never come into existence, either because businesses refused to consider older consumers as worthy of innovation or because they rushed too readily to fulfill demands that fit some stereotypical idea of age without stopping to assess whether those demands matched reality?

Among the vast preponderance of businesses that are wholly unprepared for an aging world, there are a few bright spots—and not just in the industries you might expect, either. It should come as no surprise that pharmaceutical and financial services companies have taken a relatively proactive approach toward studying how population aging will affect their bottom lines. But so have companies that, at first glance, seem to have little to do with age. BMW, Audi, and Volkswagen plants, for instance, are now experimenting with exoskeletons in order to retain their highly skilled, aging factory workers, something

I discuss in Chapter 7. Harley-Davidson, whose average consumer is nearly 50 years old, appears to be quietly doubling down on a strategy that makes motorcycling more pleasant for smaller riders—which is to say, women—as well as older riders by invoking lower seat heights (easier to mount if you have stiff joints) and more manipulable hand controls. In 2008, Harley introduced its first "trike," a three-wheeled motorcycle of the sort that is increasingly popular among late-career road warriors.

But examples like these are the exceptions. For the most part, companies that are demonstrably unready for an older world seem to be either complacent about their status or blissfully unaware. In the many articles and books about this fact—at this point, nearly a genre of economic journalism unto itself—a hectoring tone is the norm. *Businesses,* the implication goes, *just need to wake up, smell the Ensure, and start courting older consumers with all the fervor they currently lavish on millennials.*

What no one seems to be willing to acknowledge is that there may be a reason for why businesses are acting the way they are. Think about it this way: if businesses did in fact knowingly work against their own best interests by refusing to give older adults the attention they deserve, that would constitute a spectacularly large, systemic failure—the kind that could only happen if everyone in business were either an absolute moron or ageist bigot or both.

I don't think that explanation quite describes what's going on. Rather, the apparent failure of the business community to act in its own best interest hints at something deeper.

The Source of the Problem

Imagine you're sitting in a hotel lobby and you see a businessperson in an expensive suit approach the front door. He pushes on it; nothing happens. He pushes harder, grunting—until he finally realizes that he has to pull to open it. He does so and walks through, looking sheepish.

From your perch in the lobby, you might, if you're anything like me, chuckle a little to yourself and turn back to your newspaper. But wait— now another businessperson in a sharp suit comes up to the same door. Once again, she struggles mightily before figuring out how to work it. *Hmm,* you might think to yourself. *Businesspeople aren't very bright.*

Now imagine sitting in that lobby every day for a week and witnessing the same struggle every time anyone tries to use that door. At a certain point, you'd have to stop blaming the people involved. You would have to surmise, *Gee, there is something strange going on with that door!*

Gee, there is something strange going on with old age. From my perch at the AgeLab, I've observed all sorts of businesses wrestling with it: pushing, pulling, trying to get a grip on an exceedingly powerful group of consumers who just don't seem to be behaving as expected. And those are the smart companies—more concerning are the ones who fail to see the door for what it is and walk headlong into it, only to emerge with a sore nose and a red face.

None of the businesses involved recognize that their struggles are not their fault. Rather, the problem is our very idea of old age, which is socially constructed, historically contingent, and deeply flawed—as falsely defined as a pull-to-open door with a "push" sign on it.

Oldness, in this misleading definition, is bad. Any disinterested reading of the facts would suggest otherwise: older populations are a good thing, the natural result when societies keep their members healthy, out of danger, educated, and in command of their reproductive rights. And yet, there is an overwhelming tendency to view old age and the aging of populations as a slowly unfolding crisis. I can't tell you how many times I've seen the aging of one group or another—nations, workforces, the *entire world*—referred to as a "ticking time bomb." I can still recall one issue of *The International Economy* magazine that I stumbled across in an airport bookstore in 2004. Its cover story, "Aging: The Next Ticking Time Bomb," was accompanied by an illustration of a figure in a bathrobe, crouched over a walker, attached to an intravenous bag filled with blood. The head of the "person" was planet Earth, which the artist had somehow managed to make appear wrinkled, with waves of planetary flesh rippling indiscriminately across land and ocean. Stuck in the top of the globe, naturally, was a burning fuse. When I saw that picture of that old-person-world-bomb, *my* head almost exploded. If that's seriously how we think of older people as a group, how could someone who comes across as "old" ever hope to land a competitive job? How could she ever get funding to start up a business? And how could companies ever take her demands as a consumer seriously?

Dig into this sort of age-fearing literature, and you'll quickly discover that the growing older population is up there with planet-killing asteroids and nuclear war as one of the great threats to the human race. You'll soon learn that Social Security (or the equivalent pension scheme outside the United States) will fail, medical care will become too expensive for societies to manage, taxes will double or triple before today's kids reach middle age, and the baby boomers will spend their later years surviving on cat food because they haven't saved enough for retirement. In fact, if you think I trotted out some big numbers earlier in this chapter, they're nothing compared to the figures the doomsayers of age have readily at hand. It's been suggested, for instance, that the US government's interest-and-all "bill" for taking care of its elders, when extrapolated out to the indefinite future, will come to more than *$200 trillion*. That's the message that tends to stick, not rebuttals from other economists explaining that that estimate fails to take into account future economic growth or that extrapolating debts to year infinity is a meaningless exercise. As these frightening messages sink in, an air of fatalism starts to take hold. In both the United States and Japan, there are now serious public intellectuals talking about how if older people could just "hurry up and die"—an actual quote from Tarō Asō, Japan's finance minister—many of the problems we face would be solved. Implicit is the idea that life in old age isn't worth the cost of keeping older people breathing. While most wouldn't go quite that far, it is extremely common to hold a negative view of older people as a group—and of old age in general, never mind the fact that psychological well-being rises with every year of life after middle age. Implicit bias—prejudice so deeply ingrained that you might not even know you harbor it—against older people is the norm across age groups. It's very hard to fool an implicit bias test;* even I have tested positive for a moderate implicit preference for young faces over older ones, a prejudice I'd hoped I'd shrugged off years ago.

If you're like most people, when you picture "the old," a remarkably specific impression comes to mind. With some variation by country, we tend to think of this group as a singular, homogenous population that depends on the largesse of others to survive because it can't provide for itself. We expect older people to live apart, quietly sequestered away in retirement communities, assisted living facilities, and nursing homes, surfacing to shop and dine only when everyone else is at work. We consider their natural role to be that of the consumer of goods, services, and ideas, never the producer. Most important, we assume that they like it that way. Because we're taught to think of retirement as the reward for a long working life, we suppose—often despite personal experience—that to be not working and separate from other age groups is to be living the dream. In this all-too-common reading of age, older people are somehow simultaneously *needy,* because they're considered constitutionally unable to provide for themselves, and *greedy,* because they are at their most conspicuous when they're out in the world, having fun, and—the default assumption suggests—spending other people's money.

Taken together, these ideas about oldness add up to a picture of a consumer that feels complete. Leisure products and relaxation must be what older adults want, while medical and accessibility-oriented

---

* If you're curious, it's easy to test yourself for implicit bias. "Project Implicit," a website run by researchers from a number of universities, allows you to test for a variety of biases (https://implicit.harvard.edu/implicit/takeatest.html). It only takes about 10 minutes, and I bet you'll be surprised by what you find out.

products for the deteriorating older body must be what they need. With both needs and wants covered, businesses, nonprofits, and even policymakers need perform no additional mental legwork to understand their commitments to the older population. The idea of the needy, greedy "senior" is so comprehensively drawn that hardly anyone thinks to wonder which aspects are true to life.

And, to be fair, some aspects of the picture are grounded in fact. We do tend to become sicker as we grow older, which makes us less independent, and many of us eventually require care. Though most will never experience dementia—and the implications of non-dementia-related cognitive decline are seriously overblown—it's true that when dementia happens, it almost always occurs in old age. The same can be said for death: in 1900, when most people in the United States died before age 50, death was a constant threat that stalked everyone, all the time. Today, by contrast, 81 percent of US deaths occur after the age of 65, which represents a great victory over a world that is always conspiring to kill us. In the process, however, age has taken on morbid overtones. It is now the only time when we expect to die.

The fact that old age is also the only time in life that routinely sees new years *added* to it, meanwhile, gets lost, as do many other possible reads on aging. "The old" make up a population so diverse that it almost defies characterization. Depending when you decide old age begins, the group can be said to account for people found anywhere along a 50-plus-year span of life, with every imaginable level of physiological health, cognitive ability, and wealth represented, along with every type of personality; ideologies of every stripe; and every race, nationality, creed, gender, and sexual identity to be found on this blue Earth. Yes, many things become harder with age, and biological reality eventually limits what we can achieve as we grow older. But aging unfolds differently for everyone. We all enter the process at unique starting points and then proceed through a wild variety of physiological experiences at rates that vary from person to person. The idea that there exists one single state of older being that kicks in at age 50, 65, or at any other single age, defies all logic. So does the idea that there is one single, normal way to live a later life.

If the way we conventionally think about old age is not tied fast to the facts of biology, economics, or sociology, it must contain elements of fiction. My preferred term for what's considered the normal way to live up to and through late life, given our limited way of thinking about oldness, is our *narrative* of aging. It's a story that's been passed down from generation to generation.

We tell ourselves stories because they teach us lessons. We tell ourselves stories because they make us feel certain emotions. And we tell ourselves stories because they help us make sense of the gift of life, because it's the sort of gift that comes with no accompanying instructions. Several generations ago, especially during the late 19th and early 20th centuries, we found ourselves endowed with bonus years of that precious gift. It was more than we knew how to handle. We turned to story in an effort to make sense of it, and it just so happened that, as I describe in Chapter 1, the narrative that emerged taught us to think of our new gift as a burden.

As we've continued to add more years to the average life, this framing has had wide-ranging effects on everything from policy to how older people think about themselves. It has also prevailed over how businesses have addressed old age—or ignored it—in products. It continues to hamstring innovation for older adults, because "solutions" for older demographics are almost always limited to leisure products (for the greedy) and bodily needs (for the needy). What older people today might aspire to become, or hope to accomplish, falls by the wayside. And in terms of defining *new* aspirations—as companies routinely do for every other age group—businesses simply fail to show up.

Our narrative of old age has already cost businesses untold losses in terms of failed launches, missed opportunities, and off-target products. Worse, because products and marketing reinforce social norms, the narrative's prophecy becomes self-fulfilling. Products that treat older adults merely as a needy, greedy headache to be taken care of, not an enormous group of people with diverse goals and motivations, remind us every day to be old is to be always a taker, never a giver; always a problem, never a solution. Even more troublingly, subpar products restrict what we can do with ourselves. When we grow old, we simply don't have the tools we need to stay competitive in the work-force, or contribute culturally, or stay connected, or remain independ-ent for as long as possible, because those products either don't exist yet or are built for younger users. Or—though intended for older users—they are presented in such a way that many find them embarrassing or alienating to use.

Such failures to connect with older consumers, however, are about to come to an end. Our new, older world is arriving, and the going narrative of aging will soon give way. It couldn't happen at a better time. Should the current, dysfunctional narrative remain in place, the approaching demographic swell of older adults would mean that many of the worst assumptions of old age's doomsayers—the wrinkly-time-bomb-planet crowd—would come true. Old age would become an anchor dragging down society, just like our narrative of aging predicts.

But it won't come to that, because the approaching older world contains the seeds of that narrative's demise. You might have heard of these agents of change, since they've run the world for the past 30 years or so. They are known as the baby boomers.

The People Our Parents Warned Us About

In a twist of poetic justice, the baby boom—a force responsible for much of the explosiveness of the "demographic time bomb"—is in fact poised to significantly improve the experience of old age—right in the nick of time before the world grows older for good. Throughout their lives, the boomers have applied their economic demand to the world around them like a sculptor's chisel, and the very landscapes of nations have conformed to their whims. Worldwide, on the boomers' watch, energy use has increased by a factor of 6, fertilizer consumption by

20, water use by 3, and the rate of major dam construction has grown sixfold. Since 1975, the world's total mileage of paved roads has more than tripled. In the United States alone, starting in the 1950s, boomer children provoked their Greatest Generation parents to purchase free-standing, single-family houses in the first mass-produced suburbs, which grew along the corridors of interstate highways like grass in sidewalk cracks. The shopping mall was born in such environs, where it soon multiplied. When the older boomers purchased their first homes in the late 1960s and 1970s, they overcame a stagnant economy and drove the construction of apartments and condominiums. Malls grew bigger. In the 1990s, larger homes appeared throughout the United States as boomers traded up. The big box stores such as Walmart took hold, and vast new fleets of minivans and SUVs ferried the boomers and their progeny between them. Whatever your impression of this mode of life, one thing is certain: what the boomers wanted, they got—and it didn't matter if it squared with what prior generations said was good or right. In the humble words of Jimmy Buffet, the baby boom generation's mixologist-in-chief (and my favorite waterlogged poet): *We are the people our parents warned us about.*

Now, however, the boomers are facing a future that is not set up to give them what they want. Today's products have been built in the context of the going narrative of age, and that monolithic, homogenous story diverges wildly from the lived existence of the many varieties of older people. As a result, today's older adults don't exactly have a finely tuned relationship with the businesses that make products for them—to the limited extent that industries outside of pharma and financial services even bother. They suffer the indignities imposed by these products or the lack thereof, sometimes in silence, sometimes loudly, but rarely with any real hope of changing anything.

Enter the boomers. Technology permitting, businesses and products have always attended to their every whim. When they discover that old age isn't like that, I don't expect them to take it quietly—I expect a revolt. They will demand products that dovetail with their wants and needs, and punish companies that fail to provide them. As I explain ahead, these products must work with the boomers' aging bodies and respect the mental models that they've built up over the course of decades. These products will also need to leverage cutting-edge technology and make it available in a way that is highly usable without ever seeming blunted or dumbed-down. Most important, the baby boomers will demand products that simply excite and delight them in old age, just as products have at every other stage of their lives. Objects in institutional shades of beige and grey, services suggested because "they're for your own good"—that kind of approach is simply not going to fly anymore.

The baby boomers, in short, will act as a sorting mechanism in the longevity economy, ruthlessly separating the companies that solve their real demands from those acting on a tired, false idea of oldness. The ultimate effect will be profound: a new, emergent vision of later life—reflected in and normalized by the myth-making apparatus of the private sector—which hews closely not to an antiquated vision of old age but how people actually want to live. In some ways slowly, and in some ways with astonishing speed, a new, better story of life in old age will replace our current narrative of aging.

The chance to write the beginnings of this new narrative falls squarely to businesses, which simultaneously presents one of the most profound opportunities and liabilities that the private sector has ever faced. The main purpose of this book is to help businesses understand this brave, old world and succeed in it: to enable them to harness the heightened expectations of baby boomers craving a better old age and to avoid being left in the dust of creative destruction as others do the same.

First, in Part I, I'll describe how we arrived at our current narrative of old age and the people who will guide us out of it. Chapter 1 describes how our singular—and singularly inaccurate—myth of old age got its start in 19th-century medical practice and how social institutions etched that idea into narrative stone. Chapter 2 continues the thread by delving into how the narrative of aging has led to some of the most disastrous product flops in history and how it continues to limit the imaginations of designers, engineers, inventors, and others. Chapter 3 is about the agents of change: the people who will blur the line between consumer and producer to identify products capable of solving the true demands of tomorrow's older adults. By and large, these innovators will be older women. And in Chapter 4, we'll take a break and go for a not-so-relaxing trip to Florida, home of The Villages, the world's largest gated retirement community and strongest bastion of the prevailing narrative of old age. Then we'll travel to a different sort of village run by older adults and compare notes. What aspects of the current vision of old age are absolutely essential for businesses to hold onto as they move forward? And which constitute existential threats to intergenerational coexistence?

In Part II, I'll take the insights from Part I and describe how to translate them into products. Chapter 5 is a guide to navigating design pitfalls and other issues that can prevent a product from exciting and delighting an older audience. In it, I'll introduce the concept of *transcendent design*—making things not just accessible for all types of users but so wonderful to use that people go out of their way to obtain them, even if they don't strictly need them. In Chapter 6, I'll delve into how to serve older adults' healthcare and eldercare needs in a way that treats those solutions not as the end goal but rather a stepping-stone on the way toward the accomplishment of older people's aspirations and goals—which are the topic of Chapter 7. Finally, Chapter 8 will address legacy—a concern of many individuals facing a finite span of life, and of the baby boomer generation itself.

How history will remember the baby boomers remains an open question. Will they be seen as the generation that gave rise to the environmental movement, for instance, or the one that ended the environment? Will they be the generation that closed the curtain on the Cold War or the one that killed off trust in institutions?

The answer will probably be "all of the above." What's more, I believe that the boomers have one additional legacy left in them. Thanks to their ingenuity and economic demand, the boomers have the potential to open up possibilities for older adults across the economic spectrum, across nations, and even far into the future.

Old age, as it stands, is ridiculously unequal. Although populations in most countries are growing older due to a dearth of births, the gains in extreme longevity I mentioned earlier are enjoyed mainly by wealthy societies and often high-education and high-income populations within those societies. In the United States, higher-income groups generally live longer, and life expectancies for African Americans and Native Americans, despite recent increases, trail those of white, Latino, and Asian Americans. Meanwhile, in 2014, life expectancy dropped for white women—a rare and disconcerting demographic surprise—and between 2014 and 2015, the US population as a whole followed suit, the result of increased midlife mortality among white men, white women, and African American men. This average decline—unique to the United States and still little more than a blip in a decades-long upward trend—masks a disturbing divergence: wealthy and highly educated Americans are reaping the bulk of our continued longevity gains, while poorer, less-educated groups are taking on major longevity losses. A metric called healthy life expectancy—how long you can expect to live without frailty and disability—tells a similar tale: wealthier, better-educated people not only live longer but enjoy better health in late life.

Of the causes of death that have climbed in the United States in recent years, most are at least somewhat preventable, including heart disease, stroke, type 2 diabetes, suicide, and drug and alcohol poisoning. The fact that prevention is *not* happening—particularly among lower-income, lower-education populations—is both horrifying and mystifying. All told, we are staring at a possible future in which the gift of extra years of life is diverted straight to the wealthiest people in the world, while those less fortunate get sick and die earlier—sometimes far earlier. Historically, wealth has always made it easier to live longer, and yet the fact that things are somehow getting worse, not better, for certain low-income populations is beyond dismaying.

There are many things that can and must be done to reverse this course. Changing the fundamental rules of old age is among the most important. By building a vision of late life that is more than just a miserable version of middle age, companies won't just be minting money, helping older people and their caregivers, and making aging societies more viable. They'll also be creating a cultural environment that values the contributions of older adults, which may make it easier for those who need employment to find it. They'll be building better tech products that, as they inevitably become commoditized, stand to improve life across the income scale. Most important of all, they'll be giving young and middle-aged people a reason to hope for their future—no insignificant step, given the outsize toll that preventable and self-destructive behaviors are taking on public health.

It all starts today, with companies finding the vision needed to invest in the burgeoning older market. It starts with businesses recognizing older consumers, listening closely to their demands, and building them better tools with which to interact with the world around them. It starts with bold leaders willing to erect a new narrative of possibility in old age.

It starts, in a word, here.

PART I

1

Vital Force

"OLD AGE," AS we know it today, seems like an idea that's been around forever—perhaps because it feels inevitable and therefore the consequence of natural, not human law. Or perhaps because the people whom we consider old seem like *they've* been around for a long time, and so our idea of oldness must be just as venerable. But in reality, it wasn't so long ago when a completely different idea of age was taken for granted. Our current narrative—the story we tell ourselves about the normal progression of life, culminating in a needy, greedy old age—is a relatively recent invention. Historically, in many different cultures and time periods, growing old was something experienced on an individual basis—not at a set age for everyone and not always according to the same set of rules. However, in the second half of the 19th century, this began to change as the first pension plans, old-age homes, and other institutions dedicated exclusively to older people first appeared in Europe and North America. Together, these institutions would lump older individuals into a single, monolithic category—"the aged"—and convince the public that this population constituted a problem in need of a solution.

Shaping the development of these institutions was the still-adolescent field of medicine, which was in the throes of transition from ancient, humoral theories of the body to the modern practice of pathology. As physicians began to conquer once-insoluble problems through vaccines, anesthesia, sterile surgery, and public health measures, the physiological effects of old age remained stubbornly resistant to medical intervention. For the first time, doctors began to regard their older patients' ailments as distinct from complaints arising at other ages, and, in the process, the older body as fundamentally different from the young.

Medical Vitality

In the middle of the 19th century, the public was learning to place its trust in science, despite the fact that the practice of empirical research was still, from today's perspective, primitive. Within the field of biology, a term that had only been coined in 1802, almost everything we now take for granted had yet to be discovered. The ideas that reigned instead were as influential as they were (often) unsupported by scientific evidence. It was in this time and research climate that social Darwinism and phrenology flourished. And so did a medical theory of old age that, though now thoroughly disproven, continues to influence how we view later life today.

In the mid- to late 1800s, Western medicine agreed that to be old was to be someone who had run out of "vital energy"—which, at the time, was no mere metaphor. Scientists and physicians believed the stuff to be tangible, literally present in the body and its fluids. Everyone had a finite reservoir of vital energy that gradually became depleted over the course of a lifetime. When you began to run low on vitality, you were old; death followed when the tank was empty.

The concept dovetailed with the worldview of Victorian-era doctors in several ways. For one, it explained why illness seemed far more curable in the young than the old, a fact that had largely gone ignored in early 19th-century medical texts. Physicians supposed that the loss of vitality created a "predisposing debility," making the older body vulnerable to illnesses it could have staved off in youth. The theory also fit with American religious thought as influenced by the Second Great Awakening, which peaked in the 1830s. The amount of vitality you were endowed with at birth was simply your lot. Whether you used it well or squandered it, however, was your personal responsibility.

And which activities spent vitality most profligately, leading to premature disability and death? All the fun ones, of course. The specifics varied depending on which expert you consulted. "Some endorsed the use of wines; others demanded abstinence; still others debated the merits of vegetables or red meat," writes historian Carole Haber. Regardless of whom you asked, moderation was always the key: "If death resulted from an exhausted supply of energy, then the goal was to retain it at all cost . . . by eating the correct foods, wearing the proper clothes, and performing (or refraining from) certain activities."

This was a society, remember, that had yet to behold the shining example of Keith Richards.

Sex—specifically, sex of nonprocreative or self-pleasing varieties— was to be avoided at all costs. For men in particular, it was evident when one's vitality was on the wane: things stopped working as they once had in the marital bed. Doctors inevitably told these poor fellows that it was all their fault. Personal indiscretions—whether of recent vintage or way back in semiforgotten youth—had added up. "By the 1850s physicians supplanted preachers as the leading anti-masturbatory crusaders," writes historian Carolyn Thomas de la Peña. "Concerns over the state of one's internal reserves became a more pressing question than the state of one's soul." Self-styled experts even went so far as to quantify the vitality lost through such exertions. One decreed, "The male excretion embodies forty times more vital force than an equal amount of red blood right from the heart."*

---

*He had good reason to be making such claims: he was selling "electric belts," a device that promised to top off one's depleted reservoirs of vitality by delivering jolts of all-healing electricity directly to the genitals. The mainstream medical community, which believed vital energy loss to be irreversible, never fully endorsed this approach

In continental Europe in the 1850s and 1860s, vitality theory began to wane as French and German pathologists realized that the lesions, fibrous tissue, and calcium deposits they discovered in older people's cadavers could provide a physiological explanation for some of the complaints of old age. But in the United States and Britain, even those aware of the European findings doubled down on their existing belief system: any wasting observed in cadavers was simply due to the loss of vital energy. Perhaps the best evidence for that point of view was the moment in a patient's life when vitality began to appreciably decline, which English-speaking physicians named the "climacteric period" or "climacteric disease." In women, the climacteric period was believed to begin between ages 45 and 55 and was associated with menopause; in men, it took place between 50 and 75 and was indicated by such signs as wrinkles, white hair, and complaints of feebleness. In some cases, this "extraordinary decline of corporeal powers," as one physician termed it, seemed to progress rapidly, even violently—surely the result of vitality levels reaching dangerous lows. If you were in the right age bracket and betrayed any signs of the climacteric, the implication was clear: you needed to immediately drop whatever you were doing in order to conserve what was left of your energy—avoiding "excesses and undue exertions," as one doctor wrote in 1853. And unfortunately, if you were a living, breathing human, you probably exhibited several of the warning signs. "Headache, vertigo, faintness, 'heat flushes,' emotional waves, phases of moral perversity, irritability, querulous impatience, even intellectual disturbance (especially of memory and of attention) prevail," a doctor catalogued in 1899.

"By far the most serious sign of climacteric disease was the tendency toward insanity," Haber writes. The umbrella of climacteric "insanity" covered the constellation of conditions we know today as dementia but also included the far milder cognitive symptoms that

---

or others like it, such as physiologist Charles Edouard Brown-Séquard's famed elixir, which included extractions of ground-up guinea pig and dog testes.

can arise in the course of normal aging. During and after the climacteric period, physicians noted, insanity could appear suddenly, sometimes as early as one's 50s or, more commonly, gradually in one's 70s or 80s—a disparity they attributed to different-sized reservoirs of vital force. Earlier, at the start of the 19th century, physicians had attempted to differentiate abnormal dementia from the more standard cognitive effects of aging, but by century's end, most agreed that almost all older adults experienced the same sort of insanity, differing only by degree.

Worse, though not every older person would experience the most severe symptoms of insanity, experts warned doctors to watch for subtle early warning signs. "Even in instances where the aged person seemed healthy and active, the brain could be undergoing progressive and irreversible decay," Haber writes. As a result, mentally robust people who merely *appeared* old found not only their physical strength but also their soundness of mind called into question. The centuries-old vision of the aged as fonts of wisdom went out the window; oldness was now synonymous with the loss of mental flexibility, *joie de vivre*, and self-control. One writer blamed the Crédit Mobilier scandal—a massive case of railroad graft that rattled American politics in 1872—on the advanced age of the participants. Even Sigmund Freud, who was otherwise busily upending all conventional wisdom about the human mind, insisted in 1904 that "old people are no longer educable" and that those "near or over the age of fifty lack . . . the plasticity of the psychic processes upon which the therapy depends." Tellingly, he was 48 years old when he delivered this pronouncement.

Only the family doctor could attest to whether an older person was in his or her right mind, giving family practitioners outsize say on such legal matters as wills and testaments. The main criteria for diagnosing insanity in aged adults were noticeable changes in attitude or behavior. In a catch-22, older people, constantly faulted for mental rigidity and stubbornness, could also be accused of insanity if any of their habits or beliefs changed in any appreciable way. The only way to be deemed mentally competent was to act "old," and, as physician T. S. Clouston wrote in 1884, "In the old man there is an organic craving for rest."

Once the climacteric period seemed to be underway, you were presumed to be running on the fumes of your reservoir of vitality. Doctors could do nothing for you—and you could do nothing, period, or else risk not only disease but also accusations of mental incompetence. In the eyes of medicine at the dawn of the 20th century, once you'd become visibly old, no matter your apparent health, no matter how sharp your mind seemed, all you could hope to do was withdraw and rest, saving your vitality for that final sprint. Crucially, you could no longer work. "The notion of a healthy old age was erased in this mode of discourse," writes critical gerontologist Bryan Green. Old age now changed you from an economic producer to a consumer, from healthy-as-a-default to a patient-despite-health. And it was only a matter of time until charities, businesses, and government reacted to the news.

Medicine Changes, Institutions Remain

As the 20th century progressed, insights in the medical field of pathology would eventually discredit the vital-energy theory of old age. But first, vital energy would mold the development of a robust set of social, cultural, and economic institutions, all built on the idea that once old age struck, the only recourse was to withdraw from work, rest, and prepare for the worst. One field strongly affected by the ideas coming out of the medical community was charitable poverty relief, which then turned around and demonstrated to the public how bad life could be once your vital energy gave out. By the outbreak of World War I, poverty-relief institutions had redefined "the old" in the public imagination. Aging, once something experienced by individuals and their families, became a problem to be dealt with on a mass scale—a mode of thinking so deeply ingrained that many today find it hard to consider older people in any other way.

"The old," as a monolithic group, couldn't have been defined as a problem any earlier. Mid- to late 19th century was when demographic metrics such as death rate, birth rate, and unemployment first emerged, and these led to the statistical discovery of a concept that had hidden in plain sight since the dawn of history: population aging. For the first time, writes Green, "population aging could be 'seen' in statistics and made a visible political problem."

And once you're part of a population, people start deciding what to do with you. "The emergence of 'population' as an economic and political problem," poststructuralist philosopher Michel Foucault writes, is "one of the great innovations in the techniques of power." In the case of the plight of the older population, the loss of individual agency would be tangible. A tipping point occurred between 1909 and 1915, when a number of institutions set their sights on the older population for the first time. This span of years saw the first public commission on aging, significant survey of the economic condition of older adults, state-level old-age pension system, and federal-level pension bill in the United States. Meanwhile, the medical term "geriatrics" was coined in 1909, and the first geriatrics textbook was published in 1914. In the space of a handful of years, old age as a population-sized phenomenon had officially become something people thought about—and a problem they wanted to solve.

The question was, how? Would society hold needy, sick older people responsible for their own condition and extend help only grudgingly? Or would misfortune in old age elicit not blame but rather the kind of big-hearted helping hand reserved solely for the deserving?

Ultimately, the latter framing would win out. In the United States and around the world, older people today are treated as uniquely worthy among adult groups claiming aid from tax revenues. But at the turn of the 20th century, that conclusion was far from foregone. In fact, if there was one force more responsible than any other for driving home the older population's problem status, it was the institution of the almshouse, a potent instrument of shame aimed at the "undeserving" poor.

For over a century, it stood as a symbol of what could happen when old age went wrong.

The almshouse arose together with the industrialized American city in the mid- to late 1800s. Earlier, in rural 1700s society, most older people who received economic assistance from outside their family were given "outdoor relief": money, food, and firewood, provided by their community or church. In terminology that carried over the Atlantic from the original Elizabethan Poor Law of 1601, "outdoor relief" stood in contrast to "indoor relief": incarceration in a work-house. In the young, bucolic United States, Elizabethan-style indoor relief was rare. Those who couldn't physically care for themselves and had no family were typically placed into the homes of their neighbors, not institutions, a practice subsidized by local poor taxes. As American cities grew, however, almshouses became more common. They were unpleasant, Dickensian places: poorly heated, filled with rough characters, manned by disciplinarians devoted to the character-building value of grueling work. Older people unable to support themselves could easily find themselves bunking next to criminals or the town drunkard. That unpleasantness was there by design, part of what became known as "scientific charity." The harshness of indoor relief was meant to serve as a deterrent from reliance on the public dole, and it caught on in cities despite costing more, on an individual basis, than outdoor relief.

As the 19th century progressed, however, "homes" for specific groups of people appeared, and the almshouse began to change. Soon there were separate homes for those unable to see, hear, or speak; and then for juvenile delinquents. Orphanages, distinct from almshouses, became more common. Dedicated workhouses sprung up for poor people who were considered unwilling yet able to work. The oldest residents of the almshouse were left behind. Soon, the almshouse accommodated more older adults than any other group.

Meanwhile, theories about waning vitality dominated contemporary medical thought concerning the health of the old. Doctors in hospitals and insane asylums could do nothing for their older patients because the root cause was incurable: depleted vitality. In response, almshouses, once a last-ditch stop for the indigent of all ages, became places where poor older people with dementia or other diseases could be treated like patients, if not cured. In 1903, the New York City Almshouse, acknowledging that its original mission had shifted significantly, renamed itself the Home for the Aged and Infirm. Many others followed suit.

Changing the name of the almshouse did not eliminate its stigma. While the vast majority of the older population didn't live in an almshouse, anyone who walked by one could see it was brimming over with older people. A new fear developed. Since loss of vital energy would eventually come for everyone, preventing self-sufficiency—and the presence of the overcrowded almshouse served as a constant reminder of what could happen to you when you became non-self-sufficient— then the implication was clear. This, dear worker, dear mother, could happen to you.

Worse, the new concept of unemployment, a term first coined in 1887, had demonstrated that macroeconomic caprices could steal jobs from perfectly diligent, capable hands. The potential for bad luck to lead to ruin was hardly a new concern, but the identification of massive, heretofore unseen forces controlling the labor market changed the way people thought about work. Now even the most assiduous, strong-bodied worker could end up penniless through no fault of his own. And everyone knew where the destitute went when they grew old.

The effect of the looming threat of the almshouse on popular culture was profound. It inspired D. W. Griffith, the groundbreaking (and infamously racist) silent film pioneer to make the 1911 drama *What Shall We Do With Our Old?*, which showed a white-haired carpenter and his wife starving after he loses his job to a younger worker. Perhaps even more resonant was Will Carleton's 1872 poem *Over the Hill to the Poor-House*, which appeared on the cover of *Harper's Weekly* and later inspired a popular song, and then silent film, of the same title. To this day, we still worry about the implications of what it means to be "over the hill"—a phrase that likely descended from the Carleton poem— and whether that journey will take us to the modern poorhouse: the government-funded nursing home.

But there was a solution in the air: the pension. If you lived in the late 1800s or early 1900s and weren't independently wealthy, a public or private pension was your best chance to ward off eventual penury and institutionalization. Demand for pensions, which had been rare prior to the Civil War, soon snowballed. By 1932, 17 out of 48 states had old-age pension laws on the books (although California, Massachusetts, and New York accounted for 87 percent of the money these plans paid out). The terrifying threat of indoor relief and the almshouse, created to deter people from living off the fruits of others' labor, had ironically become a rallying cry for increased financial assistance in the form of public pensions. Burgeoning public support for such measures was one of the first hints that society, finding the needy old a uniquely deserving problem population, would prefer to provide it with financial support, not censure.

And it would be those pensions—particularly Social Security, which didn't start out as a pension but became the de facto pension to rule them all—that would give us the final piece that was missing from our current narrative of old age. Leading up to the 1930s, the public understood "the aged" to be, as a rule, incapable of work, sick, and pitiable. But it wasn't until retirement became widely accepted as a stage of life that this idea of old age would become second nature: what everyone expected to become after 65.

Efficiency Takes Over

Our current vision of retirement is now so deeply ingrained that it's considered a life stage on par with middle age and childhood. Meanwhile, 67 percent of workers said in 2015 that they planned to "work for pay in retirement," a seeming contradiction in terms that shows just how confused we are about what retirement really is. Part of the issue is that retirement is actually not one thing but two. First, it's the cessation (or scaling back) of work, typically around age 65. And second, it's what you do with yourself afterward—the expectation being the pursuit of leisure activities. In our current idea of retirement, the normalization of the first led to that of the second.

One pervasive myth regarding how we came to see 65 as the age to stop working dates the turning point to 1875, when German Chancellor Otto von Bismarck created the world's first nationwide old-age social insurance program in an attempt to diminish pressure from leftist agitators. Bismarck supposedly decided on age 65 as the plan's trigger because that was his age at the time, and the rest of the world followed suit.

The story isn't all wrong: the United States did look to Germany and other countries as models when it set up its Social Security program in 1935. But Germany actually set 70 as the age of retirement in 1889, when Bismarck was 74, a requirement that would only change to 65 in 1916, 18 years after his death. Well before then, in 1890, the United States had already instituted a widespread old-age insurance plan of its own that kicked in in one's 60s: the Union Army pension, which provided payments to Civil War veterans and their widows. By 1900, the program was the most widespread form of governmental assistance in the United States, consuming almost 30 percent of the federal budget and paying out to about a quarter of the population 65 and over—an unprecedentedly comprehensive program, especially considering that immigrants and Confederate veterans weren't eligible.

Prior to these programs, retirement was not something older workers looked forward to. At the very least, it entailed what could be a crippling loss of income, and it usually came with a loss of social status as well. People tended to put it off for as long as possible.

The Union Army pension provided the first indication that this norm might change and a subset of the older population would voluntarily stop working. Prior to 1904, Union vets had to undergo a medical examination verifying disease or disability in order to collect their Civil War pensions. But physicians, who already viewed old age as intrinsically debilitating, had trouble telling the "legitimately" disabled from the merely old. By the turn of the century, the commissioner of pensions advised doctors to simplify things by awarding pensions based on age alone. In 1904, President Theodore Roosevelt issued an executive order making it official. By dint of age, not symptoms, all Union vets were considered half disabled at age 62, two-thirds disabled at 65, and fully disabled at 70.

The order, highly controversial, was reviled especially strongly by those who hadn't yet internalized the idea that superannuation alone could make someone worthy of governmental support. Many considered it a bald attempt to buy votes. Mark Twain wrote in his autobiography: "I would want to reproach the old soldiers for not rising up in indignant protest against our Government's vote-purchasing additions to the pension list, which is making of the remnant of their brave lives one long blush." The "vote-buying" will continue, he added, "until the remains of every cat, with her descendants, that has been owned by a sutler or soldier . . . shall have been added to the pension list."

Twain feared that Roosevelt's order would create a slippery slope: soon politicians courting Southern votes would add Confederate veterans to the ranks of Civil War pensioners. That didn't happen. Instead, something truly remarkable took place: Union vets with pensions retired, while Confederates didn't. From today's perspective, that may seem unsurprising, but remember, for most people at the time, retirement was something only done out of necessity. With the guaranteed income provided by the Union pension, however, people began to retire who otherwise would have kept working. It was an early, strong indication that retirement might eventually become something that people would actively seek out—especially manual laborers, for whom work in old age was a source of literal pain.* In the decades following

---

*In the late 1800s, most workers were retiring not from desk jobs but physically laborious work—the kind that's painful to perform when you're fighting health

the Civil War, the retirement rate climbed and climbed, while the idea of working for as long as possible switched from typical to abnormal. In 1880, 75 percent of men over 64 worked, a value that would steadily drop for a century. (By the 1990 census, an all-time low of 18 percent of that age group reported working, a value that has since increased a few percentage points as people have chosen to work past "retirement age.")

Following the Civil War, not only were people starting to retire more frequently, but they were also starting to do so without involving their adult children. In 1880, only 23.5 percent of retired men over 65 lived alone or with a wife, independent of their kids. By 1900, this number had risen to almost 28 percent (and would eventually rise above 80 percent by the end of the 20th century). Retirement was beginning to morph from a family affair to a couples' and singles' retreat.

Even as some were realizing that a fully funded retirement beat hard labor, the private sector was beginning to make that choice for its employees, whether they wanted to retire or not. By 1885, the American Industrial Revolution was in high gear, and the corporation had emerged as the major form that private enterprise would take. With shareholders holding the reins, businesses began to pursue short-term profit, and high levels of production efficiency were an important way to achieve it. At the same time, economists and the medical community were urging the adoption of the eight-hour workday, which gradually replaced 10-hour shifts as the standard between 1885 and 1915. The shorter workday added pressure to increase each employee's productivity during his or her limited time at work. To further raise the stakes, factory owners who purchased new, complex, and expensive machinery needed to recoup their investments as quickly as possible. As a result, work proceeded at a feverish rate. Managers feared that aged hands couldn't keep up the pace, and the nascent field of scientific management (also called Taylorism, after the father of the field,

---

problems such as arthritis, let alone rifle and bayonet wounds. Thirty-one percent of the Union vets claimed to have sustained an injury or gunshot wound in the line of duty.

Frederick Winslow Taylor) supported their assumptions. Harrington Emerson, a scientific management pioneer and contemporary of Taylor, wrote in 1909 that the most efficient business "eliminates from its force inefficient men." Although a few efficiency experts valued the putative consistency and conservatism of an older workforce, many others agreed that the most straightforward way to weed out inefficiency would be to start with the oldest workers, producing, as Emerson wrote, "a desirable wriggle of life all the way down the line."

The moment was right for those who were seeking to reshuffle the working ranks by age. Unemployment as a concept had only recently entered common usage. The idea of a pool of young, strong, efficient workers languishing with idle time on their hands, in addition to provoking abject terror among those who saw Marxist revolutionaries lurking around every corner, added weight to the arguments of scientifically minded managers who hoped to make way for younger workers by removing the old. In short order, workers' age had become a hobbyhorse for efficiency-minded thinkers and managers.

Those efficiency experts didn't know it at the time, but the idea that labor is a zero-sum game, in which a finite amount of work is parceled out among a great pool of workers, is an example of the lump-of-labor fallacy, which *The Economist* describes as "one of the best-known fallacies in economics." Chief among the reasons why it is wrong is that the amount of work to be done in an economy isn't fixed, and so the number of available jobs can change. Obvious "solutions," such as shortened workdays and early mandatory retirement, tend to decrease overall economic efficiency. Meanwhile, we now know that population aging does not affect the employment of younger workers, and older workers do not rob the young of jobs; in fact, they failed to do so even during the unemployment spike of the Great Recession. "This horse has been beaten to death," write researchers from the Center for Retirement Research at Boston College.

In the early 20th century, however, the belief that older workers crowded out the supposedly more efficient young became widespread.

Meanwhile, as a result of the rise of compulsory education, older, out-of-work adults seeking new employment found it harder to compete with younger job seekers armed with high school degrees.

Whether older workers who were laid off simply gave up on work or tried and failed to find a new job, the result was "retirement"—a word that, at the beginning of the 20th century, meant nothing more than dismissal from work due to age and had yet to pick up its connotations of sunshine, cruise ships, and golf courses. The plight of older ex-workers unable to support themselves didn't go unnoticed by the companies letting them go, however—at least, not always. The American Express Company provided the first private pension in the United States in 1875, and over the course of the ensuing 35 years, railroads, public utilities, banks, metal industries, and larger industrial corporations followed suit. By 1910, dozens of firms were adding pension plans annually. Some of these pensions were bestowed as a result of genuine managerial largesse, others were hard won by unions, and still others were adopted by managers who used the promise of pensions in the future to justify paying employees less in the present. But most importantly, private pension plans served the goal of efficiency. With a pension in place, a manager who once might have refused to cut loose a 65-year-old worker would be free make the more "efficient" decision to retire him, unencumbered by that troublesome ethical factor.

By 1932, 15 percent of workers—mainly those employed by the largest corporations and government—were promised pensions. That was enough to ensure widespread understanding of the concept of the pension as a form of relief for the older individual, regardless of wealth or health, but it wasn't enough to cover much of the population. And suddenly, much of the population needed coverage. As the Great Depression set in, the unemployment rate ballooned across age brackets. In older age groups, over half of all people lacked the income to support themselves. For both of these reasons, what little had been done in the private sector in terms of providing funding for retirees was about to be scaled up in a way never before seen in the United

States. With Social Security, old age would change, and retirement would become one of its defining features.

The Social Security Era

By the period between the world wars, the United States had come most of the way toward its current narrative of old age. "The aged," most younger people now understood, was a homogenous population characterized by ill health and poverty. Incapable of work, it would always need resources provided by younger generations, passed upward through families, companies, and the government. Though this new story made intuitive sense to many, the fact remained that there were still great numbers of perfectly capable older workers who had been laid off or fired throughout the 1920s, and then dramatically more of them in the 1930s, who hoped in vain to regain employment. It was one thing for younger workers, many of whom saw their elders as inefficient, to view the retirement of older workers as normal, but quite another for older adults themselves to accept this state of affairs. The shift in collective thinking necessary for this to take place would only be made possible by the signing of 1935's Social Security Act. By the middle of the 20th century, as Social Security expanded in coverage and dollars awarded, retirement became not only something workers did when forced but also something everyone looked forward to—or at least was expected to look forward to. With the normalization (and later, glamorization) of retirement-the-life-stage, the older population would learn to subscribe to an idea of themselves defined by their consumption, not capabilities. Only then would our current narrative of old age be complete: a time of life the story of which would be characterized by needy, greedy, useless otherness.

Social Security didn't come into being spontaneously, however, but rather grew in the fertile soil of a nation that had become obsessed with efficiency, an ethos that had escaped the world of mechanized business and made its way into other aspects of life. "Historians have labeled the message 'the gospel of efficiency,'" recounts public-policy historian Robert H. Nelson. "One said that the Progressive movement was characterized by 'an efficiency craze' that amounted to 'a secular Great Awakening.' Another historian spoke of 'the efficiency movement' that was offered 'as a panacea for the ills of mankind' and exhibited 'a moral fervor that had all the earmarks of a religious revival.'"

This widespread preoccupation with efficiency, combined with the pervasive idea that older adults were anything but efficient, led to the common belief that society as a whole would benefit if older adults could be removed from positions of importance, not only in business but also in such fields as research and government. For instance, in 1914, US Attorney General Clark McReynolds argued that federal judges above age 70 "have remained upon the bench long beyond the time that they are able to adequately discharge their duties." He even went so far as to suggest that for every justice over 70, the president should appoint a counterpart judge "who would preside over the affairs of the court and have precedence over the older one." It was an idea that would come to haunt him.

Meanwhile, in the world of research and development, I'll use one voice to illustrate the prevailing wisdom about age: Thomas J. Midgley Jr., one of the most celebrated applied scientists of the 1920s, 1930s, and World War II. When making his 1944 year-end address as president of the American Chemical Association, he was emphatic that retaining older workers in the field of chemistry and beyond, at the expense of hiring young, would cramp overall innovation and efficiency. "Youth is original and creative, while age is simply experience," he said. "Every executive who has lived beyond 40 is guilty, to some extent, of not getting out of the way of younger men."

It was a sentiment that had become widespread in the labor market, especially as jobs became scarce during the Great Depression. Thirty to over 40 percent of American companies had age limits for new hires in place in the 1920s and 1930s, and "We make 40 our deadline in taking on new people" was a common refrain among hiring managers. John

Steven McGroarty, the poet laureate of California, represented the situation well in a 1934 editorial when he wrote, "The white-collar man, the artisan, and the other classes of men, are not wanted after they are even forty-five years of age. They are ditched by employers just when they are the most capable."

In Midgley's case, if the concept of the intellectual productivity of youth came from the culture around him, his own experience confirmed it. In 1921, at age 33, he had made his name in industrial chemistry by inventing leaded gasoline, which prevented engine knock and increased an engine's power. Then in 1928, at age 40, he invented Freon and other chlorofluorocarbons, a class of nonflammable refrigerant gasses that also served as aerosol propellants, which replaced the various toxic, explosive ingredients then in use.

By the end of World War II, Midgley was considered an American hero. Although leaded gasoline fueled both Allied and Axis aircraft, the Allies had found a way to use it to greater effect in the form of ultra-high-octane gasoline. Allied airplanes running on 100-octane, as this gasoline was known, could take off in one-fifth the runway space, climb faster, fly higher and farther, and carry more bombs than Luftwaffe aircraft running on the relatively lackluster 87-octane. "We wouldn't have won the Battle of Britain without 100-octane," Britain's petroleum secretary, Geoffrey Lloyd, claimed after the war. Meanwhile, the Allies relied on aerosol DDT bombs containing Midgley's propellants to keep malarial mosquitoes at bay, and crews used related compounds to put out fires in tanks.

By the end of the war, however, Midgley was not well. He had contracted a rare, late-in-life case of poliomyelitis in 1940 at age 51, against odds he equated to "the chances of drawing a certain individual card from a stack of playing cards as high as the Empire State Building."

As he approached the podium to deliver his 1944 address, mortality was on his mind. He ended with a poem he had composed, which concluded as follows:

When I feel old age approaching, and it isn't any sport,
And my nerves are growing rotten, and my breath is growing
    short,
And my eyes are growing dimmer, and my hair is turning white,
And I lack the old ambitions when I wander out at night,
Then, though many men my senior may remain when I'm gone,
I have no regrets to offer just because I'm passing on,
Let this epitaph be graven on my tomb in simple style,
This one did a lot of living in a mighty little while.

Because Midgley, like many of his contemporaries, didn't think much of the mental acuity of the aged, he took comfort in the idea that he'd only miss out on dull and enervated years if he passed away in his 50s. It was exactly the sort of thinking about the second half of life that had made employment a vanishing dream for so many adults in the Great Depression. And, arguably, it was also the line of thought that had inspired Franklin Delano Roosevelt to push as hard as he did for the passage of the Social Security Act during the depths of the Great Depression.

From the earliest days of its development, Social Security was meant to be both more inclusive and more robust than traditional welfare programs. In fact, the 1935 Social Security Act contained 11 sections, called titles, several of which created new and improved versions of traditional welfare measures for a variety of groups, including needy mothers and children, the blind, and the unemployed, all of which were funded from general federal revenues. The Old-Age Insurance component of Social Security—the part most commonly referred to today simply as "Social Security"—was different, however, and was meant to do more. Anything else would be the "same old dole under another name," FDR said. His plan, which would unyoke old-age financial support from the stigma of a handout or the almshouse, was the logical consequence of the events that had begun at the turn of the century, when the population of "the old" was first conceived as a problem and then deemed uniquely worthy of government assistance. It was also, more pragmatically, something that would last a long time while growing in scope. The Social Security Act represented "a cornerstone in a structure which is being built but is by no means complete," he said as he signed the 1935 Act into law. His long view meant that any money raised by the program needed to be hermetically sealed against thieves within the government—future budget-slashing or coffer-raiding politicians—and his method of politician-proofing Social Security was elegant in its simplicity. By creating a sense of ownership among its recipients, he and his team made receiving one's Social Security check feel like a right, not a handout. The way he did this was to tell the nation that Social Security was "contributory": that the money workers paid into the program would be, for all intents and purposes, the same money that they would receive years later, should they find themselves out of work in old age.* As long as the funding for the program came solely from its beneficiaries and not from general revenues, the reasoning went, it would be politically fatal for anyone to even suggest raiding the Social Security trust fund for any purpose other than paying out Social Security benefits—and that's still the case today. "We put those payroll contributions there so as to give the contributors a legal, moral, and political right to collect their pensions and unemployment benefits," FDR said in 1941. "With those taxes in there, no damn politician can ever scrap my social security program. Those taxes aren't a matter of economics, they're straight politics."

If it's clear why FDR wanted old-age insurance to be contributory, it's harder to say why the program needed to pay out to all older retirees and not merely the neediest among them. In fact, in addition to its

---

* Whether that remained true after the program shifted from a reserve-fund model to pay-as-you-go in 1939 is a matter of semantics. In its long history, the program has received next to no funds from general reserves, although due to demographic trends, recipients have until recently received far more on average from the program than they paid into it during their working lives.

old-age insurance titles, the Social Security Act contained a separate old-age assistance program, which was funded from general revenues and awarded monthly payments only to the poor elderly, not to every retiree above a certain age. Why not simply stick with this approach for old-age insurance and make poverty, as opposed to retirement, the condition the program insured against? It would have certainly cost workers and employers less per paycheck.

There are two answers: for one, paying out to every retiree, not just the poorest, made the plan feel less like the "same old dole" and helped guarantee a sense of righteous ownership among its recipients—a sense that would continue to protect the program as the decades marched on, and Social Security became the indispensable part of later life it is today.

But it's also reasonable to argue that FDR also wanted to create a permanent source of funds for all older people, regardless of need, for a far more cynical reason: because he, like Midgley,* believed that to be old was to be incapable of good work and therefore inherently economically disadvantaged. If so, it would have been a line of thought traceable straight back to the 19th-century theory of vital energy. It also might not have been wholly humanitarian in its motivation. In fact, there is a school of historians who suspect that FDR thought so little of older workers that he hoped to use Social Security not just to provide for their welfare but also to actively push them out of important roles in the US economy. It was for this reason, the thinking goes, that, until 1950, Social Security recipients were allowed to go out and earn no more than 15 dollars per month, a measure put in place to make sure they had fully retired, thereby opening up jobs for younger workers. As Barbara Armstrong, a UCLA law professor who led the effort to draft the Act's language concerning old-age insurance, said

---

*FDR knew of Midgley, who was an important wartime figure, and wrote to him to express sympathy for his polio diagnosis after being told about it by Vannevar Bush, who headed the US Office of Scientific Research and Development during World War II.

in her 1965 oral history memoir (italics are hers): "The interest of Mr. Roosevelt was with the younger man . . . that's why that little ridiculous amount of $15 was put in . . . Let [the retiree] earn some pin money, but it had to be on *retirement*. And retirement means you've stopped working for pay."

The Social Security Act makes no mention of pushing older workers out of the economy, however. It was written in a way that, its proponents hoped, would earn it safe passage through a Supreme Court that had recently proved all too happy to squash New Deal legislation. For Social Security to have a hope of making it past the Court, its wording would have to downplay the sense that the government was seeking to tamper with the economy, stressing instead how its special payroll taxes would improve citizens' general welfare.

But in the two years after FDR signed the Social Security bill into law in 1935, the Supreme Court continued to strike down piece after piece of New Deal legislation—including three such rejections in one day. It appeared that no amount of careful phrasing would prevent the Social Security Act from going down in flames as well. Then, in 1937, FDR called for a change to the makeup of the Supreme Court. The bill he proposed, commonly referred to as his "court-packing plan," is often held up as one of the most significant examples of executive overreach in US history. It is also probably responsible for the fact that Americans enjoy the protections of Social Security today.

FDR's scheme was simple: since five out of the nine sitting Supreme Court justices voted against his New Deal bills more often than not, he would simply add allies to the court's roster, swelling its ranks to as many as 15 and swinging decisions his way. Students of US history know what happened next: Associate Justice Owen Roberts, previously an FDR opponent, cast his lot in favor of the Social Security Act. At the time, Congress heavily favored Social Security but otherwise opposed FDR's intention to tamper with the Court. In declaring Social Security constitutional, Justice Roberts diminished the appeal of FDR's court-packing plan in Congress, where the bill shortly thereafter met defeat. For this reason, Roberts's vote is colloquially known as the "switch in time that saved nine" justices.

But perhaps what's more interesting than that sequence of events is how FDR justified his extreme actions. His stated reason for packing the Court should sound remarkably familiar: he argued that that older people aren't good at their jobs—not even Supreme Court justices. The court-packing plan called for a fresh face to be added to the high court for every sitting justice older than 70 years and six months. And why was age, of all criteria, the deciding factor?

The gospel of efficiency certainly played a role. "By bringing into the judicial system a steady and continuing stream of new and younger blood, I hope, first, to make the administration of all Federal justice speedier and, therefore, less costly," FDR said in his March 1937 fireside chat, syndicated nationally by radio. "This plan will save our national Constitution from hardening of the judicial arteries."

But perhaps FDR was motivated by a sense of poetic justice as well. The specific wording of his court-packing plan mirrored almost verbatim the 1914 argument of Attorney General McReynolds, who, please recall, had favored supplanting older federal judges with new presidential appointees. McReynolds had been in his 50s when he wrote those words, but now, in 1937, he was well over 70—and sitting on the Supreme Court, where he was a known antagonist of the president. When FDR suggested that age 70, give or take, was when Supreme Court justices became less efficient, he was literally using McReynolds's own words against him.

In hindsight, the stakes of FDR's gambit boggle the mind. His humanitarian concern for the aged—combined, arguably, with a powerful societal narrative that suggested that they were unable to contribute to the American workforce—was significant enough for him to risk both his personal legacy and the separation of powers in the US government. When Justice Roberts blinked, FDR finally had his politician-proof old-age insurance, contributory and unassailable from pols of all stripes.

But in the beginning, the program was small. The old-age insurance component of Social Security covered less than 60 percent of the American workforce at its outset and didn't include spouses or dependents. That would soon change. For decades after its signing, the program would expand—usually in election years—in terms of professions covered and money paid out. Eventually, it would even disburse to older people who were still working—a complete reversal of the program's original purpose, which was to insure only those who had been "retired" from their job.

That reversal took place gradually, starting with the self-employed. From the start, Social Security was compulsory: if the Social Security Act covered your profession, you were required to contribute. But as the program expanded in 1950 to include self-employed workers, it became clear that there was something unfair about that arrangement. Despite being required to make a lifetime's worth of Social Security contributions, the self-employed didn't have a boss to "retire" them and were therefore more likely to continue working well past 65. It didn't seem right for a group to pay into Social Security according to the same contribution rate as everyone else, only to expect far less in return—that would be like charging a low-risk driver the same auto insurance rate as a habitual speedster. Rather than charge different professions different contribution rates, which would have been politically and logistically infeasible, Congress took a different tack. The 1950 amendments to Social Security provided full benefits to everyone over 75, regardless of retirement status, so that even the self-employed could eventually get a bite at the Social Security apple.

That was the first of many measures that would diminish the strength of the requirement that Social Security recipients not work, known as the "retirement earnings test." In the decades that followed, politicians would take virtually any opportunity to defang the earnings test. Amendments made in 1954 dropped the age at which the test no longer applied to 72, and then 1977 amendments decreased it further to 70. Meanwhile, the test changed from a cutoff to a sliding scale in 1960, and the amount younger Social Security recipients were allowed to earn increased more-or-less continually for decades on end. At the same time, Social Security coverage expanded to include more and more professions, until the program applied to the vast majority of Americans.

Ultimately, the earnings test would be dropped entirely. Social Security, in this mature (and in my view, optimal) form would effectively function not as an insurance policy but as a national pension. More fascinating than what Social Security became, however, is the reason why it changed forms. "I believe we should eliminate the limits on what seniors on Social Security can earn," President Bill Clinton said in his 1999 State of the Union address. In 2000 that wish became reality. The measure was sponsored by Representative Bill Archer of Texas, who had been fighting against the earnings test (which he termed an "earnings penalty") since he was first elected in 1971. At some point before Archer began his crusade in 1971, the earnings test, once seen as the only way to ensure fair distribution of old-age-insurance benefits, had morphed in the public's eye into a punishment for working. It's impossible to overstate the significance of this distinction: it signaled a fundamental shift in the meaning of retirement. Social Security was still a program for "retirees"; its most fervent advocate was the American Association of Retired Persons,* after all. But somehow in the 1950s and 1960s, the public had begun to believe that you could be both retired and employed at the same time, which meant that "retirement" was no longer synonymous with the state of nonwork. Now it was something else: a stage of life.

Enter Del Webb

By the middle of the 20th century, the prevailing idea of oldness was close to its current form. The monthly generational handoff of money in the form of Social Security payments lent constant credence to the

---

* I am a proud board member of this organization, now known simply as AARP.

longstanding notion that "the aged" were unsuited to economic production. Still missing, however, was the final piece of today's narrative:
the idea that older people *prefer* to be consumers taking support from
society, as opposed to producers adding to its strength. Retirement,
the supposedly fun, final life stage, would supply the key. It was an idea
that only the private sector could have come up with.

First, the growing influence of private pensions in the midcentury
United States swelled the ranks and increased the financial security of
retirees. During World War II, salary caps prevented companies from
competing directly for scarce laborers, but they could one-up each other
by offering generous pensions. After the war ended and Social Security
began paying out more money to an increasingly comprehensive set of
people, the expectation of private pensions remained. When Social Security expanded in the 1950s, companies that had initially balked at higher
contribution rates realized that the more the government paid out, the
less they'd have to provide labor unions in the form of pensions. As a
result, leaders in business clamored for increased government payouts.

As the 1950s wore on, retirees received more funding than ever, but
they didn't yet know what they wanted to do with it—or themselves.
It was part of a broader problem society was facing: finding meaning
in consumerism. In his 1952 essay "Some Observations on Changes in
Leisure Attitudes," sociologist David Riesman wrote:

> Whereas the explorers of the last century moved to the fron-
> tiers of production and opened fisheries, mines, and mills, the
> explorers of this century seem to me increasingly moving to
> the frontiers of consumption . . . And frontier behavior is awk-
> ward: people have not yet learned to behave comfortably in
> the new surroundings. There is formlessness, which takes the
> shape of lawlessness on the frontier of production and of aim-
> lessness on the frontier of consumption.

The aimlessness of a population learning to define itself in
terms of what it bought, not built, was doubled in the case of those

who had recently retired outright from production. "Had Riesman chosen to apply this analogy specifically to retirement, he could only have concluded that the retired, existing on the new frontier of leisure and consumption, would soon learn to 'behave comfortably,'" writes retirement historian William Graebner.* "The problem of leisure, as Riesman defined it, lay not in leisure itself but in twentieth-century man's awkward responses to it." Take, for instance, this 1949 essay, by Julius Hochman, manager of the International Ladies' Garment Workers' Union Joint Board Dress and Waistmakers Union of Greater New York:

> The "old man" himself is bewildered. He appreciates the fact that his span of life has been increased. But it is difficult for him to understand why the powerful forces of society that shape and control economic life have marked him a useless man to be discarded. He does not like it even when it is labeled "retirement." He wonders. Retire on what? Retire to what? To what in terms of life's content? To what in terms of that vague and yet so meaningful word "happiness"? He is disturbed and depressed. He wonders why he should have to retire at all.

On the frontier of retired life, there were now inhabitants but no institutions or instructions for how to live, no economic production roles to differentiate one retiree from the next, and nothing to tell them what to do with their time. But if retired life seemed to have no natural purpose to it, perhaps one could be invented. "Perhaps," said historian of technology Lynn White Jr., while serving as chair of a 1951 roundtable on retirement hosted by the Corning Corporation, "we have to glamorize leisure as we have not."

---

* Graebner's 1980 book, *A History of Retirement*, was a key resource for this chapter, and is perhaps the best articulation of the revisionist theory of FDR's motivations for setting up Social Security.

And that's exactly what the private sector did. Life insurance companies, among the first to sell retirement financial products, painted a rosy picture of what retired life could be. As one 1950 newspaper advertisement read, "Today the average child at birth can expect to live eighteen years longer than his grandfather lived. Are these years to be some of the best of your life . . . or will you miss your chance to have your dream come true?"

Figuratively and literally, employers (especially insurance companies themselves) and individuals bought what the insurers were selling. But still, the terminology of a new, positive vision of retirement was lacking a certain indescribable something. Graebner writes: "The editors of *Retirement Planning News* chose the first issue, published in 1956, to express their dissatisfaction with the word *retirement*, since it was 'likely to mean retirement from life, a withdrawal from the active world.' Why not 'the fulfillment years?'"

Why not, indeed? Because living out "the fulfillment years" sounds about as sexy as watching milk curdle. But the sentiment was close—very close—to a vision with infinitely more potential: three words that would paint the end of life not as the slow gathering of a purple dusk but rather the explosion of a glorious sunset, warm and brilliant and blazing with crepuscular rays.

The golden years.

A vision which could be obtained together with a bungalow and a plot of land in Sun City, Arizona, the world's first major retirement community, for a small down payment to one Delbert Webb, its builder. The resort-like destination, which began selling homes on January 1, 1960, represented a new way of thinking about retirement: not as something bad that your boss did to you, or an aimless limbo before death, but rather as a well-deserved reward for a long, hard career. The framing was immensely appealing. Supposedly, on that first day of business, Webb expected 10,000 potential homebuyers to tour the community. One hundred thousand showed up, causing a traffic jam that extended far into the desert.

With the invention of the golden years, a happy retirement became something that consumers would pay for and, in funds provided via Social Security and Medicare, voters would demand. Within decades, it would become hard to even think of following up one's primary career with anything other than the pursuit of leisure.

Taking a step back, what was the stroke of genius that visited Del Webb and the other early architects of the modern myth of retirement, such as the salespeople of the first retirement plans? They realized that although age strikes everyone at different times and in different ways, oldness as defined by government, industry, and culture had become monolithic and occurred at the same age, give or take, for everyone. Healthy people over 65 with money in their pockets didn't need to rest then (and they don't now, for the most part), but they would need to do *something*, and they'd pay for that privilege—not just for leisure but for a coherent idea of how to live that made sense at a gut level. Webb and the rest took a new, positive, concept of retirement, put a bow on it, and sold it back to us. And we've been buying it ever since.

As leisure became an inextricable part of later life, the broad cultural narrative of aging assumed its current form. At the beginning of the 20th century, it was understood that older people weren't supposed to work; their job, if anything, was to buy things. Then, following the passage of Social Security, it became clear that they weren't expected to contribute financially to society. Far from it—they claimed a monthly check from the government. Sun City and its "golden years" rounded out the picture. Older people, the new dream of retirement suggested, no longer belonged in even the same zip code as everyone else. Rather, they belonged in a beautiful place where they could play games and spend other people's money and try not to think about the inevitable.

A Narrative Whose Time Is Done

Thomas Midgley Jr. did not die well. Although the chemical engineer compared the odds of his developing polio to pulling a specific card from an impossibly large stack, perhaps, unbeknownst to him, the deck had been rigged. In his long history as an advocate for tetraethyl lead, he had often attempted to demonstrate its safety by washing his hands with the colorless liquid and inhaling its sweet-smelling fumes. The resultant lead exposure likely compromised his immune health. By the time of his 1944 speech, he was paralyzed from the waist down and relied on complicated string-and-pulley systems of his own devising to get into and out of his bed, swimming pool, and wheelchair.

A few weeks later, his wife found him entwined in the ropes and pulleys attached to his bed, strangled to death. He was 55.

Today, Midgley is known mainly for his effect on the environment. In the United States alone, before it was largely phased out in the early 1980s, leaded gasoline caused scores of millions of children to experience toxic lead exposures and was directly responsible for many factory workers' deaths. Chlorofluorocarbons, meanwhile, turned out to not only comprise some of the most potent greenhouse gases known but were also largely responsible for the late-20th-century perforation of the ozone layer. Thanks to these breakthroughs, Midgley has been described as having "more impact on the atmosphere than any other single organism in Earth's history."

But his inventions also contributed to the downfall of some of the most reprehensible regimes in history. His research provided exactly what was needed at a certain point in time, even if it later proved to have major drawbacks. In this sense, it has something important in common with our current narrative of old age.

Through most of the 20th century, the idea that "the aged" are inherently unhealthy and uniformly incapable of economic production achieved far more good than harm. Indeed, from the perspective of older people, it led to some of the most cherished government programs in US history, including Social Security, Medicare, and the Older Americans Act, which created the first comprehensive set of federal services and legal protections for older adults. There are a great many older people who have avoided what would have been extreme, unconscionable deprivations had these programs never existed—and they never would have existed if not for the story of old age that began with the medical theory of vital energy in the mid-1800s.

But now, that narrative has become a liability. It has taken us as far as it can, but it is now holding back innovation in a way that's proven hard for many to recognize, let alone solve. Like leaded gasoline, the invention that once served us so well must be replaced. Our narrative of age has always been arbitrary: a social construct that is equal parts historical hangover and marketing ploy. But now more than ever, it's limiting how we think about solutions for older demographics. If we want to live better in tomorrow's older world, this mental constraint must—and will—give way.

2

Myths

I WASN'T ALWAYS SO hell-bent on dismantling our narrative of age. The founding idea behind the AgeLab was simpler: to correct a dangerous scarcity.

In 1995, as a private-sector transportation wonk, I was asked to contribute to a policy project for the US Department of Transportation and the White House concerning the mobility needs of the US population, which was about to start aging rapidly. From the start, the tea leaves didn't look promising. In fact, they kind of resembled a mushroom cloud. The more I crunched the numbers, the more it became clear that we weren't ready for the baby boomers to grow old. Paratransit systems in cities and towns would be wholly inadequate to contend with the impending influx of aging boomers as they chose to limit their driving or lost the ability to drive. And in rural and suburban areas that lacked such services, the situation was substantially bleaker.

I was even more dismayed by the fact that we should have seen the flood coming: the aging of the boomers was perhaps the most predictable large historical event of the last century. Ever since the end of World War II, when Americans started procreating like they hadn't seen a member of the opposite sex in years—which was more or less the case during the war—demographers had preached that the oversized generation they produced would eventually turn grey in unison.

Now that that date had arrived, it was painfully obvious that little had been done in preparation.

But beyond the sheer inadequacy of the scope of our mobility systems, another issue began to trouble me. If you were lucky enough to have access to a municipal paratransit system, you could count on it for the kind of service I privately refer to as "mobility triage." It would readily take you to the grocery store and the doctor's office. But if you wanted to meet some friends for an ice cream cone, you'd better hope they could pick you up, because the system wouldn't take you there. (Even today, such "premium" trips, distinct from "priority" rides, must typically be booked too far in advance for anything resembling spontaneity.) That bothered me, because I like my ice cream. Life, liberty, and the pursuit of happiness are supposedly unalienable rights, but services for older people were only set up to support life. Liberty and happiness just weren't a priority.

For my contribution to the White House report, however, I had to focus on the issue at hand: the lack of seats in moving vehicles intended for older adults. The solution I proposed involved a sort of air traffic control for ground transportation, which would have allowed older adults to summon the closest vehicle in a roving fleet of taxis, vans, and buses. (The only thing missing was the technology needed to make it happen, which wouldn't arrive for another decade.) What I proposed might have addressed the scarcity issue—but still, the question of how nondriving older people could meet friends for ice cream vexed me. If you couldn't have fun once in a while, then even if you were living longer than generations past, you certainly wouldn't be living better.

After the paper was published, my phone rang. Yossi Sheffi, a professor and former military pilot who now headed the Massachusetts Institute of Technology (MIT) Center for Transportation & Logistics, was on the other end. He said he needed someone to manage the New England University Transportation Center, a Department of Transportation-funded research hub, and to teach some transportation courses. Was I interested? It meant a substantial pay cut, but I said yes without hesitation. (Well, some hesitation.) The fact was, we were looking at a demographic crisis, but I had a feeling there was a fix. We could invent our way out of it, and MIT was the key.

Consider radar, the safety razor, email, and the Internet Archive. The electronic spreadsheet, GPS, and concentrated soup. The transistor radio and the World Wide Web. All of these inventions owe part or all of their existence to MIT. It's where the "Tech" in Technicolor comes from. At MIT, we could rebuild old age. We had the technology. We could make it better than it was. We could take products that helped older people and ramp up their effectiveness—make them better, stronger, faster.

And so I left the private sector in great part because of what MIT offered: tomorrow's technology, now. If there were a way to get me to my ice cream at age 85, I figured, it would come only through technology. We could scale up and engineer our way out of the scarcity we were facing. And it was with that goal in mind that, two years after joining MIT, I founded the MIT AgeLab.

I can still remember the moment when I realized that engineering more of the same solutions wouldn't be enough. The year was 2004. Industry was beginning to increase its production of technologies for the older crowd, and the AgeLab had made a few of its own too. Together with my architect and designer friends Gui Trotti and Mickey Ackerman at the Rhode Island School of Design, we started developing gadgets and gadget ideas, such as a pen that could remind forgetful users of key information. We made a newfangled medication adherence tracker. We even prepared at one point to build a Furby- or Tamagotchi-esque virtual pet, which looked sort of like the furry Tribble of *Star Trek* lore, except with a small grayscale screen on one side. The idea behind PillPets, as we called them, was that they came in pairs. One went to a grandparent; its counterpart went to her grandchild. Every time Grandma took her medicine, she would get to virtually "feed" her PillPet—and if she didn't, both her PillPet *and* her grandchild's would get sadder, sicker, and eventually die. The idea was to tie emotion to medication compliance, but today I look back at that idea and wonder what we were thinking. Although it made sense on one level, it was also undeniably twisted! More important, I didn't recognize at the time that it was the sort of idea that comes out of the going narrative of old age, which was built on the assumption that the older population is, by its very nature, a problem. Only when you view older adults as something broken to be fixed, not human beings, does it make sense to treat the things that matter most in life, like family, merely as a means to a medical end.

The moment my perspective began to change was at a conference in Volterra, Italy, hosted by Pisa's Scuola Superiore Sant'Anna. The event, at which I'd been invited to speak, provided a wonderful excuse to visit one of the most beautiful cities in Europe, and I brought my family with me.

The day of my lecture, my friend Giuseppe Anerdi picked us up at our hotel in a green Alfa Romeo. From the start, we were running very late. Luckily, he was a former designer for Ferrari and he drove like it: first, through switchback after switchback in the rolling hills of Pisa, and then through the narrow streets of the city of Volterra itself. The roads in that beautiful, ancient community, which is the world's historic epicenter of alabaster goods, had developed organically over the course of centuries. As we screeched around impossibly tight corners, doing a solid impression of Michael Caine in *The Italian Job*, my eldest, in the backseat, turned a pale shade of green. And then biology took its course.

Finally, after driving on two wheels through a narrow alley, launching off a ramp, and performing an aerial barrel roll—that's what it felt like, anyway—we arrived at the lecture site, which was a medieval church: echoing, cavernous, and, on that sticky summer's day, noticeably unventilated. As I rushed up to the podium, hoping not to succumb to my own lingering carsickness, I observed the beauty of the setting in a detached way. All I remember from my time at the podium—which was actually a pulpit—was the sweat falling from my face and into my computer's keyboard.

At that moment, no one could have faulted me for saying that physical comfort was a more important design consideration than aesthetics. *Install air-conditioning ducts in every cathedral!*, I might have said. *Straighten out the roads of Volterra! Pave over the cobbles!*

And yet, it was in this place that I realized that that was the wrong approach. Volterra on a planned-out, grid system of roads just wouldn't have been Volterra, and ductwork would have ruined the soaring airiness of the church's architecture. Sometimes a comfort-at-all-cost approach does indeed come at too great a price.

But, unfortunately, that was exactly the sort of approach that the engineers at the Volterra conference were applying to technology for old age.

The principal theme of the conference was "domotics"—domestic robotics—which, as a field, was theoretically capable of providing improvements for all aspects of home life, from base-level needs like physical safety on up to higher-level desires such as active social lives, mental health, and productivity. That's what the high-tech, prototype "smart homes" of the time, such as the MIT's House of the Future project, proposed to accomplish for residents of all ages—allowing them to do things like consume and produce media throughout the home, learn a new language, prepare new meals, and move walls to do more with less space. Today, although companies are now rapidly churning out individual smart-home doodads, we're still only starting to understand how tomorrow's highly connected houses will coordinate their components and how the technologies involved will affect our daily lives. It's shaping up, like my family's trip through the streets of Volterra, to be a wild, bumpy ride.

But, in 2004, there was nothing exciting about the smart home for older adults, which, as conceived by virtually everyone discussing it at Volterra, would be less a tool to be used at the resident's discretion than a life-support system. It would be filled with pill reminders and telehealth devices, stroke rehab aids, smart scales, and stair lifts. Which was, in one sense, wonderful. Very often, the needs of people with disabilities get left behind in tech design, and here was an entire subfield devoted to finding solutions for them. But it was also disturbing, because it showed how utterly synonymous old age had become, in the minds of young, whip-smart engineers and designers, with its associated physiological and cognitive problems. Just like my experience in the senior transportation field, in senior tech there were well-intentioned provisions galore for the base-level, bodily needs of older adults. But if anyone wanted an ice cream? Forget it. The kinds of solutions being discussed sacrificed the experiences that make life worth living in order to keep people alive.

It's worth restating that within the tech sector and without, far more consideration is needed in product development and marketing for users with disabilities—something I delve into in the chapters ahead. But when it comes to users of old-age tech, the issue isn't that "disabled" is their assumed condition. It's that "managing disability" is their assumed *goal*—as opposed to getting out and doing things, despite disability. That's a crucial distinction.

For one thing, this framing limits creativity in terms of what you can do for older people with technology. At Volterra, there was absolutely no mention of the F-word: Fun. Or, equally concerning, the other F-word. Human sexuality doesn't fit into most young people's preordained, infantilizing idea of old age—at least, not until they get there themselves. And so, whenever younger engineers proudly unveil, say, a sensor that goes under someone's mattress that can send nighttime heart rate, breathing, and movement data to her doctor, many older members of the audience find themselves thinking about how disruptive such a device would be to their sex lives.

And, I thought, what about aesthetics? In a place like that church, in a city like Volterra, it was especially jarring to see presentations parading grey or beige, injection-molded plastic doodads with rounded edges, big buttons, and oversized displays that, in terms of overall design, resembled those gigantic universal remote controls advertised during *Golden Girls* reruns. Surrounding us, marble columns stretched heavenward, rhyming strength with beauty. And yet in their midst, the gadgets we were learning about threatened to whisper to their users every day: *You are frail. You are incompetent.*

In a small way, the conference's Italian setting may have helped explain some of the presenters' idea of old age. Italy was, and remains, the oldest-on-average major economy in the world after Japan. It's also, like Japan, a place where family matters. To the extent that it continues to survive, the Italian multigenerational household is a tremendous asset—in terms of both cultural value and as an institution for caregiving. But there is one issue that comes up as a result: many of the younger elder-tech designers and engineers I've met in Italy seem to envision solutions not for their own older selves tomorrow but rather for their parents and grandparents today—whom they often still live with, at least on the weekend. Such an approach leads to a grandchild's view of old age reflected in technology: a focus on frailty; an assumption of leisure, not professional or volunteer activities; and the presumption that the user is no longer motivated by the prospect of romance or sex. Worse, designing for today's older adults is tantamount to creating yesterday's solutions. One enormous challenge facing the elder-tech sector is to design for a hypothetical, future older user whose idea of old age may differ significantly from what's considered normal today.

Beyond Italy, the bias I observed in Volterra was, and remains, true of the entire field of technology for older adults. A simple textual analysis of article titles in *Gerontechnology,* the journal devoted to such developments, will illustrate what I mean. I used a computer program to count the words in the titles of every article ever published in *Gerontechnology* between its 2001 launch and the end of 2015. After excluding common words like "the" and process words like "survey" and "ask," I organized the hundred most commonly used words according to the levels of Abraham Maslow's "hierarchy of needs."

Maslow's hierarchy is a useful way of thinking about human needs that organizes them by priority. It's commonly depicted as a pyramid. At the bottom are base-level needs like food, shelter, and medicine.

Only by satisfying those needs, the reasoning goes, can you move up to the second level and start to think about your personal safety. Social issues like love and belonging can be found at the third level, and the esteem of oneself and others appears at the fourth. The fifth and highest level—at least in the pyramid's traditional formulation—concerns the need for self-actualization: in Maslow's words, "to become everything that one is capable of becoming."

Gerontechnology's article titles pertained to the bottom level of needs most often, with 15 out of the 100 most common words referencing issues like food, shelter, and medical health. ("Dementia" appeared 107 times.) The next rung of needs—safety—was represented by seven of these most-used words. Four words related to social life or love, and just one referred to self-regard or ambition. (The word was "active," and I could just as easily have filed it away as a base-level need.) None of the most commonly used terms could be said to have had anything to do with self-actualization.*

Put simply, the field of geriatric technology lavishes far more attention on basic needs like health and safety than higher-level needs like the desire for human connection, personal or professional ambition, contemplation, and yes, fun. It's the sort of imbalance that can occur when you throw technology at a problem without stepping back and asking, "Why this problem, in particular?" In the case of older adults, the answer to that question is straightforward: ever since the population of "the aged" was defined as a problem starting at the turn of the 20th century, it's been hard to imagine building products for them that don't *solve them* in some way. This framing affects the development of high and low-tech products alike. In a survey the AgeLab sent out to the MIT Sloan School of Management, we asked business students what would come to mind if they had to immediately come up with a product for older adults. Although there were a few intriguing

---

* For those doing the math, the remaining 77 words couldn't be categorized according to any level of Maslow's hierarchy.

answers—self-driving cars; "a product that helps bridge the computer technology gaps"—most fell into the same old categories of health and safety. Typical responses included: "Walker." "Dementia treatment." "An app for calling assistance to walker/wheelchair." "A multipurpose walking stick." "Adult diapers."

To anyone steeped in the notion that older adults are problems to be solved, these sorts of responses might not seem overly outrageous. But imagine if I gave business students a blank slate to imagine products for a different age group—teenagers, say—and the only products they could come up with were acne creams and crutches for when teens injure themselves performing ill-considered stunts. What a colossal failure of imagination that would be! And yet, the way we think about the wants and needs of older people is every bit as blindered.

The problem status of older adults even exerts an influence over the very intellectual field facing population aging. In books, a whole genre of apocalyptic titles has sprung up. The first modern book on the subject, by Ken Dychtwald, was 1990's *Age Wave*, and the ensuing years have seen the publication of titles like *Grey Dawn*, *Agequake*, *Seismic Shifts*, and *The Coming Generational Storm*. Meanwhile, in the news media, cataclysmic wave imagery is especially well represented. I've seen references to an old-age tsunami, silver tsunami, grey tsunami, senior tsunami, and a demographic tsunami.

I don't fault anyone for turning to metaphor to illustrate an abstract phenomenon, but the trend at work here troubles me. Images used to illustrate demographic transition tend to take the form of big, inexorable, and often disastrous forces of nature. Most important, the meteorological or seismographic force in question is always *sudden*. There's a reason for that: it presents the slow creep of demographic change as something urgent that society could react to, if we only set our minds to it. We can drop what we're doing and fight back a river overrunning its banks, the reasoning goes, so why not a demographic crisis? Unsurprisingly, most books on the subject propose specific policy solutions: *The Coming Generational Storm* is adamantly pro-austerity, while others suggest smaller legislative steps. (The pioneering works of Ken and Maddie Dychtwald, a welcome exception, offer insights for the private sector.) On the whole, the recommendations made in this body of literature tend to fit the mold of top-down, pragmatic, incremental problem-solving strategies that work well in a flood or snowstorm. But demographic transition isn't the kind of thing you can solve by alerting the mayor—or even the president.

In fact, the real issue is the very reflex that causes us to envision "the aged" as a problem. The world is brimming over with phenomena that are constantly conspiring to kill us, and the extra decades we now enjoy represent a triumph of human ingenuity over nature, red in tooth and claw. But ever since we were taught to view longer life as a burden, not a gift, innovation around old age—in products, research, and policy—has been motivated mainly by the instinct to ease that perceived load, not make the most of a long, possibility-filled stage of life. And in fairness, it's easy to see why this approach has prevailed for so long. The alternative—favoring high-level desires like fun over physiological needs like medicine—seems frivolous, even dangerous. (You can't eat ice cream if you're dead, after all.) And yet, in practice, ignoring high-level desires can have a toxic effect on life in old age. Not only does it set up later life as unappealing, it even diminishes the efficacy of health and safety innovations.

Consider a classic technology aimed at the base of Maslow's pyramid: the hearing aid. In a very real sense, hearing aids work only 20 percent of the time. Now, that's not to say that hearing aids aren't perfectly functional as pieces of electronics. They are—and they're becoming more so every year. But only 20 percent of people in the United States who need hearing aids seek them out, a disturbingly low number that doesn't even include those who have hearing aids but don't wear them (a group that accounts for between 5 and 24 percent of hearing-aid owners). There are a few reasons people put off acquiring hearing aids—even those who wear them report delaying obtaining them for 10 years on average—but the main reason is that they simply don't want them.* And for all practical purposes, that's just as bad a malfunction as if 80 percent of hearing aids were to spew black smoke from people's ears. The *function* of hearing aids is not just to amplify signals entering the ear canal. Their real purpose is to help people with hearing loss live their lives however they see fit—and if those people decide that wearing (or being seen wearing) hearing aids gets in the way of that goal, then it should come as no surprise when they choose to forego them. In such cases, the higher-level desire to look and feel a certain way overpowers the base-level physiological need to maximize one's ability to hear.

Now compare hearing aids to eyeglasses. They have a lot in common: hearing aids clarify soft, fuzzy sounds, while glasses clarify soft, fuzzy images. And, yes, although more young people wear glasses than hearing aids, both become increasingly necessary with advancing age. But unlike hearing aids, glasses have it both ways: they solve a physiological problem, and they're also a desirable, high-fashion accessory. The difference has everything to do with the marketing, design, branding, and overall impression given by the technology. When was the last time you saw a Ralph Lauren or Prada-brand hearing aid? Alternately, suppose, starting tomorrow, all eyeglasses were made of flesh-colored plastic, like many hearing aids. I'd buy stock in 1-800 CONTACTS!

Meanwhile, I'm intrigued by the growing field of "hearables"— wearable technologies for the ears that stand to blur the line between hearing aids, headphones, and Bluetooth headsets. Since 2014, the Starkey Halo brand of hearing aids, by Starkey Hearing Technologies, has allowed users to pipe music and telephone audio directly into their hearing aids, no extra earbuds required. The codec that made that possible over a low-energy Bluetooth connection now resides in Apple's own wireless earbuds, the AirPods. The Here One Listening System, meanwhile, developed by Doppler Labs, a company best known for

---

* Another important reason is cost, but even in the UK, where hearing aids are paid for by the National Health Service, adoption is only 14 percent higher than in the US.

producing high-end earplugs, comes in the form of a pair of fashionable, black, electronic earbuds that are designed to reduce the volume at loud music events without a loss of sound quality. They can also increase overall volume or fine-tune the frequencies of environmental sounds via a smartphone app. Should people across age groups begin to use such augmented hearing devices commonly—simply as Bluetooth headphones, to interact with personal digital assistants like Siri and Cortana, to filter out the background sounds in crowded bars, or to tune out coworkers in shared offices and coffee shops—then hearing aids with similar functionality could rapidly lose their stigma or even become fully subsumed into the category of multifunctional hearables.

For now, however, the hearing aid remains a tough sell. But at the same time, it could be worse. Hearing aids are a resounding success compared to many other products for older adults that have been proposed and even put into production, starting many decades ago.

Epic Fails

The first complaint that advocates for older adults register about consumer-facing businesses is that companies don't seem to want older people as customers. They often design for younger presumed users or market their products only to young people. The worst part is that they don't seem to get that older people matter. In the school of product design and development for old age, these types of companies are the truants and dropouts. But even among those who do come to class, it's still possible to get an F. Such companies understand the power of the "senior market," as it's so frequently called, and actively seek to tap its wealth. But their products are built according to the prevailing narrative of old age: that to be old is to be a pitiable bundle of needs, and solving those needs alone—not upper-level desires—is good enough.

The quintessential example of a company's failure to understand older consumers took place in 1955. Denture wearers had been observed purchasing Gerber baby food for themselves because it was cheap and easy to eat, and so Heinz, the ketchup and canned-food goliath, decided to give them what they seemed to want: pre-chewed food. As *Time* magazine reported that year:

> Unlike the nation's babies, whose special requirements rolled up sales of $200 million in baby foods last year, US oldsters have no line of food especially designed for them (although a few specialty items are on the market). Last week Pittsburgh's H. J. Heinz Co. ("57 Varieties") announced a new line of canned foods for people over 60, said it will begin test-marketing it next month in Cincinnati, which has one of the highest concentrations of older people in the US. Heinz "Senior Foods" will be sold in single-serving, 8½-oz. cans, are expected to retail for 25¢ to 30¢. First varieties available: beef, lamb and chicken stews.

Heinz started developing Senior Foods in the late 1940s, and it wasn't alone in its approach. Following World War II, dairy giant Borden had introduced Gerilac, a spray-dried, milk-based nutritional supplement for older adults. By the time Heinz made its move in 1955, Gerilac had already failed. Perhaps the issue was that its "pleasant, bland taste," which the company boasted about in its advertisements, did little to stir the hearts of potential customers. Or perhaps it was that those ads implied that its older customers were too poor to afford real food. ("What Aid For the Lean Purse?" one advertisement wondered, before admonishing the reader to "Remember, Gerilac is economical because it doesn't have to be mixed with milk.")

But by 1955 as now, industry saw the rising demographic tide of older adults as a gold mine, and Heinz thought it had a way in. "By 1960," *Time* reported, "there will be 23 million people over 60 in the US. While a baby eats baby food for only about two years, an oldster could be a consumer of the new product for 15 years or more."

Despite all that demographic promise, what ensued was a major flop. Heinz scientists had spent nearly a decade developing Senior Foods, and the company had launched a well-publicized national rollout campaign. Still, jars of Senior Foods sat on store shelves, untouched. The reason came down to plausible deniability. In theory, any older adult buying Gerber baby food could have been purchasing it for a grandchild. But the same couldn't be said for Senior Foods. The act of taking Senior Foods up to the kid at the checkout counter was tantamount to a public shaming ritual. *Here I am,* the jars of stew seemed to say, *old, poor, and my teeth don't work.*

Just as important, the stews seemed gross. Heinz did its best to suggest ways to improve the appearance of the stuff: putting a lemon wedge on top added "zip to the dish," the company claimed. Chefs of even greater ambition could create the visual spectacle Heinz dubbed "Pinwheel Stew" by topping the canned gruel "with fresh or broiled tomato wedges arranged in pinwheel fashion." Heinz soon discontinued the line.

The company's experience didn't prevent Gerber itself, whose canned baby foods had inspired Senior Foods, from trying to expand into the adult market in 1974, however. Gerber Singles, as the offering was known, cannily refrained from calling out its consumers as "seniors" or "grey"—many marketing materials claimed the stuff was for college students and other single adults—but the result was the same. The ensuing flop is often mentioned as a classic example of brand failure.

These cases—Heinz's in particular—often come up as examples of how, in order to attract the older consumer, it can be helpful to market products in an age-agnostic way or even explicitly depict a younger crowd using them. Frankly—and this may rankle those who bemoan the lack of older faces in advertisements—this theory is often true. An axiom commonly attributed to at least two American auto executives from the 1950s and 1960s holds that "You can sell a young man's car to an old man, but you cannot sell an old man's car to a young man"—because not only will the young man refuse to buy it, but then his father or grandfather won't buy it either. Because old age has so many deep, negative associations, this theory goes, products that are explicitly aimed at the older user usually end up insulting and alienating the very people they're trying to woo.

But actually, perception is only part of the breakdown. The bigger issue is that solving older adults' base-level physiological needs at the expense of all other considerations leads, quite simply, to bad products.

Lynn Townsend Jr., one of those two auto execs said to have come up with the "old-man's car" quote, knew that lesson intimately. In the years before he assumed leadership at Chrysler, the company was very much in the business of building and marketing "old man's cars," and sales were flagging. TV ads in 1958 for DeSoto, one of Chrysler's makes, were hosted by a 68-year-old Groucho Marx, and emphasized not the cars' performance but rather their ease of use. "You don't have to strain to see those high traffic lights," Groucho assures the viewer. The power steering "does all the 'woik.'" The push-button gear control is the "simplest, most dependable," ever made, and the engine is "lighter, quieter, and thriftier."

But while Chrysler was making cars quiet, easy, and thrifty, competitors were pushing the envelope in terms of performance factors like acceleration and handling. As a result, the *New York Times* reported at the time, Chrysler's "car quality and profits fell," and for a moment it seemed like George Romney's American Motors would overtake Chrysler as the third-largest auto manufacturer in the United States.

When Townsend took over at Chrysler in 1961, however, he shifted the focus from ease-of-use to performance. The first line of cars that he influenced, with the help of a new lead designer he'd won over from Ford, were the 1963 models. These were considered to be of higher quality and featured more consistent, utilitarian design than prior model years. (One thing Townsend became known for was removing tailfins from his company's cars, which had grown increasingly cartoonish in appearance as the 1950s drew to a close.) Meanwhile, in an effort to win the Daytona 500, Chrysler engineers reintroduced a powerful engine type whose pistons had hemispherical heads. Chrysler's "Hemi," as it became known, developed a reputation for high performance and was included in many of the company's new offerings. In the process, Chrysler morphed in the public eye. The company that was once the go-to source for big, slow, easy-to-use cars, whose rococo styling added nothing in terms of performance, transformed into a modernized purveyor of sleek American muscle. In the early 1960s, sales of what were no longer "old man's cars" took off. By 1965, Chrysler's share of the US auto market, as a proportion of its 1961 share, had increased by 40 percent, while Ford's share dropped slightly and General Motors' rose by 9 percent. Chrysler owed its success to other factors too: Townsend changed the company's relationship with dealers, for instance, and the early 1960s were boom years for the US auto industry in general. But most important was the fact that Townsend's new cars flew out of dealer lots. During that time, the company's net earnings increased from $11 million to $233 million.

Something similar happened with Heinz, except there was no silver lining for Senior Foods. It wasn't enough that the marketing department identified Senior Foods as the culinary equivalent of the proverbial "old man's car." Compounding the effect was the fact that, like Chrysler's late-1950s', low-performance behemoths, Heinz's product was simply subpar, prioritizing mushiness above all else. (Heinz's suggested recipes, such as "pinwheel stew," didn't do much to help.) By viewing older people purely in terms of their stereotypical problems—dental issues, limited income—Heinz managed to lose sight of the main factor that motivates food buyers: taste.

Senior Foods didn't just fail as a product, sending Heinz scurrying back to ketchup. In its brief tenure, Senior Foods also managed to help poison cultural attitudes toward aging. Even though the vast majority of people who saw Senior Foods on store shelves decided not to buy them, those jars still broadcast a worldview: being a "senior" meant you couldn't chew your food and didn't care about flavor.

If Heinz alone had presented older people in this way, the damage would have been limited. But by the 1950s and 1960s, industries had already internalized the dominant narrative of age. They understood that older people made up a monolithic mass, needy and greedy, always consuming and never producing. And when they tried to sell products based on this set of "facts," it only reinforced the narrative in the culture at large. *If this is what Heinz, a trusted, well-known brand, thinks of older people,* a rational person might have thought, *then this view of older people must be normal.*

Perhaps the single most powerful example of marketing that reinforces a harmful image of old age is series of television commercials that have been airing for over 20 years. Most US residents will recognize their catchphrase: "I've fallen and I can't get up!" I have all sorts of issues with these commercials, originally produced by the company LifeCall and now Life Alert. However, the product advertised—a neck pendant that summons emergency services with the push of a button—is undeniably helpful. The personal emergency response system (PERS), as this type of device is known, works reliably. Introduced in the United States in 1974, it is hardly a new idea. And yet, like the hearing aid, there's a problem. No one wants one.

In 1992, just over 1 percent of the 65-plus population in the United States subscribed to personal emergency response services. By 2004, that number had swelled to . . . just over 2 percent. Even if the market were limited to those 65 and older living alone with a disability, the market penetration of PERS that year would still have been just 17 percent—similar to that of hearing aids. Meanwhile, even in personal-tech-loving Japan, only 1 percent of the 65-plus population used the technology. Part of the issue may have been cost, but if so, it was only a small part. In the United Kingdom, where the National Health Service footed the bill for consumers, the adoption rate was the highest of any country. But still, it was a lackluster 16 percent.

If the problem wasn't cost, it may have been that older consumers wanted not merely to stay alive but to *have a life*. It's hard to be sociable, have fun, and do things with friends when you have a testament to your impending mortality hanging around your neck like an albatross.

How can companies convince older consumers to act in their best interest and obtain a PERS? One solution that immediately comes to mind—perhaps *too* immediately—is to camouflage the device. A number of companies that have emerged in recent years have found ways to build emergency response functionality into jewelry, such as necklaces and bracelets. The impulse to do this is understandable—if users are embarrassed to be seen wearing a white, vaguely medical-looking doodad, then simply hide the device in something more attractive. But this approach misses the greater point: if you're an independent older person, it doesn't matter whether the rest of the world knows that a certain piece of jewelry can summon an ambulance. What matters is that *you* know it.

According to a 2009 Pew poll, only 35 percent of people over 75 said they felt "old." And that's a problem, because 100 percent of people understand that personal emergency response pendants are for old people. When a product is for "old people," and the user, whatever her age, doesn't think of herself as "old," she's not going to buy it. Maybe her kid will buy it for her, maybe against her wishes. But even in those cases, the user isn't likely to be personally invested in using that device every day, and so its efficacy will suffer. A 2010, German study determined that nearly a quarter of PERS subscribers never wear their alarm button, and only 14 percent wear it 24 hours per day. Most troubling, when subscribers fell and remained on the floor for longer than five minutes, they failed to use their devices to summon help 83 percent of the time.

And so, despite the demographic surge in their favor, I'm not particularly bullish on the future of PERS, disguised or not. Worst of all, on top of all the reasons people choose not to subscribe to PERS services, a cell phone can now accomplish most of what a Life Alert system can do. Sure, a single-button neck pendant will be easier to operate in a health emergency than a phone in your pocket. But that's assuming you're actually wearing, and are willing to operate, your PERS device. Even though a PERS alarm is arguably the easiest product to use in the *event* of an emergency, the cell phone is, I would argue, a better *emergency technology* for the simple reason that people actually go out of their way to own them, carry them on their person, and use them. The cell phone represents everything that a PERS alarm doesn't. Where the PERS signifies a decline into isolated dependency, a cell phone equates to a healthy social network at one's fingertips. As of 2014, 77 percent of US residents aged 65 and up own cell phones.

But even the design of cell phones themselves can suffer from an outdated way of thinking about the needs of older adults. For one notable flop, consider the Katharina das Große phone, by the small German company Fitage. The phone, introduced in 2007, was named after Catherine the Great and was, like the legacy of its namesake, large—"gigantisch," said German magazine *Focus*. (Its rubberized buttons were large as well, which always seems to be the first "innovation" tech developers come up with for older users.) All told, it looked more like a cordless landline phone from the 1990s than a cell phone. Although it was easy to use for simple phone calls, people didn't want to carry it around or be seen with it. A typical Amazon review,* written by a woman who bought the phone for her 77-year-old mother who had age-related macular degeneration, read: "Katharina is very robust, has buttons that are easy to feel, is very good to read and easy to use—nothing amiss." However, "Katharina is so big and heavy—it doesn't fit into a purse or into a jacket pocket—that my mother is having trouble accepting it, because it is obviously made for 'disabled people.' Effect: The phone will be left at home."

In 2010, Fitage went out of business. Meanwhile, Katharina's American cousin-in-spirit, the Jitterbug phone by GreatCall, has seen more success. But there is another entrant in the age-friendly-phone market that is now threatening to take over: the smartphone.

---

* Translated from German.

How can the smartphone be considered age-friendly? First, put aside the notion that older people fear technology. That used to be true, but it was more a matter of timing than anything that has innately to do with age. When the first personal computers arrived in workplaces, baby boomers had to learn to use them, while many others a decade or two older managed to slip into retirement without ever operating a PC. As a result, the Greatest and Silent generations earned a reputation for tech-phobia—in no small part because they had the misfortune of retiring just before, or while, computers were becoming omnipresent at work. But now the baby boom generation, which has used computers for much of its professional life and is also completely at home with smartphones and tablets, is marching steadily into the older age ranges. Its relationship with technology is utterly different than that of any other generation that has ever grown old. Companies that grasp this new set of facts stand to benefit enormously. Meanwhile, those that continue to treat older adults as incurable tech novices are about to enter a world of pain.

In 2000, only 14 percent of older Americans used the Internet. That number has since quadrupled, and it continues to climb. As of 2016, 58 percent of those aged 50–64 own a smartphone, as do 30 percent of those 65 and older, rates more than double what they were five years earlier. Beyond smartphones, the 2016 consumer-tech-ownership figures for those aged 50–64 and 65-plus are, respectively, 37 and 32 percent for tablets, 30 and 8 percent for game consoles, and 70 and 55 percent for desktop or laptop computers. They seem to enjoy their Internet devices more than other generations: 82 percent of older smartphone owners described their smartphone as "freeing," compared with 64 percent of those in their late teens and early 20s. The reason may be simple. When your options for connecting to others, such as driving into town and going to school or work, begin to disappear with age, technologies that enable human connection become all the more valuable.

Tomorrow's most successful products for the older consumer will feature high technology or else will embrace a consumer for whom tech is an important part of life. Yes, for a time, there will probably still be need for simplified phones. Today, some companies are even producing simplified smartphones, something of an oxymoron. But soon, as the older age ranges fill with tech-fluent consumers, the market for these devices will be limited to users with health issues that prevent the operation of a normal smartphone, such as cognitive or tactile function problems. And in the near future, voice-command interfaces will become so effective that many people who experience, say, hand tremors, will likely choose to navigate a full-fledged smartphone with their voices rather than buy a lesser phone that eschews the connected world. That will mean that, far from granting "independence to active seniors"—a typical tagline for these sorts of products—the use of "senior phones" will occur mainly among people with cognitive issues. That's still an incredibly important market to serve. But, contrary to popular belief—59 percent of people around the world erroneously think that Alzheimer's disease, the most prevalent form of dementia, is a normal part of aging—dementia is far less common in old age than the absence of it. Even among those 85 and older, two-thirds of people don't have dementia. When faced with a product that feels like it's intended for those who do have mild dementia, the bulk of the older market will run in the other direction.

But in the meantime, companies will continue marketing "senior phones" in exactly the same way that Heinz marketed "Senior Foods": by hawking a subpar product that publicly announces its users as incapable. Perhaps what irritates me most about simplified cell phones is that these devices diminish a technology that is supposed to connect people. The worst perpetrator is the three-button phone: the kind that dials home, the ambulance, the operator—and that's it. Perhaps no technology has ever been more influenced by our going narrative of old age. The cell phone, a technology originally designed to allow us to talk to each other at all times, now serves to cordon off the user by keeping older people separate from everyone except the handful of people who serve as lifelines. In a sad twist, because you're safer with your new phone, your kids may call less often to check in on you. You may no longer need to move to a community where you can spend time with friends. To return to Maslow's hierarchy, this type of technology takes care of base-level needs very effectively—at the expense of everything else.

Technology is perhaps the most important force that will make life better in the coming decades, and the idea that older adults could be left out of the march of progress would be laughable if it weren't so concerning. Maybe there was once a time when the three-button-cell-phone-for-Grandma made sense, in some cases. But that time is nearly gone. The onus is now on tech designers to come up with fully functional technologies that will excite and delight young and older users alike. As I'll explain in the coming chapters, there will still be major challenges to overcome in designing for older users, starting with considerations of accessibility, not to mention the decades' worth of accumulated mental models that older generations bring to bear on new technologies. But it will no longer be good enough to sacrifice functionality for accessibility. From here on out, it will be necessary, from a tech-design perspective, to make sure that people of all generations can use the full-fledged version of technologies.

Stuck in a Rut

Whether the tech industry is prepared to design for consumers' entire life spans isn't even a question. It isn't. It isn't even close to ready to think about what older adults want.

One of the most frustrating catch-22s about the dominant narrative of old age is that, thanks to the institution of retirement, older adults are kept out of economic production roles, which means they're not only prevented from making money but also from designing products: home goods, financial products, airplane seats—you name it. The fact that younger people hold the reins of production is a major reason why so many products aimed at older adults fail to take into account the nuances of older life.

But in one industry more than any other, the young truly run the show. And unfortunately, it happens to be the one that is every day determining the shape of life tomorrow: the consumer tech industry.

Tech firms are far younger than the general workforce. Labor market researchers PayScale assessed the median age of workers at the world's top tech companies between 2014 and 2015. According to their analysis, only 3 of 18 top companies have a median age of 36 or higher; the value for the overall US workforce, meanwhile, is 42.3. More concerning, it's the older tech companies—the HPs, Oracles, and IBMs of the world—that have the (relatively) older employees. Younger companies, including the ones responsible for some of the 21st century's most world-changing innovations, have the youngest employees of all. Google and Amazon have median ages of 30, and Facebook's is 29. As Facebook founder Mark Zuckerberg infamously said in 2007, "Young people are just smarter." Why, the then–22-year-old wondered, "are most chess masters under 30? I don't know. Young people just have simpler lives. We may not own a car. We may not have family."

As a result of the pervasive ageist atmosphere in Silicon Valley, the local cosmetic surgery industry is experiencing a bonanza. In an April 2014 issue of *The New Republic*, labor reporter and then-senior-editor Noam Scheiber described a 26-year-old Silicon Valley worker who came into a plastic surgeon's office in search of hair transplants. "I told him I wouldn't let him. His hair pattern isn't even established," the surgeon said.

Silicon Valley's age bias is not limited to the people it hires but also extends to the companies that receive venture funding. Paul Graham, a founder of famed start-up accelerator Y Combinator, said in 2012 that he could "be tricked by anyone who looks like Mark Zuckerberg." In 2010, out of 114 companies that received early-stage, angel funding, half of venture funding went to founders between ages 35 and 44.

Founders younger than 35 received twice as much as those over 45. And since, as Scheiber reported, founders age 45 and older are responsible for half of all start-ups, older tech founders are presumably competing for a pool of money that is effectively much smaller than that available to younger entrepreneurs.

That's just in the United States. In other countries with burgeoning tech scenes, such as South Korea, the ageism can be even worse. Although South Korea finally banned overt workplace age discrimination in 2010, traditionally, in an attempt to maintain hierarchical order at companies, Korean recruiters have refused to help older job seekers, and the practice has proven difficult to eject.

All told, the global economic climate, including but not limited to the tech sector, is simply not set up to produce the things and services that older adults want. Even less likely to be created are the sorts of truly revolutionary innovations that older adults don't yet *know* they'll want. And if industry has failed in this regard, government is just as complicit.

When industry can't or won't invest in work that's needed for the common good, government must step in. It's a clichéd example, but there was no way any private-sector entity could have financed the Apollo Moon missions, let alone undertaken the logistics required. That was a job for the US government. Even today's private-sector, for-profit spaceflight companies only reached their current heights by standing on the shoulders of NASA and the spaceflight agencies of other nations.

Perhaps more importantly, when it's not clear how we, as a society, will address a problem, government plays an essential role in normalizing certain kinds of solutions. Between the 1920s and 1950s, for example, the US government had to choose between train travel and the automobile. It made its choice, and today most of us drive to work. Unfortunately, however, when it comes to old age, government and the private sector alike are stuck in the railroad era. (Both figuratively and literally, considering our narrative of old age originated in the mid-1800s.) And once government figures out a way of doing something, it tends to stay stuck in that solution category.

In 1995, way back when I was still working on my elder transportation project for the White House Office of Science and Technology Policy, I was charged with bringing disparate government agencies into the same room to talk about the issue. But when the two agencies—Health and Human Services and the Department of Transportation—came in, they each sat at opposite sides of a long table, like rival factions in peace talks that might turn hostile. There were, and remain, deep differences between the two entities. At the risk of oversimplifying the situation, Health and Human Services, which is devoted to, well, health, viewed elder transport mainly in terms of the need to ferry patients to their doctors via wheelchair-accessible vans. The Department of Transportation, meanwhile, simply hoped to fit more people into existing public transit systems. The meeting went horribly. The two groups talked at cross-purposes and could agree on nothing actionable. One member of the "action" group, as it was called, literally fell asleep at the table with his mouth agape, wheezing softly.

All told, it was the most boring standoff I'd ever seen. It was also a microcosmic version of how government as a whole is stuck in a rut regarding old age. Overall, US government policy, which developed in lockstep with our current, dominant narrative of age, continues to treat the older population uniformly as impoverished medical patients. Even the transportation meeting I put together had to be chaired by a medical doctor, or it couldn't have happened. *Older-equals-patient* is simply a state of affairs the government takes for granted—and it's been that way for a long time.

After 1935, which saw the passage of the Social Security Act, the most important year for US legislative action concerning older adults was 1965, when Congress signed into law both Medicare, a single-payer insurance system for those over 65, and the Older Americans Act, a sort of omnibus law that included various antipoverty and antiabuse measures while also prioritizing, at least on paper, the "pursuit of meaningful activity" for older adults. That year, the Older Americans Act's various provisions were allotted funds totaling $7.5 million. Medicare, meanwhile, received one billion dollars. The implication was clear: government would support older adults in terms of health-care and poverty relief. All other considerations were subordinate.

I don't in any way mean to denigrate any of the crucial legislative achievements of Medicare and Social Security. They're extraordinarily important, and I don't want to live, or grow old, in a world without them. And indeed, although "a world without them" has long seemed an unlikely hypothetical, it is all too easy for politicians to become complacent on elder issues. (For one example, take Australian Prime Minister Tony Abbott, who simply neglected to fill the vital post of Minister for Ageing during his two years in office.)

But still, the way that programs for older adults' health and poverty relief dwarf all other policy concerns reinforces the idea that to be old is to be sick and poor. Policy is how government's conception of reality filters out to the public, and old-age policy, so essential to so many, is perhaps one of the most potent reality-dissemination machines of all. Unfortunately, as Caroll Estes, an important, critical voice in gerontology, writes, despite doing good work, "special policies and programs segregate and stigmatize the aged."

If businesses and policymakers alike are stuck in their respective, self-reinforcing modes of thought, what will it take to break free? What will it take to make liberty and the pursuit of happiness not just possible in old age, but normal?

A Way Forward

By the late aughts, the AgeLab pivoted away from producing health-care gadgets.

The big shift took place in 2007. Cédric Hutchings, an AgeLab master's student who hailed from France, had designed a barcode scanner that analyzed the nutritional value of food for grocery shoppers before they put a given item into their carts. I wholeheartedly endorsed the idea, because skyrocketing type-2 diabetes rates were emerging as a major threat to long-term well-being around the world. Maybe, our thinking went, we could help by making it easy for people to shop for low-glycemic-index food.

Not only did I think it was a great idea—so did Procter & Gamble (P&G), an AgeLab sponsor. So, to test out the Smart Personal Advisor (we immediately nicknamed it the SmartCart) we flew out to P&G's home in Cincinnati, Ohio, where the company had assured us we could put the device through its paces. Soon, we pulled up in our rental car to a nondescript-looking, brick-and-aluminum warehouse in the suburbs nearby. In the lobby, a lone security guard gave a bored glance at our credentials and then pointed at one of two identical doorways. I pushed it open.

Inside, taking up far more space than the exterior suggested, we discovered a massive, gleaming, fully stocked grocery store, utterly devoid of people. This was P&G's testing ground. (The other door, I'd later discover, led to a similarly deserted drugstore.)

As soon as we began consumer trials there, it became clear that we'd made a wrong turn somewhere. Again and again—so many times that it hurt—testers told us that the SmartCart wasn't . . . bad, exactly. But why didn't it tell them the one thing they really wanted to know about their groceries: the price?

The answer was simple: We'd made a mistake. We'd been caught thinking of older people only as patients, not consumers. (Worse, unbeknownst to us, the advent of the smartphone was about to obviate our SmartCart, anyway.) Today, Cédric is better known as the cofounder and CEO of Withings, a consumer electronics company currently making some of the most innovative and empathetically designed wearable and quantified-self technologies on the market. The AgeLab, meanwhile, has changed direction, leaving the production of gadgets to professionals like Cédric, while we study what's going on in the heads of today's and tomorrow's older adults—especially as they shop for and use new technologies and other products. Nearly 10 years later, if there's one takeaway from our shopping cart detour, it's this: except when they're acutely necessary to keep someone alive, consumers will reject products that treat older people merely as medical problems to be solved. They don't see themselves that way, and products that reflect that point of view come across at best as alien and, at worst, alienating. Rather, older adults see themselves for what they are: human beings with the full range of wants and needs described in Maslow's hierarchy, the top half of which is presently being neglected.

If you're still not convinced that it makes sense for industry (and government and the nonprofit sector) to attempt to satisfy these sorts of desires, I understand your rationale. The frugally responsible way for a society to deal with a problem population is to focus on its existential needs, not its frivolous wants. But in the case of older adults, the time to deal with those higher-level desires—including love, sex, self-esteem, and personal and professional ambition—never seems to come up. And as a result, we find ourselves living out a vision of later life where liberty and the pursuit of happiness always seem to be just out of reach.

That needs to change. And here's the counterintuitive thing: satisfying those high-level desires will make it easier to turn around and solve base-level needs as well. The first step is to understand what older consumers truly want.

Unfortunately, businesses, especially the youthful tech sector, don't have the requisite knowledge. They don't know what makes older consumers tick today, let alone in the hazy future. Many of these organizations turn to the AgeLab for answers. We help them to the best of our ability. But even I don't know exactly what will motivate older people tomorrow, because most older adults don't know it themselves.

But there are some who do. There is a group of consumers living out on the cutting edge of age. They're intimately acquainted with the real challenges that can pop up in later life as well as what can go right. And yet—insanely—this group is grossly underrepresented in the sorts of critical industry positions that have the potential to change the business of old age.

The people I'm talking about are women of middle age and older. Speaking generally, female consumers will define the future of old age through their personal experiences, insights, and economic demand. More specifically, within that number, there is a select set of entrepreneurs—independent operators as well as innovators within larger organizations—with the insights needed to guide us toward a radical, improved vision of later life. In the next chapter, I'll explain who they are, where their insights will come from, and why the future will be grey, female, and proud of it.

3

The Future Is Female

IT WAS SEVEN o'clock on a Wednesday night at Rockwell Table and Stage, a Los Angeles cocktail lounge, and Kathie, 60, was nervously checking her phone. It was hard to say why she felt so anxious. After all, she'd been on online dates before. She was dressed to kill. And the evening's entertainment promised to be stupendous: Jeff Goldblum, star of such films as *Jurassic Park* and *The Fly*, was due onstage at eight, where he would play jazz piano with his five-piece band.

But still, this time she'd really put herself out there. The thought of being stood up in this venue, on this night, would be the kind of defeat it would be hard to bounce back from.

She hadn't even wanted to move to California. She and her husband had raised their daughter in New Jersey. But when their kid decided to go to college in San Francisco, Kathie and her husband followed westward. They bought a 6,000-square-foot home near Pasadena. Shortly thereafter, he ended their 30-year marriage. And so the online dating began.

"I knew I was sad. I knew something was missing," she said. "I thought it was a relationship. I thought it was a boyfriend or a man."

She also knew that there were far more women than men over 50 who were looking for partners of the same age, so she decided to treat

87

online dating like the real estate market. "You put your house onto multiple listings. So I went on all the dating sites. I joined eHarmony. I joined Match. I joined all of them." As she dated, she found that the men she met were often seeking different results from the experience than she was. "Men don't seem to change. I don't care if they're impotent or not, they still want to have sex before they have anything else," she said. Although she had several female friends with no qualms regarding that approach to romance, it wasn't what she personally was looking for. What she really missed was having someone to talk to, watch TV with, and accompany her on trips. But it seemed like the only way to find that person was by way of a passionate love affair. "I didn't really want to date, but I was feeling so lonely," she said.

Around that same time, Kathie found herself attending a local cabaret where a rotating cast of young, talented men, most of whom were gay, sang every night. She was enthralled by the sheer, raw talent emanating from the intimate stage and would go twice a week or more. She wasn't the only one who noticed the performers' panache and skill. That year, several of the club's recurring entertainers signed on to compete on the eighth season of *American Idol*, and one of them, Adam Lambert, made it to the final round. The regulars at Kathie's lounge were abuzz with the news of Lambert's success, and she volunteered to host a viewing party of the season finale. Lambert lost but wound up the season's biggest star anyway. More importantly, the party was such a triumph, and her guests had such a good time, that some of the performers joked about moving in with her. She surprised them by telling them to go right ahead—and soon, she was serving as den mother and too-generous landlady to as many as six young men at a time, including one of the cabaret's producers. "We became a very close family, celebrating holidays and birthdays and everything else," she said. "I had a Breathalyzer that I would use if I thought anyone had been drinking too much to drive. That always caused a little friction, but truly, we all got along famously."

Even later, after she'd downsized her home and the cabaret migrated to a larger venue, she kept in touch with them. It was through these showbiz connections that she'd come to know about Jeff Goldblum's piano performances—a weekly gig, and a reliably wonderful night out. "He's so quirky, and so funny, but he just commands the stage," she said. By now, she was trying out a new dating site: Stitch.net, a start-up that catered exclusively to the 50-plus crowd. She decided that one of Goldblum's performances would be the perfect way to bring out the fun in whomever she met on Stitch.

Once she set up the date online, her friends worked behind the scenes to reserve her the best table in the house, right in front of the stage. She sincerely appreciated the special treatment, but there was one small drawback. If she did get stood up—not uncommon, in her experience of online dating—it would be in front of both her friends and Jeff Goldblum. That would be beyond mortifying.

And indeed, for a moment that Wednesday night, the worst seemed possible. Kathie arrived early to reassure herself that everything was proceeding as planned. But soon she was sitting alone at her prominent, empty table, fidgeting, thinking about what might have gone wrong.

Then, finally, her dates began to arrive—all seven of them, all women.

The Ultimate Consumer

As I've discussed in prior chapters, products for older people tend to reflect an arbitrary, outdated narrative of how old age should progress. Today, however, the experience of old age is changing. A new class of people is noticing that the 20th-century story of how to live after age 50 or 60 is no guarantee of satisfaction in later life. And so they are striking out on their own. They're finding new ways to live and new ways to support those narrative twists—sometimes with the help of cutting-edge new products and sometimes, when the cutting edge isn't sharp enough, by creating their own.

This pioneering consumer class has a few salient characteristics. It controls vast swathes of personal wealth. It's innately tech-fluent.

And, because it's made up mainly of baby boomers, it's been long accustomed to shaping the economic and physical world around it.

One thing this class is not is male. Women's notions of *what old age is* tend to be further flung from the current narrative than those of men. As a result, traditional products aimed at older adults tend to serve female consumers especially poorly. And, unfortunately for the companies providing those products, when it comes to the older market, women are responsible for the vast majority of consumer purchasing decisions.

Worldwide, among all age groups, women influence 64 percent of consumer purchases. In many specific cases, not limited to categories such as household goods but also regarding big-ticket items such as cars and houses, they wield far greater sway. In the United States alone, women decide where between $5 trillion to $15 trillion goes every year.

Within older age groups, the power of the female consumer is even more profound. If anything, the real question is not which purchasing decisions older women make but which are left for their husbands—to the extent that their husbands are even alive. One hard, unassailable fact about aging is that the older you get, the less likely your contemporaries are to be men. For those aged 65–69 in the United States, there are 96 men for every 100 women. For those 85 and over, that number drops to 60. (In some countries, the sex ratio is far more severe. For instance, due to a host of issues including alcohol-related mortality, for every 100 women in Russia over age 64 there are just 44 men.)

In addition to their greater numbers and tendency to dominate household spending, women's influence in the older consumer market is magnified geometrically due to the simple, unfair fact that women provide far more than their share of eldercare. Most older people who receive care of some kind get it solely from their family and friends. (To be abundantly clear, when I talk about "care," I don't just mean all the typical things that the term brings to mind, like toileting, dressing, and picking up medications at the drugstore. I'm also talking about changing a light bulb, giving a lift to the library, helping pick out a new phone, lending a hand with paperwork, updating a computer—even just spending time with someone who could use the company.) Most women will have undertaken some form of caregiving by the end of their 40s. Women make up 66 percent of the informal (i.e., family or nonprofessional) caregivers in the United States, and spend as much as 50 percent more time providing care than caregiving men.

In heterosexual marriages, when one spouse cares for the other, it's usually the woman caring for the man. And when an older person's adult child is the one providing care, that child is usually a daughter. In many cases, that adult daughter is in the middle of a dependency sandwich, providing care not only for an older parent or in-law but also her own children.

As is the case with so many things regarding aging, American trends are amplified elsewhere in the world. In Japan, women absolutely dominate informal care. The Land of the Rising Sun has one of the lowest women's labor participation rates in the high-income world to begin with, and, of the over 100,000 Japanese people who quit their jobs each year to care for elderly parents, 80 percent are women. In rapidly aging Western Europe, meanwhile, women are estimated to provide as much as two-thirds of all informal eldercare. These global caregiving trends have serious, deleterious effects on women's ability to earn a living, pursue a competitive career, finance their own retirement, and, in a self-perpetuating loop, take care of their own health.

One of the major, unsung roles caregivers often take on is that of Chief Consumption Officer for two, three, or even four generations of people in their families. Add to that the sheer numerical advantage older women have over men and how women of all ages tend to control consumer spending, and you've got a strong argument for why many products should be aimed at women as a default.

When marketers and product designers understand that, and hear that older women in particular are not well served by the vision of old age currently reflected in today's products, dollar signs should appear in their eyes. And yet, that doesn't always happen. I've experienced firsthand the challenge of convincing some companies to act in their best interest and cater to female consumers. In 2013, I was speaking to a large group of doctors, health insurers, and hospital administrators in North Carolina when something unusual happened: the audience turned against me.

I spend enough time behind podiums to know the typical warning signs of disengagement. When an audience gets bored, you see more forehead than chin, because people are looking down at their feet, or worse, their phones. This was different. Throughout, I saw heads thrown back and chins thrust out, their owners observing me down the length of their noses. Many had crossed their arms on their chests, and some had even leaned back far enough that their chairs were balanced on hind legs. My ideas weren't being tuned out—they were being actively rejected.

Why? Because I'd started in on the topic of the all-important female consumer, who is especially influential regarding the sort of spending that the healthcare crowd cares about—even in households supposedly run by men. I talked about how women live longer and provide more care than men. I trotted out hard data regarding household spending. I told what I thought were charming anecdotes to help the medicine go down. Then I reached the heart of my argument. Men, I said, take a backseat when it comes to making some of the most important decisions in their own homes.

The room revolted. And the director of the conference—who had convinced me to speak as a personal favor—shouted from the back: "Our women have more respect than that. They would never behave that way in public."

Despite the sweat now accumulating on my brow as I tried to wrap my talk up, I managed to make one mental observation. Almost everyone in the audience who was now glaring at me had one thing in common: a Y chromosome.

Meanwhile, though some of the women in front of me were also visibly upset, just as many seemed to be smiling to themselves. And that gave me the small breath of hope I needed to scuttle offstage with my ego intact.

Men, Women, and Innovation in Later Life

I want to live in my old age like the old rules don't apply. The straightest path to a future where a new, better narrative of age prevails is for companies to innovate in service of the *true* wants and needs of the older consumer and not just churn out the same kinds of stuff that older people have hated for a century or more.

But for that to happen, companies need to see eye-to-eye with their customers in a way that they currently don't. Given that the older consumer is more often than not an older *female* consumer, that kind of insight may be hard to come by for companies run mainly by men under age 65. The tech sector, more likely than any other to shape our collective future, fits this profile precisely.

Tech is not only young, as I discussed in the previous chapter, but also overwhelmingly male. Men make up 83 percent of the tech-oriented parts of Google's workforce, and that's typical of the top firms in Silicon Valley. The 10 largest companies in the Valley are 70 percent male, and in top managerial and executive positions, that number rises to 83 percent. (California's overall workforce, by contrast, is just 55 percent male.)

More damningly, only 3 percent of all venture-backed tech companies have female CEOs. Throughout Silicon Valley, women hold just 11 percent of all executive positions. This disparity has led to wave upon wave of technological products that are emphatically male oriented. To pick one instance of many, take the first iteration of Apple Health, which was supposed to be a comprehensive health-tracking app. Apple Health would "monitor all of your metrics that you're most interested in," said Senior Vice President of Software Engineering Craig Federighi at a launch event in 2014. The first version tracked not only common health metrics like heart rate but even obscure ones, like chromium

intake. And yet, despite recording nearly every possible bodily meas-
urement, the product's designers somehow managed to omit the one
cycle that humans have been carefully observing for millennia: men-
struation. As Arielle Duhaime-Ross wrote at the tech blog *The Verge*,
"In short, if you're a human who menstruates *and* owns an iPhone,
you're shit out of luck." Apple rectified the omission in a later version
of the app, but, unfortunately, Health is far from the only tech product
that has reflected a built-in gender bias. As tech writer and podcaster
Rose Eveleth has pointed out: "Phones are too big for many women's
hands. The newest artificial hearts are designed to fit 80 percent of men
but only 20 percent of women. Drop-down menus show "male" over
"female" even when the rest of the menus are alphabetical."

If gender could prevent the folks at Apple—Apple!—from incorporating the most obvious source of health data of all time into its
tracker, then one wonders how smaller companies facing far less public scrutiny will perform. But even if the young men of Silicon Valley
were to somehow come up with a product that satisfies the demands
of older women, the chances of their marketing it successfully would
still be abysmal. That's because, once again, a whopping 3 percent of
creative directors at marketing firms are women. No, I'm not missing
a zero. Three percent.

Between tech's built-in age and gender biases, it couldn't be better
set up to utterly ignore the problems of older, female consumers. However, fortunately for those consumers (and unfortunately for many
existing companies), change is in the wind. To paraphrase the great
New Orleanian songwriter Dr. John: if one company won't do it, you
know somebody else will.

Kathie's story is telling. Following her divorce, she found herself on
the dating circuit simply because it was expected of her. Traditionally,
if marriage number one fails, conventional wisdom tells us to go for
marriage number two—or in the case of many baby boomers, number
three. The many dating sites she tried were built according to that idea.

Dating sites and apps "all announce themselves under the guise of being ultimately for marriage or ultimately for a romantic relationship," she said. On those sites, "I met a few wonderful people that I dated for different periods of time." But, "it was just like, this is what you're *supposed* to do. When you're single, you date. You find a relationship."

In Stitch, however, she found a dating site built on a different set of priorities, which enabled her to seek connections outside of the traditional idea of one-on-one romance. At first, "when I was filling out my profile, I was still thinking that I wanted a boyfriend," she said. But she soon realized that users could set up group events and invite multiple others to attend. Her mind immediately went to Goldblum's weekly revue—"He'll do trivia games, or he'll do 'six degrees of Jeff Goldblum'"—and so she sent out an invitation. Sometimes, no one shows up to these kinds of things, she explained, which can make "you look like an idiot," but in this case, she was saved by "the draw of Jeff."

The concert was a smash success. Goldblum took individual photos with each person at Kathie's table, who all stuck around until after the final encore at nearly midnight. And so, later that month, when Stitch invited its LA members to a movie night it was hosting, Kathie didn't think twice about trying again and posted a note telling anyone interested where to grab dinner before the movie.

At that meal, something clicked. Again, only women showed up, and they ended up forming the nucleus of her current, tight-knit group of friends. "It's hysterical because there's probably ten of us in this little posse," she said. "We all text each other good morning. We text each other goodnight when we go to bed. We're like 15-year-olds."

Today, she values the female platonic friendships she's made on Stitch above almost everything else. (That is, other than perhaps her new grandson, whom she refers to as "my baby.") "I realized, almost instantly, that it wasn't a relationship that I needed so badly in my life—I needed a connection. And that was the big turning point—the big 'ah-ha' moment," she said. "I realized that it wasn't necessarily that

I needed a man in my life to make me feel important or loved or cared for. It was just the connection with other people."

Stitch, it should be said, is still a dating site, just as devoted to fostering romance as platonic friendships. For Kathie, however, it provided what she really wanted, even if it was outside the industry's normal bounds. This sort of story—delivering what the older, female consumer truly desires, not just the same old products—is something every company facing older age groups should strive to emulate. But the kind of insight needed to do so can be hard for businesses to come by.

The fact is, it's still a man's economy—a *young* man's economy, in many sectors—and although many men think they know what women really want, it's hard for men to get it right. That's especially true when it comes to what older women want, because of the stark, fundamental differences in how men and women view later life, which is something we pay close attention to at the MIT AgeLab.

In one pilot study, the AgeLab used a novel, open-ended surveying method to prompt people between ages 25 and 60 to describe what they anticipate and fear in terms of life after 65. Participants chose from a large pile of photographs representing various things that can happen in old age—fishing trips, hospitalization, a quiet dinner out, money troubles, and more. Then they placed these photos into a bullseye, the innermost rings of which represented what they eagerly anticipated in old age, while the outermost represented their greatest worries. (We called it the "ring of fear.") As they made their decisions, we asked them to talk about their choices.

In these monologues, which we recorded, there were stark difference between men's responses and women's. Men were more fixated on pleasant outcomes in old age than on the process of how to achieve them. They used outcome-oriented terms like "independence," "leisure," "vacation," and "enough" more often than process-oriented terms like "plan," "investment," "mortgage," "bond," "stock," "annuity," "Social Security," "savings," "insurance," and "finance." For women, the exact opposite was true; the process of succeeding in old age ruled their discussions. *"How to fulfill my wants and needs?"* seemed to describe their thinking, not *"What will be my reward?"*

At the same time, men's responses were generally more positive than women's. Men said "happy" and "good" twice as much; "nice" and "enjoy" three times as much. Women said "worry" and "stress" twice as often.

Put simply: our male study participants were approaching old age with a fuzzy, optimistic mindset, while women were coming to it with a much more precise conception of the challenges of later life. Men were *looking forward* to a relaxing few decades. Women were *planning* to grow old.

That clarity on women's part may help explain why they are at the front of the large, ongoing march toward work in old age, a phenomenon that's been accelerating since about 1990. In the United States, the older labor force participation rate (i.e., those either working or seeking employment) first plummeted starting in the late 1800s, when Union Army veterans decided it would be nice not to work until they dropped. The rate bottomed out between the late 1980s and early 1990s at about 11 percent. It has been climbing back up ever since. Today, 18.6 percent of people over 65 participate in the workforce, a number that the US Bureau of Labor Statistics expects will increase to nearly 22 percent by 2024. Yes, it's still true in the United States and many other countries that working men outnumber working women across age groups. But between the 1990 and 2010 US censuses, women's labor force participation rates climbed faster than those of men for every older age segment.*

---

* This trend is inextricably tied to the fact that half of American workers haven't saved enough to support their standard of living after retirement. But need isn't the only reason older people are pursuing work. Yes, many boomers plan to delay retirement or never retire because they can't afford 30 years of leisure, but many others plan to do so simply because they like working. A 2013 study by the Center for Retirement Research at Boston College revealed that the main reason most people continue to work after 65 is that they prefer it to retirement, a line of reasoning that becomes more true as education levels rise. College graduates over 65 are twice as likely than

There are a few probable explanations for why women are leading the charge toward work in old age. One may be that that they seem to internalize less indoctrination regarding the stage of life we've been taught to call "retirement."

In another, larger study, AgeLab scientist Chaiwoo Lee conducted a survey of 10,000 people across age groups, income levels, and locations in the United States. In one section, she asked them to provide five keywords describing their life after completing their primary career. We avoided the term "retirement" in our instructions, in an effort not to provoke any responses associated with decades of retirement marketing. Nevertheless, the word most closely correlated with maleness among our respondents was "retirement," followed by "relax," "good," "hobbies," and "travel." Men were repeating the party line of retirement back to us so consistently that it was like someone had been playing Sun City ads to them in their sleep.

Women were another story. The keyword most associated with female respondents was "fulfilled," followed by words like "peace," "calm," "accomplished," and "family." These results, combined with those of the study I mentioned earlier, suggest that women don't just approach old age with a relatively detailed understanding of the challenges those decades will bring but also incorporate more nuance into their aspirations than men.

Part of our female respondents' insight may also have come from personal experience. Not only do women of middle age and older provide far more eldercare than men, but the care they provide is more likely to be intimate, involving activities like bathing, toileting, and

---

those without a high school degree to continue work after 65, and the number of college grads crossing the age-65 threshold increases every year. "We conclude that the increase in the labor force participation of older persons is largely a favorable development that reflects the desire by more educated and healthy members to remain in the work force," the study's authors write. Even those not significantly impacted by the recent recession intend to work longer. Many older workers, especially those with desk jobs, might need a change of pace or a change of colleagues but don't physically need a rest, and they simply prioritize leisure below meaningful work.

dressing. That is, men tend to volunteer to change their parents' light bulbs and clean their gutters. Women step in to clean their bodies. In the process, they learn what can happen to the older body and the amount of work that can be required just to keep it running.

The fact that men have built their very conception of old age around the fuzzy, positive fiction of a leisure-centric retirement, while women see old age in a clearer, if harsher, light, is a crucial distinction. It suggests that when consumers vote with their pocketbooks against the current narrative, it will be women who lead the way. Across age groups, they have a better idea than their male counterparts of which issues they will want solved in later life. They will be the first to recognize where existing solutions are inadequate or address the wrong questions. They will know the difference between products that attempt to solve the problem *of* older adults and those that solve problems *for* older adults.

And, in the cases of certain female entrepreneurs, they will be the first to create new, better products that blow incumbent companies out of the water. It was exactly that kind of insight that led to the creation of Stitch, the dating site.

Marcie Rogo is one of those rare, wonderful people born with a love for older adults—as she puts it, she's "more at home in a retirement village than a pre-school." After graduating from the University of Pennsylvania in 2007, she traveled to Sydney, Australia, where she pursued a business master's at the Australian School of Management and decided to go into the business of aging. Soon, she was all-but-living in retirement communities in California and Australia, talking to residents, finding out what made them happy or sad and what they still needed in their lives. She identified social isolation as the archenemy of healthy older living.

"For the past five years, I've been trying to help put off social isolation among people over 50, because that's when it becomes detrimental to your health," she said. "When you're in your fifties and sixties, it's more of a preventative thing." But once you're significantly older and frail? Social isolation will "kill you immediately."

To lengthen lives by fighting isolation, she founded a company called ConnectAround, a private social network for residents of active-living retirement communities. The way she was thinking about isolation at the time was typical, perhaps *too* typical, of the aging field at large. Because "old" is virtually synonymous with "unwell" in our current narrative, often the best way to justify something fun for older people is by claiming that it has health benefits. It was a line of thought that proved persuasive to the retirement communities Rogo approached. ConnectAround grew and was soon acquired by Tapestry, a company that served as a sort of simplified social network for older people, which gained some limited traction in Australia and California.

During this time, Rogo continued to work hard to understand how to promote social connections among isolated older adults. "What I thought, in the beginning, I wanted to do was to kind of make them be friends with each other," she said. But she kept getting the sense that the older people she was working with found the idea somewhat forced.

"And so finally, in 2014, Andrew and I"—that is, Andrew Dowling, the founder of Tapestry, who would become Stitch's chief executive—"looked at each other, and we were like, 'Whoa,'" she said. "As much as we're trying to force this way for them to connect with their families and friends and neighbors, they want it in a different package. They want a little more sexy, a little more cool."

That is, a little less meet-and-greet at the local senior center, a little more Jeff Goldblum in a nightclub.

A dating service of some kind was the logical way to make the promotion of healthy social connections sexy. But there was a problem. The people Rogo was talking to already had access to dating sites galore but shied away from them. For this crowd, she and her partner would have to rethink the very concept of the dating website. "Stitch was built, from the ground up, for people that are no longer reproducing," she said.

The company's headquarters, housed in a hip, converted factory in the Potrero Hill neighborhood of San Francisco, looks out over homes and offices toward the three-legged, three-pronged Sutro Tower, a distinguishing feature of the city's skyline. As Rogo spoke, a dense layer of fog hung around the structure's legs. The antenna emerging from the cloud suggested the conning tower of an immense submarine, about to breach.

Other dating sites, Rogo said, are built for people looking to get married and have kids. Success in the eHarmonies and Match.coms of the world is measured in the number of marriages achieved and soul mates discovered. "With Stitch, we don't even say the word *marriage*," she said. Rather, Stitch would dump the goal of finding "the one" entirely. The fact was, most of the single women aged 50 and up to whom Rogo was talking—people who today make up the significant majority of Stitch's user base—weren't looking for commitment. One major reason for their reticence was the looming specter of caregiving.

When the "love of your life" gets sick, explained Rogo, "you're very happy to take care of them." But what about when that same future appears on the horizon, only with someone brand new? For many, it's a deal breaker. "This is a thing you will hear a lot of women say: 'I don't want to be a nurse and I don't want to be a purse,'" she said. Many new fish in the older dating pool will have just finished long, arduous years of care for a loved one who has passed away. When you "just got done taking care of somebody, you're not willing to take care of somebody you just met."

Even for those women entering the dating pool via a "grey divorce"— the en vogue term for late-life splits, which have skyrocketed in frequency of late—there's often ample reason to pause before plunging into another committed relationship. Between 1990 and 2010, the overall US divorce rate remained roughly level. Meanwhile, the rate among the 50-plus doubled. Among heterosexual couples, it's usually the woman who initiates these divorces. One common refrain I've heard these older divorcées utter is, "I married him for life, not for lunch." That is, upon embarking on a postcareer life together, many couples find themselves staring at each other all day, which can destroy the very fabric of a relationship that, it turns out, worked better with some space built in. Add to that the additional stressor of socializing. In many married couples, women take on the majority of the work involved in building up and maintaining a couple's social network. That arrangement may work perfectly well in decades filled with work and kids, but many women in their 60s suddenly find themselves strung between a web of gregarious friends outside the home and a retired, retiring husband who prefers to stay in—with his wife keeping him company.

Indeed, Stitch has some married members, "which we totally are fine with, as long as you agree to put *non-romantic* on your settings," said Rogo. "They're almost all women whose husbands won't get off the couch." Meanwhile, "they want to travel and they want to do things."

In a series of focus-group interviews I conducted in Virginia, New York, Nebraska, and Kentucky, I asked a number of older women what they thought the biggest problem in their marriage would be, going forward. Again and again, phrases like "bored," "boring," and "he doesn't excite me" came up. Perhaps 50 years ago that kind of failure-to-excite wasn't cause for divorce, but that's less and less the case. For one thing, second marriages are far more likely to end in divorce than primary ones. Because baby boomers were the first to really run with the idea of divorce and remarriage in their 20s and 30s, many of today's 50- and 60-somethings are in second marriages that are more likely to dissolve than those of their parents. Perhaps more important, couples in their 50s and 60s have a longer future ahead of them than their parents and grandparents did—years that are increasingly filled with possibility. The growing number of things older people can do is a wonderful development, but one side effect is the fact that being yoked to the wrong person comes at a higher opportunity cost than ever. Many choose to cut their losses and start afresh.

Whether its users are widows or widowers, divorced, or never married (the number of never-married adults in the United States has been rising steadily since 1970), "Stitch is not about finding one person," Rogo said. "It's about finding a lot of people that could be your companions. And one of them might be a romantic companion, but others might be dinner companions. They might be travel companions. They might be hiking companions."

To make it easier to connect with more people, Stitch cut back on the detailed profiles that users normally fill out on dating sites, which include parameters like age, height, weight, religion, occupation—even allergies. Just finding "someone that you're compatible with for activities and interests and location is hard enough," Rogo said. Besides, when the user is looking less for a soul mate than a dinner date—or even just a friend—those kinds of filters start to feel unnecessary. Even among users looking solely for romance, "the game changes when you're not having kids anymore, and you may even choose to live separately," she said. The point is to make those connections easier, not erect barriers.

Stitch was built from the start to facilitate a variety of social connections, including platonic friendship. Once members start using the site, Rogo describes what they hope to achieve as a "mush" of romantic and platonic aspirations. The female-to-male ratio of Stitch's 50,000 members is roughly 70/30, she explained, and so "a lot of the women are realistic that there's less men."

Still, Stitch comes across, and is marketed, as a dating site. That's deliberate, because one of the key requirements of Stitch's users is for the platform to support their self-image: not as patients who need a social-isolation intervention, as the guiding philosophy of Connect-Around had suggested, but rather as capable, fun, outgoing human beings with healthy social, romantic, and sexual instincts.

Indeed, when Kathie signed up for Stitch, she didn't know she was looking for platonic friends. She thought she wanted romance. Only later did she find out what she really needed: a group of people who will text with her every day and go with her to places like local cabarets as well as on trips to Las Vegas and Death Valley.

By wearing the coat of a more traditional dating site, and thereby operating within a paradigm that has less to do with aging than that other biological imperative—romance—Stitch is "actually much more fulfilling our mission than we ever were," Rogo said. It's a refrain that should sound familiar. In the way that the cell phone is actually a better emergency technology than a Life Alert pendant because it fits more snugly into its users' lives, Stitch is more effective than the health-oriented companionship service that preceded it. Its guiding ethos—helping vibrant people have fun—feels more acceptable to its users than the goal of helping sick people survive for longer.*

"It's this whole industry," Rogo said. If, for instance, one were to hand an older person a hypothetical device designed to prevent falls, "they'll be like, 'Leave me alone.' But if you give them something fun and amazing and cool, and that happens to help them not fall, that's a much better option."

For anyone in the business of selling anything to the older, mostly female demographic, the challenge involved in creating the kinds of "fun and amazing and cool" products described by Rogo goes far beyond engineering. The real limiting factor is one of imagination: whether companies can grasp the true needs of their consumers as the consumers themselves experience them. Only after years in the field was Rogo able to figure out what her customers really wanted. For companies run by young men, the challenge becomes far more difficult—even in the rare cases when they do seem to recognize the value of demographics beyond their own.

The Tyranny of Pink

In the previous chapter, I described the failure of a number of historical products that were designed, mainly by younger people, for older

---

* Once, Rogo said, she caught one of her web designers include a stick-figure image of a hypothetical Stitch member, holding a cane, on the site. "I was like, 'Dude! You can't put a person with a cane on here!'" The idea that older people would respond well to such imagery, she said, "is, like, super-millennial."

people. Something similar can happen with products designed, usually by men, for women.

History is full of failed corporate efforts to superficially morph gender-neutral products into "women's products." You may have heard of the most high-profile debacles: Dell, which in 2009 tried to sell pink laptops from its pastel-hued "Della" section of its website. Bic, whose infamous "For Her" line of ballpoint pens made women everywhere wonder how they'd survived using men's pens for so long. (As one Amazon reviewer sarcastically wrote, "For the past forty years, the weight and heft of a regular pen has kept me from voting.") The ePad Femme, an eight-inch "women's tablet" with recipes and multiple yoga apps included, which a blogger at Jezebel.com described as "preloaded, so as to not bewilder miniature lady-brains with complicated 'downloading' procedures and 'human agency and choice.'"

The history of cars marketed explicitly to women is perhaps even more painful. Between 1955 and 1956, Dodge introduced La Femme—that is, "the wife"—which came with dedicated interior compartments for accoutrements including a complementary lipstick holder and handbag, both of which matched the pink upholstery. The model (technically a trim option for the Custom Royal) was discontinued after two years. Later, in 2013, Honda tried its hand at the same approach, with the Honda Fit She's. Released only in Japan, the Fit She's came in pink, with air conditioning technology that was supposedly good for passengers' skin and special window glass that was impervious to UV light, or, as *The Globe and Mail* termed it, "the sun's crone-inducing rays." Once again, like the La Femme, it spent only two years on the market.

To take an even deeper dive into the past, there's a centuries-long tradition of products billed as aids for womankind that have, in point of fact, prioritized the needs of men. In her extraordinary book *More Work for Mother,* Ruth Schwartz Cowan describes a number of ways in which products, theoretically designed to help women, have ended up adding to their workloads in the home. For instance, cleaning carpets was once an occasional, even seasonal, affair that required the collaboration of the entire family. With the advent of the vacuum cleaner, however, one person could get it done alone—and suddenly, that person was expected to do it far more frequently. At the same time, the vacuum cleaner released "the stronger members of the household from the obligation to move the rugs outside, or the younger members from the obligation of beating them," Cowan writes. In that new light, "The question of whether cleaning a rug has been made easier or faster by the advent of vacuum cleaners becomes considerably more difficult to answer. Easier for whom? Faster for whom?"

The effects of the vacuum cleaner and other products like it, such as washing machines, added up. Household laborsaving devices effectively helped only men escape housework, which had once been split evenly between the sexes or outsourced to hired help. As a result, the early 20th century's increases in wealth and available consumer products did not come with a commensurate "increase in leisure for housewives," Cowan writes, "but, rather, by increases in the amount of work that some housewives had to do, and in the level of productivity that others were able to achieve."

One of the major questions raised in Cowan's book is why women throughout history seem to have willingly bought or advocated for products that would ultimately make their lives more difficult. In one sense, the motivation was obvious: the new tools of housework made what Cowan terms "a minimum standard of health and decency" accessible to wide, new swathes of people. It was "small wonder then that these women . . . viewed the modern tools . . . as liberating, rather than oppressive agents," she writes.

Another way of saying that is: there was a march toward domestic health and hygiene that took place between the mid-1800s and mid-1900s, and women shouldered the brunt of the labor involved. Arguably, they have never made up what they lost as a result of that sacrifice. Today, something similar is happening. More of us are living longer, and new technologies will once again make it possible to push forward a frontier in terms of quality of life—this time in old age. The question is whether history will repeat itself, and women will end up constrained by products designed for a world envisioned by men. After all, women are already shouldering the burden of the vast amounts of caregiving that will need to be done for an older society to function. Will tomorrow's products and marketing reinforce that norm—perhaps by depicting mainly female caregivers in marketing materials or equating "care" with the color pink?

Perhaps, but if there's one sign of rebellion against that idea, it's that women are rejecting products that would foist an unasked-for caregiving burden onto them. To many, dating websites that would match women with potential care-recipients-for-life simply feel less attractive than a site built on a more casual, short-term idea of human connection. That lesson applies across economic sectors. Ideas that make a sense only to young, male product designers might still find success among the all-powerful, older, female consumer group—at least, in the absence of a better alternative. But once that better alternative appears, those consumers will jump ship.

It's that possibility that should worry major, incumbent companies. When it comes to future products for the older consumer, there's every indication that today's companies are lining up to make the same sorts of products that they always have, perhaps juiced up with new technologies, but otherwise built on a similar conceptual foundation. In a sense, they would be crazy not to. Broadly, in fields from economics to ecology, systems achieve stability by perpetuating the status quo. Companies that are good at one thing successfully innovate most reliably by producing variations and improvements on that theme. But underlying that mode of innovation is the assumption that one's consumer market will continue to demand the same sorts of solutions indefinitely.

Consider the kitchen of tomorrow. Appliance companies have been building futuristic, concept kitchens since the 1950s, and, as tech writer Eveleth has explored at the food blog Eater, the animating priorities of today's future kitchens are still stuck in that decade. Early concept exhibits, which appeared in midcentury commercials and World's

Fair-type events, showcased, say, a kitchen built entirely out of plastic, made by Monsanto; or one that allowed you to bake a cake with the push of a button, designed by GM.

Today's kitchens-of-the-future are strikingly similar. Instead of an all-plastic kitchen (Monsanto was primarily known in the 1950s as a plastics giant), Corning Inc., the glass manufacturer, recently created a video exploring the possibilities of an all-glass one, with helpful touch-screen displays everywhere. Helpful, that is, until a chef actually has reason to touch one. "Imagine the smudges on your iPhone blown up to kitchen-size, usual fingertip oils replaced with cooking grease. None of the work of maintaining that cleanliness is apparent—or even hinted at" in Corning's vision, Eveleth writes. Meanwhile, what do people who actually use kitchens want? How about a self-cleaning option? "Here's how many times I saw anything about keeping the kitchen clean in all the future-home videos I've watched," Eveleth writes. "Not once."

More often than not, even forward-looking product designers will direct their focus toward the kinds of problems that are convenient for them to solve—that is, those that make use of technologies that are readily at hand and that require little adjustment of the designer's worldview. It's said that when all you have is a hammer, the world looks like a nail. If all you have is Gorilla Glass—Corning's scratch-resistant material commonly used in smartphones and tablets—then perhaps the world looks like an iPad.

For a different approach, consider the Swiffer, a wet-wipe-on-a-mop-handle introduced in 1999 for the cleansing of hard floors. The Swiffer isn't a self-cleaning kitchen, but it's a start, and has been an unalloyed success for Procter & Gamble since its introduction. And yet, how is it possible that no one thought to put a disposable cleaning wipe on the end of a pole until 1999? The disconcertingly simple answer: for decades, cleaning-products companies took it as given that the only way to clean hard floors was with a bucket and mop.

This kind of systemic failure of imagination is holding back products for tomorrow's older consumers. The insights needed to break through, however, do exist. They're out there, sitting in consumers' brains. The idea of harnessing them may sound like an opportunity—and it is. But it's also a threat. The insights that occur to this particular consumer group are powerful enough to raze major companies to the ground—and raise new ones out of the rubble.

The Job of the Consumer

There is an important business concept that I've been using implicitly up to this point, and it's time to make it explicit: the job of the consumer. What the atom does for chemistry and the gene does for biology, the job of the consumer (or user, or customer) does for capitalism. It's the single smallest possible unit that makes everything else happen.

The concept was originally popularized by Theodore Levitt, a legendary Cold War-era Harvard Business School professor. Famously, Levitt told his students again and again: "I don't want a quarter-inch drill; I want a quarter-inch hole!" That is, when consumers have a job to be done—the creation of a hole in the wall—they "hire" a product to do it. Manufacturers often forget this and think of their customers not as people who want holes but as people who want drills. But because consumers are wedded to the job, not the product, there's always the possibility that a new product will come along that does the job better. The moment that, say, the Hole-Puncher 5000 comes onto the market and makes it easier or cheaper to poke a hole in the wall than to drill one, drill manufacturers will find themselves in trouble.

One of Levitt's students who went on to become a Harvard Business guru in his own right is Clayton Christensen. (Famous in management circles, Christensen came up with the concept of disruptive innovation—more on that later.) An illuminating, nonfictitious example of the job of the consumer comes from Christensen's 2003 book, *The Innovator's Solution*. He describes how one fast-food chain discovered that 40 percent of milkshakes were being purchased in the morning hours. Milkshakes were supposed to be a dessert bought after lunch or dinner. What was going on? A member of Christensen's team interviewed the morning milkshake drinkers to find out. These people usually came to stores alone, didn't buy anything else, and drank their shakes as they drove off in their work clothes, often to embark on a long, boring car commute where the milkshake could serve as both food and entertainment. Although the shake drinkers tended not to be very hungry at the time of purchase, they told the researcher that they needed something that would keep later, midmorning pangs of hunger at bay.

Put simply: they required a delicious, calorie-dense food that took a long time to consume and that they could eat with one hand without making a mess. Traditional breakfast products didn't fit the bill. Bagels shed seeds and fillings onto drivers' laps and required an accompanying beverage, while a banana or doughnut wouldn't stave off midmorning hunger for long enough. Health wasn't a factor—as Christensen and coauthors write, "Becoming healthy wasn't essential to the job they were hiring the milk shake to do." Perhaps most crucially, it didn't matter that a milkshake was a "dessert" food. It got the job done, so that's what customers bought.

Older adults, like all consumers, weigh factors like these constantly. But unlike other consumer age groups, marketers and designers consistently fail to wrap their heads around older adults' jobs-to-be-done. In the previous chapter, I described how denture wearers in the 1950s bought Gerber baby food but refused Heinz Senior Foods. That was because the job of the consumer in that case was not only to avoid chewing food but also to preserve her dignity in the checkout line. In the case of Stitch versus various other senior-isolation-abatement programs, the job of the user is similar: to interact with others in a normal social setting, such as a date, not in a forced, medicalized simulacrum of one.

Only by accurately understanding the nuances of the job of the consumer will it be possible for companies to avoid major flops in the longevity economy—a big ask for young, male companies and industries. In fact, the dominant narrative of old age is so powerful that even *older* would-be innovators can fall prey to it. There are ways through, however. It is possible for firms to achieve a breakthrough in empathy, perhaps by dispatching researchers to spend years scrutinizing older adults, like Marcie Rogo did. But there is a faster route to understanding.

Consumer Hacks

In Christensen's breakfast milkshake example, what's especially revealing is that "breakfast" is not the intended usage of the product, which was supposed to be a dessert. To borrow parlance common here at MIT, in using the milkshake in an unintended way, consumers had "hacked" breakfast. If you look around, you'll start to see this kind of thing happening everywhere. One common example on college campuses is what's known as "revealed preference paths," the bane of groundskeepers around the world. You've probably seen these bare, dirt pathways worn through the grass in otherwise manicured campuses and parks. They occur in places where people want to get from points A to B quickly, and the prescribed walking routes are too circuitous. The job of the pedestrian, it turns out, is not to walk on a hard surface but to get where she needs to go.

Historically, companies have been delighted to find consumers using their products in unexpected ways, because it reveals an opportunity to sell to a new market. Take Kleenex: first marketed by Kimberly-Clark in the 1920s as a makeup wipe, consumers (and the manufacturers themselves) soon discovered that the soft paper sheets served admirably as disposable handkerchiefs. Kimberly-Clark changed its marketing tune and packaging, and "Kleenex" became synonymous with "snot receptacle." Overnight, the way people blow their noses changed—forever.

If you were to take a close look at today's older consumers, you'd see them quietly hacking away, using products in unexpected ways that conform closely to their otherwise unmet needs. In every one of these cases, the true job of the older consumer is revealed. To use an example from the care setting, have you ever seen an older adult's walker with cut-open tennis balls stuck onto the ends of its legs? That hack allows rubber-footed walkers to slide. Recently, walkers with small plastic skis on their legs have become fairly common, which take advantage of the job of the consumer revealed by the tennis-ball trick. But that kind of hack is just the beginning—a modification of something that's already intended for an older user. Far more interesting are cases where older adults and their caregivers find new uses for products that were never explicitly originally intended for them.

Sally Lindover, 88, is one of the stalwart members of the AgeLab's 85-plus group, a consumer workshop that meets every other month to discuss all kinds of topics ranging from technology to politics to death and dying. She is also a user par excellence of on-demand and sharing economy services.

Her apartment, perched on the eighth floor of an 11-story building in Cambridge's Central Square, looks out over Cambridge and across the Charles River to Boston. In the afternoon, sunlight positively floods in. She's lived there since the 1990s, and she regrets not buying a home then, when prices were low. But then again, so was the cost of rent at the time. Besides, more often than not, she was out of town—far out of town.

For nearly three decades starting in 1983, Lindover served as an officer in the US Foreign Service. Prior to joining, she'd been a clinical psychologist and managed an art gallery, but by her mid-50s, she felt it was time for something new. She joined the Peace Corps and then the Foreign Service a few years later, at 56. According to Lindover, when she signed up, she was the oldest junior officer ever to join. "I broke the age barrier," she said.*

When she started renting her Cambridge apartment, it served mainly as a home base in between foreign postings in countries ranging

---

* Elements of this section originally appeared in an article I coauthored with Luke Yoquinto for the *Washington Post*.

from Lithuania to Yemen to Rwanda. At first, the rent was "very reasonable," she said, and then, when the price went up, she kept it anyway because she liked the location, and then, when it increased even more, she justified it as a good place to care for her mother, who lived with her for about a year.

"Time went by, and my rent is now tripled," she said. Meanwhile, after her retirement from the Foreign Service at age 81, Lindover's income, now fixed, wasn't quite enough to cover her expenses. So she took on a visiting MIT professor as a lodger for a year. It went just fine—"He was so wonderful," she said, in part because he lived in New York most of the time, and so "he was never here!"

At the same time, her children were using Airbnb. "I thought, why don't I try that? And I did!" she said. "It worked very well. And I really had very successful experiences."

Today, Airbnb is far from the only sharing-economy or on-demand service Lindover relies on. After hurting her lower back on a walking-intensive Paris trip with a younger group, she stopped walking to her local Trader Joe's and started ordering groceries via Instacart, a service that sends personal shoppers into local grocery stores. For heavier household goods, she uses Jet.com (now a subsidiary of Walmart), whose prices, she noted, are competitive with Amazon's. For entertainment, she's a Netflix devotee. *Ray Donovan*, the ultraviolent Liev Schreiber show, is her current preferred binge, but she waxes poetic about *The Wire*, HBO's widely adored—and also disturbingly violent—take on Baltimore's gangs, cops, politicians, and communities.

Although the stream of people who come to her apartment and help her meet her daily needs is now nearly constant, she doesn't see her situation as anything overly novel. "Communities have always done this—have always shared, have always helped each other," she said. "The concepts have been there." Now, "they're just organized in a different way."

Though her use of online services may feel wholly natural to her, Lindover is an example of what I call a "lifestyle leader"—a sort of early adopter, not necessarily of a new technology but rather of a new way of living. Although she's at the forefront of on-demand and sharing-economy usage for people her age, she's not alone. Currently, 22 percent of users of such services are 55 and older, a figure that will grow rapidly in the coming decades. As it does, it will stand in stark contrast to the accepted way of doing things.

Traditionally, when older adults evince a need for help with periodic, unavoidable tasks, the list of remedies has been small: hired aides, family caregivers, senior facilities. By piecing together needed services using the on-demand and sharing economy, Lindover and others like her are demonstrating a new, viable way. When her lower back prevented her from walking a mile to her usual grocery store, that alone might once have prompted a move into some kind of care facility or at least increased reliance on various senior services. Instacart, Jet, and other online companies allowed her to delay such steps. In doing so, she not only continued to live her fiercely independent lifestyle but also possibly saved money, because independent senior living, even at its most minimalist, offers a number of services that come bundled together: building maintenance, housing, meals, cleaning, fast emergency response on the premises, and more. Many people move to an assisted living facility when they require just one or two of those services and end up paying for the bundle. But now, in the way that Netflix and other streaming services have made it possible for "cord cutters" to avoid paying for bundled cable television programming, new sharing and on-demand services have allowed Lindover and others like her to become "care cutters," fulfilling their jobs as consumers on an à la carte basis.

In fact, in one AgeLab analysis, we determined that a hypothetical 75-year-old Greater Boston homeowner could avoid thousands of dollars per month in independent senior living fees by living at home, supported by online services. These included a home security system, personal emergency call system, meal and grocery delivery services, medication delivery service, medication adherence app, occasional use of a laundry service, and, via TaskRabbit, housekeeping and home maintenance as needed. For transportation, we envisioned the frequent use of the MBTA, Boston's transit system, but allotted 10 Uber trips per month. For fun, we threw in a book club, dance class, and YMCA membership. Total monthly costs, which included standard homeowner costs such as utilities, Internet, insurance, and taxes, fell in the low $2,000 range, well below the monthly cost of many independent living facilities when meals and housekeeping are included.

Much as Kimberly-Clark was pleasantly surprised to find that its Kleenex wipes were being used for more than makeup removal, the young companies in the on-demand and sharing economies are finding this kind of unprecedented usage by older adults to be a very welcome development. Take Airbnb. Its cofounders, 20-somethings at the time, originally named their start-up Airbed & Breakfast, after the inflatable berth they rented out in their too-expensive San Francisco loft. Soon they turned their innovation into an Internet service, targeting people like them: starving young adults who hoped to make a little extra rent money; peripatetic travelers looking to slumber somewhere on the cheap. But older users soon flocked to the service. At the time of this writing, most of Airbnb's hosts are older than 40. More than 10 percent of them are over 60—the company's fastest-growing demographic of hosts. Nearly two-thirds of these older hosts are women.

In signing up, these hosts identified a use case not initially on the young company founders' radar. Throughout history, a typical way for older property owners, widows in particular, to make money was to take on boarders in their homes. As times and expectations changed (and regulations tightened), however, that became harder to do—at least in single-family homes without dedicated, standalone apartments. With the advent of Airbnb, however, unused bedrooms once again became a source of revenue for older adults looking to convert real-estate wealth into liquid money. In a sense, older users "hacked" Airbnb, benefitting both themselves and the company. Other sharing and on-demand companies that have noticed the strength of the older market include ride-hailing companies like Lyft and Uber as well as the personal butler service Hello Alfred. One-quarter of Uber's drivers are now 50 or older, and Lyft's older drivers are among its most popular, in part because, as longtime residents of the cities where they drive, they can impart knowledge of local roads and amusing geographic anecdotes. "Number one, they love driving, but number two, they love talking to people and engaging with people," said Mike Masserman, Lyft's director of government relations.

Instacart's case is especially telling. Traditionally, food-delivery options for older adults have been couched in the language of disability and poverty. The service provided by Meals-on-Wheels and other similar organizations is *absolutely essential* to millions who would find themselves in dire straits without them, and in no way do I advocate cutting or defunding this critical lifeline. But it's curious that there's never been a major, upmarket version of the service for older people who are unable to shop but still want to live at home and eat their favorite foods from the grocery store. Instead, those potential customers had to wait until age-agnostic versions appeared. Instacart was founded not by someone with seniors on his mind, but rather a 25-year old who told the *New York Times* that he had the idea for his company because he "had this problem of never having groceries in my fridge and never having the motivation and energy to go to the store."

Hello Alfred is another intriguing example. The company, named after Batman's ultracapable butler, assigns Alfred Client Managers—Alfreds, for short—to its customers, who can instruct them to do any variety of task, from folding laundry to paying bills to setting up other online services—including, for instance, Airbnb. Like Airbnb and Instacart, it was originally created by two 20-somethings hoping to improve their own home life. While students at Harvard Business School, Hello Alfred's cofounders Jessica Beck and Marcela Sapone hired help from Craigslist to keep their domestic worlds in order; soon neighbors asked to take part in the scheme, and they turned it into a company. A year after Hello Alfred's launch in Boston in 2013, it won San Francisco's TechCrunch Disrupt, the world's most prestigious annual start-up competition.

Beck said that the company remains oriented primarily toward busy people—and that includes "folks that have had a life change," such as a shift in family composition or dependency status, which can cause needs to increase even as the hours in a day remain the same. Although Hello Alfred doesn't market itself as an eldercare provider, once you broaden your definition of "care" to include doing things like changing light bulbs, helping with paperwork, and carrying heavy things upstairs, it's easy to see how a company with its business model could fulfill an important gap in the market. Old age certainly counts as the sort of family change that Hello Alfred can help with, said Beck. "We're one place with a trusted relationship for people to come and get help with things that go on in the home."

To lean, consumer-facing start-ups like these companies, the prospect of being discovered by an enormous older market might sound like a dream come true. To established companies already operating in the older space, however, such developments are a source of peril.

Tom Grape, a good friend of mine and chief executive of Benchmark Senior Living, the largest provider of senior housing in New England, views encroaching on-demand and sharing economy services as a looming challenge facing his industry. "Technologies better enabling seniors to stay at home longer are an exciting development," he said, but they will likely cause the senior-living resident population to skew older and frailer. And although the march of technology will help his industry in some ways, such as by allowing firms to offer new services and cut down on staffing inefficiencies, "These technologies are truly going to transform the ability for seniors to age in place in their homes."

Lead-User Innovation

The economic demand of people like Sally Lindover and Kathie has the power to rewrite the way we live in old age. It wouldn't be the first time such a narrative emerged from human minds, but it *would* mark the first time older adults got the chance to author their own destiny. Our current story was written by doctors, almshouses, and efficiency experts at the turn of the century; then government officials in the 1930s; and then the retirement industry in the 1950s and 1960s. The story that resulted was useful once-upon-a-time, but it's now holding us back. Innovation that creeps along one beige, injection-molded, medicalized device at a time will not help us achieve better, longer lives. Rather, the visionaries who will help build a better old age will be those who understand, at a deep, intuitive level, where *what older adults want* diverges from the current narrative. The products that bridge that gap will empower older adults. They will help them continue to participate in society—economically, culturally, and socially. And as cultural objects, these products will send forth the message that personal agency in old age is normal. As older adults grow more connected to everyone else, the way we think about old age will change. In a virtuous cycle, as their capabilities become more obvious than their limitations, older people may find it easier to land meaningful work. Better employment opportunities, together with savings vehicles more closely aligned with their new demands, may increase the amount of money flowing through the new older market, which will incentivize the creation of even better products. And so on.

The question, as with most hypothetical virtuous cycles, is how to get the process started. The idea that someone from the tech world could come along and hand down the kinds of revolutionary products I'm calling for seems unlikely, especially given the tech sector's current demographic blinders. But the opposite approach, wherein companies put an ear to the rails and ask consumers what they want, is just as fraught. To paraphrase Steve Jobs, when you want to create something utterly new and transformative, the one thing you can't do is ask consumers what they want. As he famously said in 1998: "It's really hard to design products by focus groups. A lot of times, people don't know what they want until you show it to them." Sometimes, I wonder if the Internet itself would have made it past a hypothetical focus group.

In the case of today's middle-aged-and-older consumers, you can't just ask them what they'll want in old age, because their ability to picture new, better ways to live is utterly constrained by our current, pernicious narrative. More often than not, you'll find that most people—men, especially—repeat the party line back to you.

As part of the AgeLab study I mentioned earlier, my colleague, Chaiwoo Lee, asked 1,000 survey respondents to provide five words that describe what they think about life after their primary career. These were people from all throughout the United States—men and women of a variety of different ages, races, and economic backgrounds. Of the just-under-5,000 words we received, there were 918 distinct terms. Just 28 of them accounted for half of all responses.

Put another way, there are *parrots* with larger vocabularies than most of us have concerning life in old age. This is how we've ended up with people saying they want to "work in retirement," a logically inconsistent idea. But people who want to keep working after their primary careers say it anyway, because they can't imagine a life in old age that doesn't incorporate "retirement," one of the central plot points of our current narrative.

But notice how I said "most of us," not all.

In the older market, there are people—mainly older women and younger, usually-female caregivers—with piercing insights into what the jobs of tomorrow's older consumers will be. Better yet, within that group, there is a subset with the know-how and wherewithal to build groundbreaking solutions themselves. These individual tinkerers, entrepreneurs, and "intrapreneurs" within larger organizations have the ability to change the very fabric of old age.

The process through which they will do it is known as "lead-user innovation." The concept comes from Eric von Hippel, a professor who works down the street from the AgeLab at the MIT Sloan School of Management. In a profound departure from traditional models of innovation, lead-user theory posits that in certain industries where rapidly changing products are the norm (i.e., certain high-tech sectors), customers, not companies, are the ones who come up with many of the most useful ideas and advances. Not just any customers, however. Only a select few users have both needs that precede those of the bulk of the marketplace (making them "lead users") and also enough technical sophistication to come up with solutions on their own (making them lead-user *innovators*).

Outdoing even those who hack new use cases out of existing products, à la Sally Lindover and Airbnb, lead users go so far as to prototype new products, either by modifying existing ones or making new ones out of whole cloth. One classic example von Hippel uses is the case of early windsurfers in Hawaii. In the late 1970s, a group of extremely skilled windsurfers discovered that they could rocket off of huge Pacific waves to great heights. But landing was a problem, because their feet would lose contact with the board. At best, surfers would fly off to the relative safety of the water, but all too often the rider's limbs, head, sail, mast, and board would return to sea level in a painful and damaging mass. It was these human-flight test subjects, not the board manufacturers, who first affixed foot straps to wind surfboards. "All of a sudden not only could you fly into the air, but you could land the thing, and not only that, but you could change direction in the air! The whole sport of high-performance windsurfing really started from that," one of them recalls in von Hippel's book, *Democratizing Innovation*.

In this example, innovator and consumer are one and the same. It's a pattern that appears again and again. When von Hippel studied the development of scientific instruments in the 1970s, for instance, the bulk of useful innovations came not from instrument manufacturers but from the scientists themselves, because only they fully understood the specifics of the next thing that they would need to measure. Similarly, the first people to come up with an electrolyte-rich sports drink were not beverage companies but scientists at Florida State University, whose football team needed a competitive advantage while playing in hot, dehydrating conditions. Today, that beverage is named Gatorade, after the Florida Gators.

For lead-user innovation to make sense in a given market, consumer demands must be constantly, rapidly evolving. That is emphatically the case in the older market, due to both ongoing technological advances as well as converging demographic and economic forces. As narrative and demands change in the coming years, yet products remain the same, lead-user innovators will emerge to reconcile the difference.

Perhaps no class of consumer has ever been better equipped to do so than the baby boomers. They are the wealthiest, most highly educated generation ever to achieve old age, and in their lifetimes they have experienced the effects of technological change more profoundly than any other age cohort in history. They will expect nothing less than for that process to continue to into their later life, even if they have to make that happen themselves. Consider the people involved: retired or semiretired engineers, computer scientists, designers, CTOs, doctors, nurses, venture capitalists, and others who have spent their entire professional lives getting problems solved. When an obstacle affects them personally and they can see a way to solve it, they will innovate. In many cases, they will form start-ups of their own. And yes, venture funding is notoriously difficult for start-up founders as old as even their late 30s to obtain, an impediment that looms even larger for older women in particular. But that may soon change. I'm already seeing the beginnings of a self-supporting ecosystem of older start-up founders, angel investors, and venture capitalists, who will be ready to turn emerging lead-user insights into lean, competitive companies.

According to Encore.org, one quarter of Americans between 44 and 70 hope to start businesses or nonprofits in the coming 5–10 years. The Ewing Marion Kauffman Foundation, which is devoted to studying new business formation, reports that the rate of entrepreneurship among those aged 55–64 has nearly doubled since the mid-1990s, from 14.8 percent in 1996 to 25.8 percent in 2014. Older entrepreneurs now have the highest rate of any age group of opportunity entrepreneurship.*

---

* That is, new business creation undertaken by people who think they see a competitive opening, as opposed to "necessity entrepreneurship," which occurs when there are no other jobs available.

Still, the world of venture capital can be inhospitable to good ideas that come in unconventional (read: not young or male) packages. This is especially true of Silicon Valley, where there are but a few bright spots in an otherwise desolate venture-capital landscape. A handful of advocate funds are devoted to shepherding aging-related health companies into existence. Stitch benefited, for instance, from early, seed funding provided by Generator Ventures, which is affiliated with Aging2.0, an organization whose noble mission is to "accelerate innovation to improve the lives of older adults around the world."

But gaining the support of funders devoted less to improving old age and more to cold profit can be impossibly difficult. Regarding the funding challenges she's faced as a female entrepreneur targeting older consumers, Marcie Rogo laughed. "I think the question is what *aren't* the challenges. In this space and as a woman, it's . . . ," she trailed off. "If it's traditional VCs, it's almost impossible." For one thing, "the aging space is not sexy." Old age just isn't something investors spend much thought on, perhaps, Rogo mused, because they "don't like to think about their own mortality." Then there's the widespread misconception that older adults fear technology. But most devastatingly, investors like to back companies that resemble their past successes, which often equates to products made by, and sold to, guys who look like a young Mark Zuckerberg. Systems, remember, tend to perpetuate themselves.

Although at this time of writing Stitch has yet to receive a major, Series A round of financing, it has received smaller chunks of early-stage funding from a handful of well-known venture capitalists in addition to Generator Ventures, including Structure Capital, an early investor in Uber. Without the help of her well-connected, male cofounder, Rogo said, "We would not have raised any money from traditional venture capitalists, because you already have the subconscious bias to me as a woman."

The separation of women from positions of economic influence isn't limited to the United States. To return to Japan, where innovation happens more in large, entrenched companies than in scrappy start-ups, women hold just 11 percent of managerial or supervisory positions. In 2013, in a policy nicknamed "Womenomics," Prime Minister Shinzō Abe tried to boost women's presence in Japan's shrinking workforce using methods including a new national employment target, which large companies could meet by raising the number of female managers to 30 percent. By 2015, it became apparent that that was unlikely to happen, and Abe's officials halved the target figure.

There is cause for hope, however. In the United States, Japan, and most of the high-income world, we live in a capitalist system. And in capitalism, when something is undervalued for no good reason, as seems to be the case among start-ups with non-young-male founders, smart operators eventually sniff out the opportunity.

Pirc

Perhaps the most notable of these smart operators is an angel investor named Dan Scheinman. The "angel" designation means that Scheinman invests his own money, not that of a fund, in brand-new start-ups. He usually focuses on business-facing, or enterprise, companies. But in two cases, he's found compelling reasons to place bets on consumer businesses. One of them, called Tango, is a near-profitable videochat app that works across national borders and mobile platforms. It currently has "about 350 million people who've downloaded the app, and tens of millions of people are using it on a daily basis," Scheinman said. If it needs to, he said, Tango has enough cash in the bank to run as-is for more than a century. There was a hint of pride in his voice at the company's success, but it was clear that he thought there was still room to grow.

The other consumer-facing start-up, named Pirc, serves a more specific niche: dedicated couponers. Scheinman lives and works in Burlingame, a small Silicon Valley city. In his mid-50s and clad in an unassuming polo shirt that hinted at a recent, crumbly meal, he looked exactly like what he is: the best-kept secret in Silicon Valley investment.

At a local sandwich joint over Diet Cokes—"this is my poison," he said—he described his investment strategy. Although it may sound like there's no single theme running through Scheinman's portfolio, Tango, Pirc, and the rest have one thing in common: their founders are almost all old by Silicon Valley standards. That's not to say that Scheinman is an altruist, generously seeking to help older people trying to make a living, or even an advocate hoping to make the world a better place for older adults. "I'm not in the old-people-building-products-for-old-people business," Scheinman said. "I'm in the *tech* business." But because most other tech investors and venture funds are competing to woo the same pool of young, male founders, by broadening his search to include the older crowd, Scheinman has found a competitive edge.

"Every company I'm involved with has trouble raising money in Silicon Valley from traditional seed," the earliest stage of start-up investment, he said, thanks to the tendency of other investors to invest in Zuckerberg lookalikes. "They say, 'I made all my seed funding money when I funded kids out of Stanford, and so therefore that's what I want to fund, kids out of Stanford.' Or whatever variant of that," he said. "It's not like there's an iron bar" preventing non-young-male founders from succeeding. "It's more that you're in a room, and it's that subtle bias—a 'you're going to have to be twice as good in order to get half as far' kind of thing."

Because such demographic factors have little bearing on the ultimate ability of a company to deliver a good product, however, founders rejected by biased investors present what Scheinman has described to *The New Republic* as "the mother of all undervalued opportunities." "If you follow the herd," he said, and go after the same pool of young, male, Stanford-educated founders as everyone else in the venture community, "there's obviously billions of dollars of opportunity." However, "If you go the other way and you get it right, there may be *tens* of billions of dollars in opportunity. And so, I'm playing for that."

Fiddling with his Coke bottle, he reckoned that since he started angel investing in the late aughts, he'd made a return of three times the capital he's invested, not counting the assets he's still holding. If he were to suddenly liquidate those, the return would be more like a multiple of 10 or 15. But he's holding out for far more.

In the case of Tango, the video-call app start-up, one of the founders is older than Scheinman. "He was an Israeli tank commander but had done a bunch of start-ups. Very experienced guy." His cofounder, a veteran of both Hewlett Packard and several start-ups, was also old by Valley standards. With Tango, they were targeting the consumer, as opposed to enterprise, market, which some early-stage funders told Scheinman was foolish. Enterprise is widely seen as friendlier to older founders, he explained, because they have a long work history and often know their clients. But the consumer market is another story. "Some seed funders said to me, 'It is ridiculous that a 55-year-old-guy is going to be able to capture the consumer market.'" But Tango did, "because they understood peer-to-peer technology so well, they actually could build a product that consumers liked."

The Tango founders' deep knowledge of their customers was something they had in common with the other consumer-facing entrepreneur whom Scheinman had staked: Danielle Barbieri, founder and CEO of Pirc. Talking to Barbieri is like speaking to ball lightning, crackling with human energy. And yet at 43, Barbieri is ancient by Silicon Valley standards. In addition to running a demanding start-up in California, she also takes care of her 83-year-old mother, who lives alone in North Carolina. Barbieri flies there monthly, checking in and performing various health- and paperwork-related tasks. Typically, these kinds of duties end up on the plate of the oldest daughter of the family, and, though Barbieri is the youngest of four, "I'm single, and I'm female," she said with a laugh. Before her father died, she cared for him as well. "I lived half my life in a senior community," she said.

When she and her siblings grew up on Long Island, their family wasn't exactly wealthy. But "we never felt deprived or anything like that," Barbieri said, because her mother "was one of the smartest shoppers I ever met in my life." Barbieri would often spend time at her mother's elbow as she made her way through newspaper supplements, hunting for coupons and sale notifications. "She would do this all on paper—going through the papers and just trying to get the best deal on whatever. On chicken and fruit, or cereal . . . She worked tirelessly on going through the ads."

Barbieri's father first became ill in 2011. At the time, she was working in a small, consumer-facing section at Cisco, a major tech firm that sells networking equipment and services, mainly to businesses. That year, Cisco killed her section. "My whole team left," she said, including Dan Scheinman, who had been her boss.

She was laid off shortly thereafter, "which was great," she said, because she needed more time to spend caring for her father. But she had also lost her regular source of income. She said to herself, "Hey, I probably need to think about saving money now."

One constant source of consternation was the price of contact-lens solution. "I use a lot of contact-lens solution—like, a ton of it for some reason. Vats of it. And it's expensive, and it's basically like throwing water"—and money—"down the drain." As a result, she would try to only buy it on sale. "You save five dollars. It's not like chump change!"

But it was always an open question which store would have her ReNu or Clear Care on sale. "So that's essentially how it got started," she said. "I was like, well, this is really silly that I have to either go into the store, or do a really long search, and look for these digital circulars online—that, at the time, weren't very easy to navigate—just to know if something was on sale."

Pirc, the company she founded with another former Cisco colleague, aims to change that. What it does is so obvious that it's surprising no one's done it before: it tells consumers which of their favorite products is on sale in their local area and rounds up relevant coupons for them. "I get emails—I spend half my time doing customer service, which is always fun—saying, 'oh, I'm so glad someone's finally doing this. I thought of this idea ten years ago,'" Barbieri said.

Though Pirc is not explicitly aimed at the older female population, Barbieri estimated that that cohort probably constitutes a plurality of its current customers. ("Our first comments from users actually came from older males, saying, 'Oh, this is great. I can buy booze, like really cheap Jim Beam, at CVS.' Which is actually true. CVS has really great liquor deals.") It was knowledge of that older female consumer that initially inspired her. "I really did it with my mom in mind," she said. The service makes sense not only for people on a fixed income like her mother but also for people long accustomed to planning their shopping trips around sales. "They're very used to that behavior," she said, "and the fact that they now get it delivered to them—they like it."

Challenges remain. When first founding her company, Barbieri was lucky enough to know Scheinman, who was looking for undervalued, atypical company founders to back, and so she was able to get Pirc off the ground with the help of his seed investment. But finding the funding needed to move forward has proven a problem.

Regarding Barbieri's need for a round of Series A funding—the larger stage that comes after seed—"I think that if she was 25, doing the same pitch, I think she would have been funded, personally," Scheinman said. "Somebody would have rolled the dice, because she's very compelling, she's very smart." Not to mention, the product works—"It's a pretty good proof of concept," he said—and Barbieri's customers have proven remarkably loyal while keeping up their demand. What she hasn't been able to convince venture funders of, however, is that she will be able to bring more users on board without spending too much money.

It's a chicken-and-egg problem, said Scheinman. "It's a strange situation because here's what happens. The things that I think should have gotten funded,"—start-ups that never quite made it off the ground—"they don't work, and then the community said, 'See, I told you it didn't work.'" But, he said, raising his voice, "It didn't work because it didn't have any funding!"

Innovation: Disruptive and Sustaining

Happily, there's one powerful economic reason to believe that support will soon increase for entrepreneurs closely in tune with older adults' demands: *disruptive innovation*. First described in 1995 by Clayton Christensen, the source of our aforementioned breakfast milkshake example, disruptive innovation involves the selling of a simplified, more portable, or lower-cost version of an existing product, either to new customers in an existing market or in a new market context altogether. Typically, this process occurs to the detriment of established, incumbent companies. In the late 1960s, for instance, Toyota, Nissan, and Honda's cheap, subcompact cars found a fertile market in Americans seeking low-cost, reliable personal transportation. American manufacturers had been ignoring the needs of these customers as they made each year's model bigger, more powerful, and more expensive, and they lost a huge chunk of business to the Japanese firms as Americans began to buy the cheaper imports. At Chrysler, for instance, the early-1960s' sales gains Lynn Townsend had made by focusing on performance fell sharply by 1969. The company refused to introduce a truly subcompact car until 1978. By the next year, the company's new chief, Lee Iacocca, was asking Congress for the auto industry's first-ever bailout.

When Christensen introduced the concept of disruptive innovation as an explanation for upheavals of this sort, the timing couldn't have been better for the concept to catch fire. By the late 1990s, the first dot-com boom was shaking things up everywhere, and the entire business world was questioning old assumptions and making new leaps of faith. To established companies sensing the dot-coms nipping at their heels, Christensen's insight came as a welcome, if ominous, articulation of the threat they felt.

Even as late as 1995, the group of people who used the Internet could have been considered a "small or emerging market," the soil in which Christensen's disruptive innovation flourished. But Internet use soon exploded. And so "disruption," once something that happened only to an unlucky few companies, became the rallying cry of hungry Silicon Valley upstarts and panicked Fortune 500 execs alike. The term lost some of its specificity as it resounded, and people began to use it to refer to any idea that could shake up a status quo. "The theory's core concepts have been widely misunderstood and its basic tenets frequently misapplied," Christensen has recently written. In its original sense, the term should refer to only two situations: when a product or company finds a foothold in the low end of an existing market or else in a new market altogether. Among poorly served, older, female consumers, both cases apply.

Low-end footholds occur when the bottom of a market wants less out of a product than what's currently on offer: a cheap, low-power car with no bells or whistles, for instance, or a (relatively) inexpensive smartphone that can perform functions that once called for a bulky, costly laptop. In the older, mostly-female market, the opportunities for low-end disruption are so ripe that companies are already performing it by accident. These include Instacart, TaskRabbit, and Hello Alfred, which offer à la carte services that were once only available to older adults as part of a bundle. In the long run, perhaps these sorts of age-agnostic companies will prove to be the most successful low-end disruptors in the longevity economy. Or perhaps entrepreneurs will see older people hacking new usage cases out of platforms like Airbnb and realize that they could make an even better version explicitly for older adults. Probably, some combination of the two will prevail.

There is also ample opportunity in the longevity economy for new-market disruptions to take place, as companies find ways to provide an older cohort with products that were once reserved for the young. To be pedantic, Christensen's model of new-market disruption refers strictly to products that find new customers because someone has figured out how to make those products smaller, cheaper, or simpler. (For instance, the first personal computers were able to reach an untapped consumer market because they were smaller, cheaper, and simpler to use than the mainframes that preceded them.) But for all practical purposes, the message also holds for products that have been kept from the older market for reasons of narrative and obliviousness and that are only now becoming available. Under this broader definition, an online dating service for the 50-plus could be considered a potential new-market disruptor, as indeed would almost *any* technological service for older adults, who have been heretofore ignored by the bulk of the tech sector. But the opportunity in no way stops there. As the baby boomers climb into older age ranges, unheralded consumer demands will emerge, creating new markets for solutions—especially tech solutions. Companies serving these novel wants and needs may achieve dramatic growth, often at the expense of long-established relationships between incumbent businesses and their customers. Thanks to Pirc, for instance, the stereotype of the grandmother clipping coupons from the local newspaper may not be long for this world.

The single factor underlying all future older-market innovations will be the job of the consumer. When a woman like Sally Lindover has a job to be done, such as stocking her pantry *without* sacrificing her independence, then the product of assisted living, with all its bundled services, is worse than too expensive. Those extra "perks" constitute a turn-off to the consumer whose job it is to avoid them. And when a woman like Kathie needs more personal connections of her own age but thinks of herself as a normal, social person, not a medical patient, her job as a consumer calls for a service that feels, well, normal. The idea of going on a date fits her self-image in a way that a medicalized, isolation-abatement program never could have.

In the near future, the products and technologies that will make old age better will, by and large, be those that work for women like Lindover and Kathie, not to mention caregivers like Danielle Barbieri and care recipients like her mother. These products, through disruption or by simply improving on what's come before, have the potential to utterly upend existing markets—in the United States and elsewhere. Even in Japan, where the large corporation reigns supreme, there is cause for concern among incumbents. In early 2016, ReadyFor?, Japan's top, Kickstarter-esque crowdfunding platform, announced that over half of its projects were founded by women, and women paid for half of all donations. ReadyFor?, founded by university student Haruka Mera while she was studying in Tokyo, owes some of its success to its website, which was designed to set at ease those who might feel shy about asking acquaintances to fund their professional goals. That is, the company that is most successfully helping female, Japanese business founders—the ones who best understand the jobs of the female consumer—was itself designed by a woman who understood how to solve the job of *her* consumers. Once again, systems tend to perpetuate themselves, but in this case, success begets success.

The mounting economic demand of older women, who are less beholden to the current narrative of old age than men, is the fuel that will drive us toward a better old age. The insights of hackers and lead-user innovators in that group, or among those who care for older adults, will serve as the spark in the engine.

Businesses, as well as governments and nonprofits, need to support this process or risk being run over. The way to do so is simple, although it involves investing real money in a class of people to whom companies often pay mere lip service. Hire and retain women, especially older women and caregivers, in important roles; fund and acquire their companies.

Slowly, change may be coming to the venture world. Dan Scheinman said that emerging funds are now following his example and investing in nontraditional founders. "There are other funds now that have cropped up, that are trying to target the same niche," he said. One thing that's changed in the last five years is "the rise of a gazillion funds that are small, but are targeting things." Major, Series-A-level funds have consolidated and scaled back on their investments at the seed level, and as a result, "micro-funds" with dozens of millions in capital, as opposed to billions, have emerged. That's "where the explosion of innovation has occurred," he said.

Inevitably, some of these micro-funds are trying out Scheinman's approach. "No one has been as bold as to steal my language yet—or borrow it," he amended. But it's still clear when a micro-fund is bullish on older founders. "They're all wary about using the same words. So, they slightly couch things differently. They say, 'Really very experienced, engineering-focused team,' or something." Regardless of terminology, "You can see them thinking the same way."

I wondered whether this new influx of action in what had been Scheinman's private pool of founders was going to be a problem for him. Far from it, he said. In fact, "More capital is better." Once upon a time, when he wanted to invest in an older founder's company but didn't want to take on all the risk personally, he had to bring together wealthy friends to form a coalition of backers. More recently, however, "I've been able to find tons of capital now that says, 'Hey, ok, this is interesting.'"

Diplomatically, Scheinman acknowledged the value of doing venture capital the traditional way and pursuing younger founders. "There's all sorts of perfectly good reasons that people do go that route." Younger founders are often more desperate, he said, and because they're new to business and in need of advice, they tend to keep the lines of communication with funders open. "The amount of value creation by young founders is astounding, right? I mean you can't argue with it."

He took a sip of his Diet Coke. "But on the other hand, you know, it's not the only way to make money. And I'm going to—I mean, I have proven it. I'm going to prove it even more."

4

A Tale of Two Villages

CRAIG LOOKED AT his feet and frowned. For hours, he had been riding in the passenger seat as his dad, Ken, drove hurriedly through a series of quiet, exquisitely manicured neighborhoods in search of a stolen vehicle that belonged to Ken's father, Ken Sr. "Aw, man, I got my flip-flops on," said Craig, a college freshman on break. "I wish I had my sneakers on. If we catch this kid, we're going to have to run him down."

Such an event was starting to seem unlikely. The sun was now hanging low in the sky, and Ken pulled the visor down to keep it out of his eyes. Neither wanted to say what they were both thinking: how their chances of finding the stolen vehicle were fading with every passing minute. How an expression of defeat would spread across Ken Sr.'s face when they returned empty-handed.

Then they rounded a corner and saw their target idling next to the road. As Ken pulled up, Craig jumped out of the still-moving car. He sprinted over and slapped his open palm on the stolen vehicle's windshield. "Don't move!" he yelled. Meanwhile, Ken wrenched his steering wheel to the right, hemming in the vehicle with his own car. There wasn't just one thief, he was surprised to find, but three. They all looked at each other.

The two perps up front were 17. The driver was small and twitchy, but the one in the passenger seat was big and mean looking. After a moment of panicked eye contact, they climbed out and scattered in all directions.

Ken hustled over and managed to grab the driver by his collar. Another kid, who had been clinging to the back of the vehicle, got away, bolting toward the town square. The big one headed toward the woods.

He never got there. Craig, a college lacrosse star, took off like a missile, tackling him in the small of the back. The kid tried to get up, raised a fist.

"Don't even think about it," Craig said. "I will drop you so fast." He meant it. This wasn't the Wild West. This was The Villages, the largest retirement community in the world. There were rules here. And the kids had stolen his grandfather's golf cart.

*   *   *

LET'S PAUSE FOR a moment at this scene of vigilante justice and rise upward through the muggy Central Florida air to take a bird's-eye view of the surroundings.

As we hover, the first thing you'll notice is the sheer number of fairways below, sprawled about like emerald amoebae. The Villages offers 630 holes of golf—more, its marketing department will gladly tell you, than any other one place in the world. The golf courses are surrounded by over 50,000 standalone houses, notable mainly for their structural homogeneity and the uniform green of their lawns. Their driveways look clean enough to slurp spaghetti from, and golf cart paths, totaling over 100 miles of asphalt, extend in every direction. They cross over highways and tunnel under thoroughfares, connecting not just courses and homes but also three master-planned town squares, a multitude of swimming pools, fitness centers and community centers, several fishing reservoirs, and a polo stadium. Nearly every household in the Villages has at least one golf cart, and residents use them to go everywhere. On the outskirts of town, the cart paths lead to supermarkets and box stores galore.

And finally, witness the ubiquity of the golf carts, 50,000 strong, crawling steadily along the paths and roads. Once, just for kicks, Villages residents made the world's longest golf cart parade and had it entered into the *Guinness Book of World Records*. Nowhere have more retirees gathered together to live out their days in comfortable-yet-active bliss, separated, for the most part, from everyone under the worthy age of 55. The growth of the community has proven extraordinary, especially in recent years. Between 2010 and 2015, The Villages' population more than doubled. At the time of this writing, nearly 124,000 people live there, and it's been the fastest-growing metropolitan area in the United States for four years running. In 2011, one of the worst years for new home sales in recent US history, The Villages announced that its sales accounted for nearly 1 percent of the nation's total.

There's a single, very good reason so many flock to The Villages: it makes its residents happy. The community is beautiful, in its way, and filled with decent people who worked hard to earn the leisure-filled lifestyle it offers.

And yet, The Villages gives me pause. Not because I have any particular problem with the way of life there: I want people to be able to decide on an individual basis how to live in old age, and it's not my job to tell them which lifestyle to choose. (Besides, as I mentioned earlier, I'm a Jimmy Buffet fan, and no true Parrothead has much compunction about easy livin'. In fact, Buffet has announced plans to open his own string of sunny, Margaritaville-themed retirement communities.) No, what worries me is The Villages' awesome narrative power. The place is so geographically large—bigger than Manhattan, and growing—and the vision of life it paints is so vivid yet familiar, that once you know it exists, it can be hard to look away. A narrative force on this scale has the power to warp our very understanding of what's normal and desirable in old age, biasing the thoughts of those considering where and how to live, not to mention companies seeking to understand what will inspire aging consumers.

Imagine having just sat down at the world's best restaurant. Without warning, all the lights go out. Although you've been told the menu is filled with all kinds of wonderful things, many of which you've never experienced before, you can't read it. Suddenly, a candle is lit at a nearby table; the rest of the restaurant remains shrouded in darkness. You turn to look and lay your eyes upon the best-looking plate of steak and potatoes you've ever seen. The steak can be cut with fork, and the potatoes are softly glowing like golden embers of deliciousness. But still, it's steak and potatoes—and you have a once-in-a-lifetime chance to try something new. What do you order?

I actually really enjoy steak and potatoes, probably a little too much. But it would be a shame for someone hoping to try quail eggs or blood sausage—or even spaghetti and meatballs—to have their options limited to steak because it's the only guaranteed item on the menu. The lifestyle offered by The Villages is like that lone, illuminated steak dinner. To many who find themselves seeking a viable way to live in old age, it can seem like the only good, reliable option, simply because it's the most *visible* choice.

The inability to perceive alternatives to The Villages' lifestyle poses a particularly serious hazard to product developers, designers, and marketers. In theory, by prioritizing the job of the consumer, longevity-economy innovators should be able to break free of the old narrative and address aging consumers' upper-level goals and aspirations, not just fundamental needs. (In some cases, companies will even compete to *define* what tomorrow's older adults will want.) But all that will be for naught if said innovators, upon first considering their consumers' aspirations, immediately seize upon The Villages as the answer. If you, as a younger product designer, internalize the notion that every older person hopes to live in a sun-drenched, leisure-oriented, age-segregated retirement community, then that idea will likely worm its way into your work, whether you intend it to or not. In this roundabout way,

The Villages may lead to products that fail to jibe with the sort of life most older adults want for themselves. Despite the place's hypervisibility, the lifestyle on offer there isn't all that popular—at least, not on a national scale. Eighty-seven percent of those over 65 would prefer to "age in place" in their own homes and communities than move to a retirement destination, as would 71 percent of those aged 50–64.

That said, the minority of people who do like what's being sold at The Villages *really* like it, and it's easy to see why: life there simply makes sense at a gut level. At a moment when it feels like there is no single, normal, agreed-upon way to thrive in old age, that coherence is spellbinding. It shines in the dark as an example of something that simply works. And unfortunately, that means that it has the potential to outshine any nascent, alternative modes of later life. Should longevity-economy businesses issue products as though all their customers were would-be Villagers, any older adult who hopes to live otherwise may find herself unable to obtain the tools she needs to thrive. The idea that older adults are a needy, greedy drain on society will only strengthen its hold on our minds. Worst of all, as I will explain, the notion that older people are frittering away generous Social Security checks in a manicured, age-segregated paradise may well set generations at each other's throats—at exactly the moment when austerity-minded politicians are likely to consider cutting back on entitlement spending.

In short, although The Villages *as a product* may achieve the commendable goal of making older people happy, The Villages *as an idea* threatens the entire project of building a better narrative of aging and may act as a wet blanket on the longevity economy. But that doesn't mean that companies hoping to understand tomorrow's older society have nothing to learn from the place. More than any other mode of later life that you could point to, The Villages' lifestyle is both coherent and compelling. It makes sense to a generation facing a protracted, unfamiliar stage of life, and it does so in a manner that draws in both widespread attention and eager, new residents.

In the future, any successful vision of later life will share these attributes. In fact, one notable upstart is already attempting to define a new way to live in old age, and some older adults are already finding it hard to resist. This community is also a village of a sort, but it lacks The Villages' most notable drawbacks. It was created by older people, for older people, and yet it presents a way for different generations to coexist in something resembling harmony. For product designers and other innovators hoping to get a picture of what an aspirational, coherent, compelling old age might look like, this second village is a great place to start.

Whether it or any other alternative vision of late life can go toe-to-toe with The Villages in a battle for narrative dominance remains to be seen, however. To find out, we must first delve into the source of The Villages' magnetism. Let's plunge back down to the level of its streets and golf cart paths. What makes retirees want to drop everything and move there? And what can go wrong when they do?

The Villages' Lifestyle

The Villages wasn't always such a gleaming testament to tiny cars and easy living. It started out as a late-1960s' mistake. A Michigan land speculator, Harold Schwartz, had been selling parcels of Florida woods, farms, and pastureland by mail order when a 1968 federal edict banned the practice. Stuck with acres upon acres of low-value land, he and a partner built a mobile-home park in what today is the oldest part of The Villages. Perhaps because the park was in the middle of nowhere, buyer interest remained low. After a decade of trying, the duo had sold only 400 units.

In 1983, at age 73, Schwartz had the breakthrough he'd been waiting for when he visited his sister in Sun City, Arizona, where Del Webb had built one of the world's first master-planned retirement communities. Like Schwartz's holdings, Sun City was an island of civilization miles away from any nearby cities—Phoenix hadn't yet sprawled so widely—although its brand of wilderness was more gila monster than alligator. But compared to Schwartz's mobile-home park, Sun City was beautiful. Its homes, pools, and roads were conspicuously well appointed, and more importantly, the community had become massive enough, and had enough going on, that its own gravitational pull kept the homebuyers streaming in, checkbooks in hand. Sun City wasn't a place where people could get away from it all, like backwoods Florida. Far from it: it was a *destination*.

That year, Schwartz bought out his partner's share in their land holdings and brought in his son, Gary Morse, to help him create a new, Floridian Sun City. The question was how to prime the pump. What could attract that first crucial wave of homebuyers who would go back up north and tell their friends, *come on down, the weather is fine*?

Morse had the answer. He instructed landscapers to plant a local watermelon field with dense, close-cut grass, and had a few ponds and sand pits installed. Finally, he had nine small holes cut in the ground, stuck flagpoles in them, and commenced a two-word ad campaign: "Free Golf!"

During the decades of meteoric growth that followed, the promise of "Free Golf!" has remained encoded in the DNA of The Villages. There are now 36 "executive," nine-hole courses, which are "free" for residents (actually covered by a monthly, $145 "amenities fee," which all Villages households pay), and eleven 18- or 27-hole "championship" courses, which charge discounted greens fees to residents. The centrality of golf to Villages life, in addition to drawing in the sport's aficionados, accomplished something far more important: it made golf carts ubiquitous, which solved a good deal of the sprawling community's elder-transportation problem. The fact that residents, even many of those no longer licensed to drive, could maintain their independence by riding their carts into town became one of The Villages' major selling points.

Today, when not whacking the pockmarked ball, residents can hit nearby pools and fitness centers; tennis, pickleball, and bocce courts;

and far more. Every week, more than 1,000 weekly activities are open to the Villages' public, organized by a dedicated Recreation Department. At night, house parties flourish, and the bar and nightclub scene resembles that of a college town, albeit one that goes to bed early. The wine flows like beer, and the beer flows like water—in fact, some restaurants pipe it underground from a central microbrewery. Martinis can be had for three dollars.

It says something about the current moment that this leisure and consumption-oriented lifestyle, though not universally appealing, is achieving such remarkable resonance among a subset of the older population. The life stage of retirement is on the wane, in the sense that more and more people are saying that they hope to work at their current jobs right through their 65th birthdays or else shift gears and find a job somewhere new or work part time. But at the same time, plenty of people are still retiring for good, and that poses the same problem of identity that has been vexing retirees for a century: *Without your job, what are you? Senior vice president of your living room? Admiral of the bathtub?* And when you don't know what you are, how do you know what to do when you get out of bed in the morning?

If anything, the sense of identity loss posed by retirement is now *more* confusing than it was in the 1950s and 1960s, when the idea of the "golden years" first emerged as a response. For one thing, those who "work in retirement" find themselves straddling categories, teeter-tottering between production and repose in a way retirees of yore rarely had to consider. For another, it was originally mainly men who faced an identity crisis upon receiving the gold watch; now, it's an equal-opportunity pickle. Add in all the other ways later life is changing—technological progress; shifting consumer attitudes and demands; increased longevity; dissolving institutions, including religious communities; geographically dispersed family structures; fewer children; heightened divorce rates—and suddenly, if you're near the traditional age of retirement, you've got an unexpected and unexplored new terrain in front of you.

For many, life on this untrammeled landscape is intolerable. "Those who move to any new frontier are likely to pay a price, in loneliness and discomfort," wrote David Riesman, the midcentury sociologist I mentioned earlier, in his 1952 essay on leisure and consumerism. And if life on any frontier is "awkward," as he put it, plagued by "formlessness" and "aimlessness," that's especially true of the retirement frontier. Having a career in middle age is like living in a town: whether you're a butcher or a baker or a candlestick maker, you know where you stand relative to your peers. But travel far enough beyond the city limits—or live long enough past the age of retirement—and those labels cease to matter. The wilderness has a way of obliterating one's socially derived sense of identity, which can feel freeing during a weeklong camping trip, but disconcerting when it's a permanent state of affairs. And so it's inevitable that some, upon discovering themselves thrust out onto the frontier of old age, hasten immediately over to the biggest settlement where life seems to make sense.

What's not immediately apparent, however, is *how* The Villages causes life to make sense. Some prospective residents see that Villagers seem to enjoy themselves, and that's evidence enough: they waltz in with open arms. Others, however, sidle in more furtively, like a cowpoke entering an unfamiliar saloon, and look around for the catch. Villages resident Donald "Smoke" Hickman belongs to this second group. Smoke (I'll continue to refer to him by his nickname because to do otherwise would be a waste) would never bring it up unbidden, but his long and illustrious career in the US Navy culminated in the rank of rear admiral. By the end of his career, he had assumed authority of the Navy Systems Supply Command and oversaw significant modernization of the Navy's supply chains. At that time, because he was a member of the military, Smoke's retirement schedule was a known quantity, and as his last day of service approached, he decided to tackle his transition to civilian life with all the planning and pragmatism of a battle plan.

Stopping full-time work "was just one of my objectives," he said. But there was more to it: a question of who he would become and what he would do with his time. "You've got this goal: 'I'm going to retire,' but, well, what are you going to do?" he said. And equally pressing: "Where did I want to live, then?"

Today, he counsels new retirees as they grapple with these sorts of questions. But 10 years ago, when he first retired, he thought he had it all figured out. He and his wife moved to a beach house in Jacksonville, Florida. Which, they quickly discovered, turned out to be a *boring* beach house in Jacksonville. "We'd get up in the morning and walk the beach, come back, look at one another, go back in the evening, walk the beach. You'd see the same people on the beach every morning and every evening. It just wasn't a lifestyle that I wanted to continue for however many years I have left," Smoke said.

So they reassessed and hit the road: traveling all over Florida looking for a place where there was more to do. "We kept coming back to visit our friends here in The Villages, and we were so impressed with, not the housing per se, because there's a lot nicer houses out in other communities, but with the activities"—that is, the long litany of club meetings, games, sporting events, and other goings-on heralded every day in the local newspaper, *The Village Sun*. It sounded wonderful, but they worried there was a hidden catch, so they hedged their bets by buying a smaller villa than they otherwise would have. "This place is almost like a dream that's too good to be true," Smoke said. "And so you keep saying, '*There's got to be something wrong.*'"

It's not hard to find reasons why someone might approach The Villages with skepticism. For one thing, the cost of living does feel too low to be true: housing is relatively cheap; the $145 amenities fee (plus a small bond) covers everything from golf to fitness centers to swimming pools; and, during happy hour, beer costs even less than soda. For another, the place gets interesting press. If you're younger than The Villages' target demographic, and you knew its name prior to reading this, it was probably because the media gleefully reported on its sexually transmitted infection rate, which spiked in the late aughts. Articles and television segments about The Villages tend to fixate on these sorts of lurid details—if not the STIs, then the colorful bar scene or the fact that The Villages has placards set up that celebrate fake historical events. There are also more significant reasons for a potential resident to worry, however. For instance, The Villages' developer runs various arms of the local media, including television, newspaper, and radio, which tend to focus on nonnews or, worse, serve as pro-Villages marketing.* Perhaps the most serious charge against the community can be found in journalist Andrew Blechman's book *Leisureville* (the source of some of the historical facts in this chapter), which contends that The Villages, with its lack of children, functions as a haven from local school taxes. Ultimately, the perhaps unfair sense you can get of The Villages by reading about it and watching the news is that it's decadent—in both the "pleasure-seeking" meaning of the term as well as in the decline-and-fall sense, which is what happens to societies that refuse to pay for the education of their children.

And yet, Smoke and his wife moved in to "check it out and find out what was wrong," as he described it 10 years ago. After six years, they upgraded to a newer, slightly larger home, and settled in for the long haul. If there was a catch to the place, they hadn't discovered it. Property values had stayed strong, even through the housing bust that had left the rest of Florida reeling. The aspects of Villages life they signed on for never diminished: the cart paths stayed clean, the grass stayed green, and the other residents remained as friendly and engaged as ever. Most important, The Villages had provided an answer to Smoke's question of identity. It wasn't that the community provided its residents with replacements to fill in the void left by their primary careers. Rather, The Villages diminished the *need* for such replacements through a form of imposed equality that, were it to occur in any other kind of community, would be considered radical.

---

* In July 2016, for example, the cover story of the newspaper's monthly magazine supplement celebrated "25 Years of Hometown Banking" by Citizens First Bank, which supplies most of the mortgages in town and which is a subsidiary of The Villages' developer.

In a world where you spend less time in your car than your golf cart, the comestibles are uniformly affordable, and houses are, for the most part, strikingly similar, conspicuous consumption falls off the map, to an extent. The most ostentatious thing a Villager can do is trick out a golf cart and hope people notice. (Everyone there has seen the cart that looks exactly like a yellow Hummer, faithfully reproduced at one-third scale.) Or if you want to, you can buy one of the community's hulking, "Premier" homes; most prospective Villagers, seeking to downsize, chose instead to live in modest, single-level houses. And that's about it: there are few other major class signifiers, at least of the sort money can buy, to be had. Meanwhile, there are many other luxuries to be enjoyed, but they're all communal in nature. Regardless of income or savings, everyone shares the gleaming roads, cart paths, health clubs, pools, and decent, cheap restaurants. The golf remains free at many courses, and it's affordable at the rest. At the polo grounds, everyone can support the imported hometown riders—an extravagance for the whole community.

"The developer here just had a vision," said Jane Boldrick, one of Smoke's neighbors. "He was going to provide a place where people who had had careers, where you have pensions and benefits, plus Social Security, you could live what he calls the lifestyle of the millionaire." Another Villager even averred that it would be possible to live on Social Security alone in The Villages, assuming you owned your house outright.

To Smoke, who had lived for decades as part of a rigid, military pecking order, the resulting sense of equality was a major part of what made him want to stay. "Everybody's the same. That's what I really enjoy," he said. "No one ever says to me: 'What did you do before you moved here?' There's no social hierarchy here that says, 'Well, I was the director of umpty-ump. Some people can get pretty carried away with those kinds of titles, or so I've found. But here, no one even cares what you did before you lived here."

In terms of its leveling effect, the closest analogue to The Villages isn't an independent living facility but rather a college dorm where the offspring of royalty intermingle with kids from all walks of life. With all that equality, all that activity, and all those material comforts, the chief psychological problem of retirement becomes far less pressing. Socially, it no longer matters if you're rich or middle-class, nor does it matter what you once did for work. When, as Smoke said, nobody cares if you were the "director of umpty-ump," the need to define yourself as what you were during your primary career falls away. Crucially, you become not who you were in the past but rather what you do in the present. And because, more often than not, "what you do in the present" becomes nearly synonymous with what one chooses to do socially, people who move to The Villages often discover that their social lives flourish. A full schedule of get-togethers is the norm; even more so on special occasions. One New Year's Eve, in the afternoon, Lee, the mother and grandmother, respectively, of the heroes of the aforementioned golf cart chase, discussed her plans for the night.

"We're going to go to different houses. Everyone has to bring something," she said. At the first house, the hostess would provide wine, "and the rest of us will just arrive with an empty wine glass. And then we'll go from her house to another house for hors d'oeuvres, then another house for coffee and desserts. And then the last house is champagne only. And we never leave the neighborhood. And it's so funny. Everybody's out walking, yelling. Some are in golf carts. Some aren't." She paused to laugh, then stopped. "We had a death once, early on. And they had a celebration-of-life party at the house. And I was walking down the street with a casserole and I said, 'It's like *Little House on the Prairie*.'"

In "The Villages life," as residents frequently refer to it, people know where they stand with their neighbors, and they know what to do on a given day. The Villages, then, is a *coherent* response to the fuzziness of postcareer existence. But is it truly *compelling*? Set aside the majority of people beyond The Villages' gates who would prefer to age in their own longtime homes and communities. To the subset of people willing to uproot in retirement, how seductive is it, exactly?

Judging by the testimony of Jodie Elliot, who lives in a neighborhood just outside The Villages, the answer is *highly*. Elliot and her husband are in their mid-40s. When her parents moved down to The Villages from a suburb of Boston, the Elliots decided to follow. But they have two kids, and children are only allowed in The Villages as visitors. So they did the next best thing to moving in—they built a house just outside The Villages' gates, where they could bide their time. Architecturally, their home greatly resembles those inside The Villages, with a screened-in, lanai-style patio and stucco walls. The main difference is that it's bigger and has a second story, where bedrooms and a dual-purpose play and study room can be found.

At first, Elliot said, "we thought we needed a better school system. We thought we needed to be closer to an airport." But once they traveled down to scope out what they thought would probably be a vacation home, they decided, "No, we can live here! Let's live here." Now, Elliot homeschools the kids while her husband, Robert, works from a home office.

"We hope to retire early. We, throughout the years, have decided like not to have cable, not to have the latest and greatest cars . . . because we'd rather save for retirement, and retire early. That would be better to us than having all that stuff. I mean, we do pretty well anyways. But if we can retire early . . . then we can play! We can ride bikes and do whatever!"

The Elliots already had golf carts and access to The Villages facilities, thanks to guest passes procured from her parents. But still, they yearned to be inside the gates.

Their daughter had just turned 10, she said. "So we can move in, like, less than nine years, because she has to be nineteen, and she's our youngest." (Adults between 19 and 55 can live in The Villages, just not own property there.) "So we're talking eight years, ten months—What time is it?—three hours. Yeah, we're definitely moving into The Villages."

Although Elliot was half-joking about counting down the days until her kids came of age, the fact remained that The Villages exerted a magnetic pull on her, even at the young age of 45. From a perspective like hers, The Villages is more than heaven's waiting room—it's the end goal.

It's hard to overstate how compelling The Villages is to people like Elliot. Prior to the release of a new Apple gadget, people will sometimes camp out for days in front of the company's stores. When the Elliots finally make it into The Villages, they will have camped outside for over a decade.

More Equal Than Others

Though Villagers find their community both coherent and highly compelling, there's one good reason why it can't be the answer to the question of how we'll all live tomorrow. Life inside The Villages may simply work, but the relationship between communities of this sort and everyone outside their gates is intrinsically unstable, and likely to become more so.

To return to our earlier analogy, one aspect of the American frontier too easily forgotten is the dozens of experiments in living that were once tried there—by transcendentalists, utopian socialists, free lovers, vegetarians (once seen as very strange), anarchists, and many others. In almost every case, the most notable exception being the Mormon settlement of Salt Lake City, these communities failed. Whether it was due to personality clashes, power struggles, natural disasters, war, disease, or simply the slow, westward creep of American society, frontier experiments died and disappeared. In the end, the only communities that survived were those that proved stable in the face of wild nature and human nature alike.

Settlements on the frontier of our new, longer lives are no different. Human nature will prevail above the best-laid plans of housing developers—even at The Villages, which isn't all happy hours and holes-in-one. There's a dark side to the place that makes me question its long-term survivability. And it starts with the kids who stole Ken Sr. and Lee's golf cart.

Immediately after tackling the biggest of the golf cart thieves, Craig, the college athlete, stood up and dragged him by his sweatshirt back to Ken's car, where a passing woman stopped to alternately berate the kid and warn Craig not to let him go. Meanwhile, Ken got a hold of his wife, Jackie, who called the police. They soon arrived in three cruisers.

"The kid's cursing, and one of the other kids are bleeding," Ken said. The third had hightailed it, and so the police asked one of the two in custody what the third looked like and headed into town to see if they could find any likely suspects.

"They picked up this big kid that was in town," Ken said, who turned out to be the wrong guy. They brought him back and got the right one.

It turned out that two of the kids were brothers whose father had just gotten out of jail that morning. The third was in his grandfather's custody. The golf cart theft was part of a miniature juvenile crime wave. "What they do is they steal the golf carts, and they either run them out of gas or until they have no more juice, and then run them into the lake or a pond or something," Jackie said.

The kids in question were apparently out to do some damage that day. The driver "was such a punk," Ken said. "As they got him, he says, 'That thing's never going to run the same. We took it over these speed bumps.'" Ultimately, a judge required the kids to write a letter of apology, which Jackie said never arrived.

"So that's basically the story," Ken said. "We got the cart back, and we're heroes." True, but one question remains: what, beyond a normal teenage appreciation for chaos, made kids in The Villages want to inflict so much damage? Clearly, there were multiple possible factors at work, including socioeconomic issues and disrupted family lives. There's reason to believe something else was going on, however. At The Villages and other retirement communities like it, although the amenities may all be first class, children are second-class citizens.

Two-and-a-half hours southeast of The Villages, there's a 55-and-over gated community called Woodfield, where children are not allowed to spend more than 30 overnight visits per year, but day visits are unlimited. Until November 2013, Bhaskar Barot, 63, lived there peacefully, occasionally babysitting his four-year-old granddaughter at his house. But on the morning of November 14, that peace was shattered. Barot woke up to discover huge, yellow letters spray-painted, in what looked like the unsteady handwriting of a kindergartener, across the hood and sides of his Toyota Camry and his wife's grey minivan. The graffiti read, again and again: "NO KIDS."

In *Leisureville*, Blechman notes a general sense of antipathy toward local kids at The Villages. "I'm always getting in trouble for trying to skateboard there," one preteen boy from an adjacent town told him. "I haven't seen a sign saying 'No Skateboarding,' but they take your skateboard away anyway." The issue isn't that people who seek out age-segregated communities are child haters—for the most part, anyway. But, as a retirement housing developer told Blechman, "they don't want somebody else's grandkids peeing in the pool. Kids can be messy."

But kids are also inevitable. Like most age-segregated communities, The Villages offered no schools during its first 17 years of operation. As it grew, however, filling up with stores, restaurants, and theaters at the same time that the developer's operations became more and more complex, enticing people to work there became an issue. In less ambitious gated retirement communities, workers routinely drive in from the outside and drive home at the end of the day. But The Villages sprawled too wide and too far from other population centers to support that model. Employees needed to be able to live within The Villages, and their offspring had to be cared for and educated during the day. The Villages, to its credit, didn't skimp on its obligation: it built charter schools for those kids—really nice ones. The multistory school buildings are gleaming edifices, and the grass on the athletic fields surrounding them is every bit as lush as the nearby golf courses.

Those schools and fields testify to the fact that no community can survive without children. But except for kids of Villages employees, resident children are still verboten there—for reasons of peace and quiet, adult conversation, and, most justifiably, a respite from an increasingly youth-focused media and commercial landscape. Villagers don't just enjoy the "lifestyle of a millionaire" by sharing luxury products and avoiding comparison to the trappings of the super rich. They also gain value by dodging the insults of a culture that unthinkingly praises youth and unflinchingly disparages age. In this respect, The Villages can feel like an island of sanity. But excluding the young comes at a price. When kids are raised in places that are intrinsically biased against them, it shouldn't be surprising that some develop a chip on the shoulder. And those golf carts look awfully fun to drive.

It may seem unfair to blame the rules of a retirement community for teenage vandalism and destruction—and indeed, plenty of age-integrated communities also have their share of young miscreants. But consider: not only are age-restricted retirement communities the only federally protected form of housing discrimination in the United States, but they are also deeply alien relative to almost every other form of community that has ever existed. Even those experimental, 19th-century frontier towns included children. When strange conduct emanates from strange social structures, it's not unreasonable to wonder to what extent those structures are responsible.

I'm not overly concerned that the residents of gated retirement communities and a handful of teenagers might wage an eternal prank war against each other. Rather, I'm worried that the antagonism on display represents the potential for something far wider-reaching and worse. Will we look back on these incidents of theft and vandalism as the first shots in a much larger intergenerational conflict—guerrilla attacks against the enemy's mode of transportation? It's easy to imagine such small acts of resentment writ large, especially as the older population expands and younger demographics change.

Ever since it was first defined as a worthy-yet-pitiable problem at the end of the 19th century and beginning of the 20th, the population of "the aged" has enjoyed one distinct advantage over other groups that draw assistance from tax revenues: at some point, almost everyone joins the club. Consequently, to the younger people paying the bills, the support of older generations feels not just altruistic but also like an investment in themselves.

For this arrangement to endure, however, younger people must continue to see their future selves in their present elders, an act of recognition that will soon come under demographic stress. As the United States becomes a majority-minority nation and similar trends unfold in Europe and elsewhere, most population growth will come from first- and second-generation immigrants, a consequence of immigration itself as well as the fact that immigrant families tend to have higher birth rates. Meanwhile, it's a deeply unfair truth that white older adults in the United States, Europe, and Australia have higher life expectancies than most* other races in these countries. The result of both trends will be older generations that are far whiter than younger ones. There's no way around the fact that when tomorrow's younger people look at their elders, the faces that stare back will appear strange to many of them.

Now, to add to this possible source of contention between generations, mix in an actual one. The Villages, as a beacon of narrative, reinforces the widespread perception that older adults are not just needy but also greedy: resource-hungry golf aficionados enjoying the "lifestyle of a millionaire" thanks to payroll taxes imposed on working-age families. Worse still is the implication, not entirely without merit, that retirement destinations function as school tax havens. Already, the more older adults living in a community, the less it spends on schools, an effect that is particularly pronounced in places where the older population is largely white and the school-age population is black or

---

* One notable exception to this trend in the United States is what demographers call the "Hispanic paradox," in which first-generation Hispanic immigrants tend to live longer than whites. This advantage, whether due to a biased sample (healthier individuals tend to be the ones able to immigrate) or lifestyle, disappears by the second generation.

Latino. These trends go back to the first major retirement community, Del Webb's Sun City. As Blechman recounts in *Leisureville,* over a dozen years starting in 1962, Sun City residents voted down 17 school bond measures, eventually causing a budget shortfall so severe that the local school district could only accommodate its students in staggered time blocks. The district ultimately deannexed Sun City in order to regain control.

Finally, add in the biggest stressor of all and pray that the contract between generations doesn't break: supporting tomorrow's enormous older population will be very expensive. Perhaps the most systematic accounting of everything that can go wrong given our upcoming demographic reality (and assuming few changes to the way old age works) can be found in economist Larry Kotlikoff and journalist Scott Burns's gloomy book *The Coming Generational Storm.* In it, they make the mathematical argument that if things continue as they have, with older ranks swelling, birth rates waning, and medical costs increasing, US children born in 2006 or later will have to pay double-sized tax rates just to keep Social Security, Medicare, and Medicaid afloat. In other countries such as Japan, where the demographics are more severe and national debt is higher, the tax situation could be far worse.

Already, there are those who would advocate extreme action—the rationing of health care for older people; the diminishment or eradication of Social Security, its equivalent in countries other than the United States, and public pensions. The effect would be catastrophic: an amplification of the ongoing, global shift of risk from the collective to the older individual. That, given the breakdown of the safety net once formed by family members all over the world, is a fancy way of saying *overcrowded, understaffed nursing homes* and *homeless elderly people in the streets.*

Currently, the "greedy geezer" image is balanced against that of the loving grandparent, the future self, and the worthy, poor senior. But given the demographic and economic trends at hand, the idea of a resource-hungry elder class, unstinting on its own comforts yet miserly toward children, has the potential to turn toxic. Should that framing of old age gain traction, it could provoke a revolt among young taxpayers. It's worth mentioning that the kids who stole Ken Sr.'s golf cart are now all of voting age.

Of course, the senior voting bloc (which is less unified than many think but will likely congeal should Social Security or Medicare come under attack) will fight mightily against any threat to its benefits—toward which, thanks to FDR's initial framing of Social Security, it feels a deep ownership. It would vote in self-defense, and soon we would have a civil war of sorts: not brother against brother but grandson against grandmother. Everyone would be so busy taking sides and defending territory that we would forget to push forward the frontier of longevity and fail to work together to make it livable. Any gains we're currently making in the fight against ageism—in the workforce, media portrayals, marketing, and product and environmental design—could easily disappear in this course of events, as the young turn their backs on the old.

The lifestyle represented by The Villages, then, though coherent and compelling to the people who live there, drives home an image of later life that is likely to lead to a poorer (in every sense of the term) old age than we want or deserve. It's unstable in the face of current political and demographic reality, and businesses should be aware that to support such a vision in products and marketing, or even to assume that typical older adults desire such a lifestyle, is to veer toward a world where their customers are having their funding, jobs, and other forms of support pulled out from beneath them. (And on a more personal level, business leaders might want to reflect on the fact that intergenerational resentment makes for awkward holiday dinners.)

Happily, for companies hoping to understand how tomorrow's older consumers might want to live in the future, there is another model that can serve as a lodestar. It addresses many of the same demands as The Villages. However, because its members still live and interact with other age groups, it does so without painting older people as "greedy geezers" desperate to escape the society they rely upon. This vision of later life is perhaps the most radical solution anyone's ever come up with to promote the care and happiness of older adults, and yet, its profile is low. In fact, it could very well exist in your own city and you might not even know it. That's what happened to me: this new sort of village first sprung up right under my nose, in a burg of Boston that I can see right from my office window, and I didn't catch on for years.

The Other Village

Joan Doucette was sipping coffee in the small café on the ground floor of the David H. Koch Center for Integrative Cancer Research at MIT, with her bicycle resting on its kickstand next to her. The Institute tends to frown on bringing bicycles into buildings, but only a hard soul could have stopped Doucette from wheeling in hers, with its ribbons streaming from the handlebars, white tires, and a front basket filled with yellow and pink flowers. The demeanor of the 75-year-old cyclist was just as sunny. Doucette peered up from what looked like, and turned out to be, a travel itinerary for a trip to Chicago.

"There's going to be 20 of us going," she said. "We're going to take a river trip. We're going to go to the museums . . . then we're going to the Russian tearoom. So we're very busy. And then we've got a tour of the skyscrapers. And then a lot of us are going to the Frank Lloyd Wright house. So very busy."

Doucette spoke with, at least to this unschooled ear, a highly refined English accent, redolent of her native Surrey, where she was born in 1938. As a young woman, she trained to become a nanny—"that was the only way we could really travel"—and became involved with the US embassy in London, which assigned her to foreign posts where she cared for diplomats' families. When the father of one of those families died, however, she moved with the mother and kids from Hungary to Dedham, Massachusetts. "I was their nanny until I married and their mother remarried. And those children are now in their fifties and we're still very close," she said.

In 1970, Doucette began a storied career at MIT, moving over the course of years between jobs in the Institute's libraries, alumni relations department, Center for Transportation Studies (now the Center for Transportation and Logistics, home of the AgeLab), industrial relations and corporate development, and more. She retired at 62, after having worked at MIT for 25 years.

"What am I going to do with my days?" she wondered. The answer that presented itself seemed merely opportune at the time. She had no idea how revolutionary it would become.

Shortly after retiring, Doucette and her husband moved to a new apartment on Beacon Hill, one of the oldest, and in many ways ritziest, areas in Boston. They moved in part because they had been living in a tiny apartment, and when Doucette retired, she came home with box upon box of possessions she'd been keeping in her office, for which she now had no room. In her new neighborhood, she didn't know anyone who lived nearby, and so she worried about her social life. Soon, however, an answer came in the mail. She received an invitation to join something called the Beacon Hill Village. "My husband said, 'This is for you.'"

The Beacon Hill Village wasn't really a village per se. Rather, it appeared to be a loose confederation of older people who already lived on Beacon Hill, who, instead of moving out to a community or facility devoted to old age, wanted to stay in their own homes, interact with their longstanding group of friends, eat at their own favorite restaurants, and attend their favorite local cultural events for as long as humanly possible.

Initially, the idea was focused on needs. Many of the Beacon Hill Village's founders had seen care gone wrong and resolved to find a better way. "Each of us had witnessed firsthand the distress our relatives experienced as they aged: a mother in a retirement community in Florida who felt lonely and abandoned; a parent in a nursing home, marginalized and overdrugged; an uncle with very limited means and no immediate family to help out," Susan McWhinney Morse, one of the founding members, has written.

In 1999, when those Beacon Hill neighbors first began to consider building something different, the instructions pervasive in the culture were clear. When you grew old, whether it was an independent or assisted living facility, a country-club retirement community or a nursing home, there was only one thing to do—move.

"Why," writes McWhinney-Morse, "should we have to pull up our roots from a community we love just to be 'safe'? Why did we need to lose our history, our friends, our identity? Why did we have to compromise our lifestyles before it became absolutely necessary, just to fit into a pre-designed community? . . . Why would we ask our children whose lives were already hectic with jobs and children to take us on, too? And what about financial considerations? Moving is an option available only to a small group of us who could afford it. Although we conceded that warmer climates and segregated communities were good choices for some people, they were not a viable or attractive option for us."

The solution they came up with couldn't exactly do everything for everyone, but it was a start. From the very beginning, the Beacon Hill Village's members agreed to help each other with the small things that come up with age and to help each other *find* help for the big things. Today, thanks to a force of dedicated volunteers comprising both members and younger folks, Beacon Hill is able to offer aid with occasional tasks like grocery shopping, home visits, pet care, light housework, and repair. For issues that pose a greater challenge, be they health or caregiving related, financial in nature, or something else, the organization curates lists of trusted service providers, who often provide Beacon Hill members with discounts.

"I've learned that if I don't know what to do about something, I just call them. The worst that can happen is that they'll do the research," said a member. She described buying a sleek new television for her home and carrying it home from the store. When she prepared to set it up, however, she realized that the big, clunky TV she was replacing, which sat on a high shelf, was far too bulky to take down by herself. So she called the Beacon Hill Village, which connected her with a young, local woman who removed the old TV and set up the new one, wiring and all. It cost an extra fee beyond Beacon Hill's annual dues of $675, but she found the experience highly satisfactory, because she felt she could trust the woman whom Beacon Hill had recommended.

Beacon Hill also provides access to vetted drivers—still helpful, even in this age of Uber, when it comes to transporting elderly individuals who require special consideration while getting into and out of cars—and far more. "They'll take you shopping for your groceries. And then if you're having an operation they'll come and pick you up and take you home," said Doucette. "When I had the new knee put in last September, somebody came and picked me up."

But perhaps the most essential aspect of life in the Beacon Hill Village is what might at first sound like the least important: the fun.

Doucette, an immigrant from the United Kingdom, has no immediate family in the United States, and so upon retiring, "I thought I'm going to be lonely," she said. As a result, when the invitation to join the Beacon Hill Village arrived, she didn't see it in terms of its potential to fulfill medical or caregiving needs but rather social ones.

She and her husband joined the first year the Beacon Hill Village became open to the public, in 2002. At that time, it was still little more than the fanciful idea of a dozen-or-so retirees. But the Village soon began building out its membership base as well as relationships with local, trusted vendors, providers, and contractors. Doucette began building as well. Her contribution was to the social schedule, which, these days, is full.

"On Mondays we have a movie group that come in my house, and we have tea, and I stream a movie. And there's about ten of us do that. And on Tuesdays, twice a month, there's another group that meets down at 75 Chestnut"—a snug Beacon Hill restaurant—"and we talk about anything we want to, mostly about theater and movies. And that's called Terrible Tuesdays. And then every Wednesday a group meets on Charles Street in one of the restaurants there. And we talk world affairs mostly . . . And then on Thursdays I got my husband to go and do First Drink, because that's for the men . . . He's not a joiner. So I managed to get him to do that." Doucette's groups are so popular, she explained, that she's started to set up satellite gatherings in other parts of the city. "And then this weekend we're off to Chicago."

My immediate response was skeptical when I first heard murmurs that something special was going on right across the river from my MIT office. Older people helping each other as needed sounded great in theory, but the pragmatist in me made me wonder how long such an altruistic collective could really last. After all, none of the many utopian frontier societies of the Pioneer Era survived as such. The Beacon Hill Village, "erected" by and for people with significant needs, seemed destined to wind up in the well-intentioned-but-naïve section of the dustbin of history.

But after a few years, the Beacon Hill Village was not exactly foundering like I had feared. Quite the opposite: it had grown in size and reputation, and almost every day people were mentioning it to me as a new model of how aging could work. As time went on, I grew quite bullish on Beacon Hill's prospects and viewed it as an alarm bell— perhaps even a death knell—for any old-style, age-segregated community that failed to take notice.

Today, however, it is clear that communities such as The Villages in Florida have done just fine without taking one single iota of notice. But so, fascinatingly, has the Beacon Hill philosophy, which has spread far from the old-money Bostonian knoll on which it spawned. In the United States, a national organization, the Village to Village Network, has emerged to facilitate the development of Beacon Hill-esque in situ communities. According to the Network, at this time of writing there are 190 villages built on the "Beacon Hill model," as it's become known, in all but four states, and 150 more are in development. The phenomenon is spreading internationally as well. At the AgeLab, I've personally welcomed groups from Singapore, the United Kingdom, Germany, and China, all of whom have dropped by on the course of pilgrimages to Beacon Hill, where they hoped to see where and how it all started.

As these Villages have sprung up over the past decade and a half, several themes have emerged. One is the spontaneous development of a pay-it-forward ethos. Paid Village staffs tend to be very small, averaging between one and two-and-half full-time employees, and so the majority of what Villages provide their members comes from volunteers, most of whom are other members. Typically, younger, healthier members—often people in their 50s, 60s, and 70s who have joined for the social aspects of Village life—provide occasional care to the Village's older members, who are often in their eighties and nineties. This care isn't usually medical in nature or extremely painstaking, such as care with activities of daily living, which usually requires help from professionals or family members. Rather, Villagers help each other with the hard-to-predict issues that inevitably come up over the course of a full life.

At the headquarters of the San Francisco Village, in the city's oft-fog-shrouded Inner Richmond neighborhood, one highly engaged member, Bill Haskell, explained that he had originally joined his Village hoping to "pay it forward" in the local older community. Fate had other plans. "Within 30 days of joining the Village, my partner found out he had to have open-heart surgery. So we needed not to volunteer, we needed help. I needed a lot of help because I'm his primary caregiver. Bob had a difficult surgery with a lot of complications. He was in the hospital for two weeks"—far longer than the three days in the hospital that doctors had told them to expect. "Then there's the home period. And so I called the Village." The San Francisco Village provided Bill with vetted referrals for home care agencies, and for times when Bill needed to run out to the store or the gym but no professional caregiver was scheduled, the Village sent over a volunteer to sit with

Bob. "People who are members of the Village brought over meals when I couldn't cook any longer," Bill said. "People we didn't know brought over dinner for us."

As appealing as this pay-it-forward mentality may sound on paper, there are drawbacks. For one thing, it's hard to market. The Villages in Florida started as a leisure community and only later added caregiving facilities and services; as a result, no one thinks of it as a place where older people go to get taken care of—although it is, and they do. Meanwhile, Beacon Hill started as an organization devoted to mutual care and only later took on its social-club vibe. That intrinsic focus on care can scare off potential members who don't think of themselves as patients. At one San Francisco gathering of members of Stitch, the dating site, the handful of people who knew about the San Francisco Village frowned when its name came up. There, and in many other cities, the most common refrain I hear is, "Oh, isn't that, you know, for '*old people*'?" This sentiment, coming from members of a dating site reserved for the 50-plus, was especially telling. Socially, Stitch performs a service similar to that of the Village to Village Network: creating new, local social networks out of whole cloth by facilitating the making of friends, socialization, and travel. And yet, there was a serious perception barrier preventing people—even those evidently quite happy to join a service explicitly for older adults—from seeing themselves in a club designed to provide care for its oldest and frailest.

Not only does the Beacon Hill ethos sometimes come across as less than compelling to potential members; it also doesn't offer an entirely coherent solution to the problem of identity in retirement. In many ways, however, this is a feature, not a failure. At The Villages in Florida, residents find themselves able to shed their former identities but only because their new community is cut off from society at large and embraces a single, specific lifestyle. Beacon Hill, in contrast, embraces complexity. Members are free to not just pursue a leisure-oriented idea of retirement but other aspirations and motivations as well, including caregiving, interacting with other generations, patronizing cultural institutions, volunteering, and working. After Joan Doucette's retirement, for instance, she returned to take on a part-time office job at the lab of Bob Langer, one of MIT's foremost luminaries. ("Oh, tissue engineering he mostly does," she said, airily.) With the active social role she plays at Beacon Hill, she said, "I don't know how I have time to come into work."

But if Beacon Hill's embrace of complexity over clarity makes sense for its members, it also poses a liability in terms of defining and marketing a new way of life in old age. It's hard for Beacon Hill's subtle, complicated message to compete with the volume, vividness, and simplicity of the story broadcast by The Villages. There is a way Beacon Hill can fight back, however: by doubling down on its own model and offering even more services and activities. Increasing the number of social events it puts on, in particular, would create the opportunity for those in the midst of a gradual transition away from a primary career to wrap themselves in new interests. And a wider variety of workshops, classes, clubs, and volunteer opportunities would increase the visibility of the model—turning Beacon Hill into, well, a beacon on a hill.

The barrier to achieving the kind of scale needed to do so is considerable, however. Joanne Cooper, part of the membership committee at Beacon Hill, said that bringing in new members is a continual challenge. "Two new members come in, four leave, one way or another," whether they're "moving to a more structured setting, or, unfortunately, passing away." The San Francisco Village, which is relatively new, has just 300 members. Kate Hoepke, its leader, said she was "very intrigued with scale. If this works for 300, it can work for 3,000." Nationwide, she said, Village memberships can be measured in the low tens of thousands. "You know, it should be ten times that many." She wonders if the issue is due to a lack of funding or the need for strong visionaries. Perhaps the Village to Village Network's perplexing pattern of growth—fast to spread across the United States and the globe, yet slow to flourish in sheer membership—may come down to the fact that "so much has happened in such a short period of time. That infrastructure isn't there yet."

She's right. For radical, new ways of living in old age, radical, new kinds of physical, institutional, and cultural infrastructure are all needed. In the Beacon Hill Village and others like it, we're probably only seeing the beginnings of that construction. Still, it's an encouraging start.

The Best of Times, the Worst of Times

Today, most older people want to stay connected to their community, often while still working, despite any disabilities or health issues that arise. The vision of old age that comes closest to providing that, on offer at Beacon Hill, has yet to achieve the comprehensive coherence and seduction sold in Florida at The Villages. The Beacon Hill ethos resembles Harold Schwartz's trailer park in the 1970s: it's got a heck of a lot of potential but isn't yet drawing in droves of people. It took free golf to launch The Villages onto its spectacular growth trajectory. It isn't quite clear what exactly will do the equivalent for the Village to Village Network or even whether that organization will be the one to ultimately prevail in tomorrow's contest to frame successful, in-home, in-community aging.

The Beacon Hill Village and others like it aren't perfect. They're too small at present. They don't leverage mobile technology as well as they could to improve connectedness, which will be an absolute must as they court tech-savvier baby boomers. They're limited mainly to urban areas, and they tend to skew middle-class-and-up, leaving a lot of people out. Still, as new generations of longevity-economy products make it easier to do more in old age than merely recreate and relax, it's easy to envision *something* resembling the Beacon Hill Village emerging from our current state of frontier chaos.

The most important aspect of that something would be its long-term stability. Recall the golf-cart chase at The Villages; the "No Kids" graffiti in the nearby Woodfield. Intergenerational tension is endemic to such visions of old age. A future built according to these age-segregationist ideals would be a poor place in which to grow old. It would also be a poor place to do business with the fastest-growing consumer demographic: its skills and insights squandered in walled-off communities, its pocketbooks depleted because no one will hire or fund people known for being consumers, not producers; takers, not givers.

At the Villages, "There's an awful lot of talent that hasn't been utilized," said Smoke Hickman, who defies the rule by serving on several directorial boards outside of the community. There, there are a handful of examples like him and Caroline Reibholtz, a *guardian ad litem* for children in the local court system. But by and large, in great part because The Villages is so insular, the world beyond its gates loses sight of its individual residents' considerable virtues and capabilities, perceiving instead the same broad, tired, narrative-constrained picture of old age.

Meanwhile, at the Beacon Hill Village, Joan Doucette recounted the ending of a simple dinner out on Boston's Charles Street. "The young waitress said, 'Oh, come back again,'" Doucette recalled. "She said, 'I really enjoyed having you for dinner, you've been such fun.' And that's nice, that a young person would say that these old geezers here were having a good time and she liked serving us."

One 2014 study found that a quarter of Beacon-Hill-model Villages are actively working to improve their communities' attitudes toward older adults, a decent rate for small organizations that rely on a largely volunteer workforce. And every day, by going out and creating a positive impression on the community around them, the members of Beacon Hill and other Villages built on its model dispel the old myth that elders are unfit to comingle with society.

If you, like me, want to live in a world where older adults and their kids aren't antagonists but rather invest in each other, work for each other, and help each other build things, then the Village movement, as opposed to the Villages, is a good guide to follow—in the United States and around the world. Villages built on the Beacon Hill model are finding fertile ground in countries such as the United Kingdom and Germany, where, as in the United States, older adults hope to avoid relying on their children. Other experiments in age integration are springing up as well. In the sphere of caregiving, for instance, one fascinating program in Germany and Switzerland, known as "Wohnen für Hilfe," or Housing for Help, subsidizes the rent of carefully vetted students who want to live in older people's homes and help out with minor chores. A similar program, Homeshare, exists in the United Kingdom. Another law provides the 82 percent of German elders who say they do not want to live in a nursing home with a grant of up to €10,000 to establish shared, community apartments, with a monthly subsidy of up to €200 per tenant.

Wherever your older consumer lives, it will be a good bet that the future will be more age integrated, not segregated. Products built with this assumption in mind are likely to fare better than their rivals, especially as connected technologies and sharing-economy services make it easier than ever for older adults to get out, do things, work, and meet people in their longtime communities and also online. If you're selling a retirement financial product, for instance, do your commercials show people walking on a beach or a golf course or involved in their community? Meanwhile, if you're *building* such a product, do you include in your portfolio real-estate investment trusts that are heavy on senior-living and retirement communities? There will of course be a market for such products in the near future, but a widespread shift toward aging-in-place may make it smaller than the raw demographics would otherwise suggest.

In terms of tomorrow's narrative of old age, there is still the potential for things to go wrong. It won't matter that 9 people out of 10 eschew retirement destinations: if business, government, and media messaging insists that normal, later-life behavior is to live in age-segregated communities while spending other people's hard-earned money, then that story could well prevail in spite of reality.

Products oriented toward a new vision of aging, however, will tell a different tale. And a more connected, age-integrated generation of older adults will act as its own cultural herald, constantly disproving misconceptions about the capabilities and motivations of older people. As this process unfolds, older adults will become more attractive as hires and business partners and more sought after as consumers. In the following chapters, I'll explain how businesses can serve those consumers and build toward this new vision of old age. Life on the frontier may feel awkward now, but it never stays that way for long.

PART II

5

Radical Empathy and Transcendent Design

Now that we have sketched the outlines of a new idea of old age, it's time to focus on how businesses can flesh out the picture. A new generation of better products will empower older adults, who will then go back and demand products that are even more useful, creating a positive feedback loop. First, however, innovators and companies must bring that initial wave of goods and services into the world, a prospect that can seem daunting. On one side, products that neglect to make allowances for older users—their aging bodies, their years of built-up experiences regarding how things work—can cause frustrated customers to take their business elsewhere. And on the other, products that *do* make these sorts of concessions often come across as patronizing or dumbed-down, and older adults reject them just as readily. As a result, filling in the new picture of old age with products can seem as impossible as staying within the lines of a coloring book using a can of spray paint.

But there is another way of thinking about products that puts success within reach: above all other considerations, they should make it *easy* for consumers to fulfill their jobs. That's not to suggest one should create "easy-to-use" products—that way lies oversized, rubberized remote controls, three-button cell phones, emergency response pendants, and all kinds of other things that no one wants. I'm talking about achieving ease not by patronizing one's customers but by exciting and delighting them. I call the most extreme form of this product development ethos *transcendent design.* As I explore ahead, transcendent design can bring new life to staid industries and generate unexpected crossover appeal as people buck demographic categories to claim the latest, greatest solutions to their jobs as consumers. In some cases, transcendent products can even have profound downstream effects, influencing anything from where consumers live to how they prepare dinner.

As obvious as it may sound to try to thrill the older consumer, however, in the face of a confounding narrative of aging, it can prove tricky to pull off. A profound understanding of one's customer's wants, needs, frustrations, and hopes is required. Sometimes, a company can purchase this kind of deep knowledge in the form of a new team, employee, or consultant. However, it's also possible to climb into your customer's head through deliberate acts of empathy—an approach that can pay out surprising dividends down the line.

But let's not get ahead of ourselves. The first step on the road to better products requires no such mental gymnastics, just a healthy dose of common sense. The most basic rule in designing ease into longevity-economy products is to avoid frustrating older consumers. That's a low bar, but plenty of products, product packaging, and marketing efforts fail to clear it. Most consumer products are built for a hypothetical, healthy, younger user, and that leads to some obvious failures, such as clamshell packaging of the sort that requires sharp scissors and a rock climber's grip to open. There are also less conspicuous breakdown points. Take web design: as communications have shifted from pulpy newsprint to backlit screens, it's become possible to invoke a wider, subtler array of colors. There's just one problem: unless you're careful, your older customers can't see them. Even without any sort of disease, the lens of the eye becomes gradually more opaque to blue light over time, meaning that the light that reaches the retina appears yellow, which is blue light's opposite number. Because this process takes place over the course of decades, no one ever notices it happening. The effect, however, is significant: The older you are, the less able you are to tell yellow from white; and blue from black, green, or purple.

Of course, accommodating consumers with varying levels of visual acuity, dexterity, strength, and flexibility, among many concerns, is no guarantee of a product's success. However, it's impossible to produce a transcendent product *without* solving these sorts of issues. The challenge is to create something that doesn't merely take away frustration but also actively delivers a measure of delight. To figure out how to cross that dividing line, however—to move from the absence of a negative to the presence of a positive—it may be necessary to try an act of radical empathy.

AGNES

The market for Mercedes-Benz's high-end automobiles tends to skew affluent, which is to say: older. In the mid-aughts, Daimler AG, Mercedes's parent company (at the time, part of DaimlerChrysler), was working with my team to try to figure out what their aging customer base wanted and how to provide it for them. To that end, the German automaker invited a group of AgeLab staff and students to a workshop at one of its facilities in Berlin, where engineers, designers, and marketers from both Daimler and Siemens, who was building car-interior components for Mercedes, were hoping to get together to try to understand the older customer.

Broadly, there are two types of high-end cars in this world: the kind focused on the human inside and the kind focused on the machine on the road. (As I'll explain below, there is a sizable older market for both.) At the risk of reducing the issue to the point of absurdity, Mercedes vehicles tend to fall into the first category, which isn't to say that they sacrifice performance for comfort but rather that its engineers and designers are well known for taking cutting-edge automotive technology and designing it as seamlessly as possible into the user's experience.

However, in my experience, they also—and here I'm referring to the people who do the actual work, not the senior vice presidents—tend to be in their 20s, 30s, and 40s. It's one thing to ask a designer or engineer a decade out of college to make a product that doesn't fail older adults. It's quite another to ask that designer to make something so delightful that it sets an older customer's hair on fire. But when someone is eyeing a Mercedes in the showroom, that's exactly the sort of experience he or she is looking for. It's a high bar, and Daimler knew that unless they figured out how to provide that experience consistently for older drivers, they could pack all the tech in the world into their cars and still be outcompeted by companies that better understood the customer. How to accomplish that, however, was (and remains) a challenge.

There is an ancient proverb concerning blind men and an elephant: one man sticks out a hand to touch the elephant's trunk and says, "I feel a tree branch." Another one touches the tail and thinks the elephant is a rope. A third touches the side of the elephant and thinks he's standing next to a wall. No one gets the complete picture. At Daimler, engineers were concerned mainly with how difficult it was for older drivers to climb into and out of their car, which could be addressed by, say, changing the weight of a door, or the placement of a handle. Designers, meanwhile, saw the older-driver issue as a tradeoff between considerations of aesthetics and functionality—which they mostly treated as a zero-sum, either-or proposition. Marketers were sure they could supply the answer with just one more focus group or one more field observation. Our challenge was to help them see the whole elephant.

Almost on a whim, my team and I decided to kick off the conference with an ice-breaker of sorts—a fun activity designed to force engineers, designers, and marketers out of their comfort zones and into the shoes of older drivers. What if, we wondered, we could dress them in some sort of age-simulation suit? It would be something along the lines of pregnancy-empathy suits or alcohol-impairment simulation goggles, which were popular teaching aids at Lamaze classes and scare-'em-straight high school programs, respectively. At the time, there were even a few goggle-and-glove systems floating around gerontologist and nursing circles, designed to mimic certain symptoms associated with old age. We decided to make a full-body version and apply it directly to the automobile experience.

We dubbed the resulting, funny-looking outfit the "Age Gain Now Empathy System." In a remarkable stroke of luck—so fortunate, in fact, that some find it suspicious—the words came together to spell out the name AGNES.

In the 1.0 version of AGNES, there wasn't much to it. I was lucky enough to have on my team an exercise physiologist with close knowledge of arthritis and aging bodies who helped us come up with the individual components. These included yellow glasses, which mimicked the yellowing of the ocular lens that comes with age. A boxer's neck-strengthening harness reduced the mobility of the cervical spine and made it harder to maintain one's posture. Bands around the elbows, wrists, and knees gave the impression of stiffness. Gloves added to the picture, reducing tactile acuity while adding resistance to finger movements.

The whole thing was a relatively slap-dash, last-minute experiment, and yet it's hard to overstate the impression it made. Part of its memorability was due simply to the hilarity that ensued as the Daimler, Siemens, and AgeLab team members tried to put the suit on. Perhaps what made the most profound mark, however, was the fact that after putting it on, we played the games Twister and Operation. As the engineers, designers, and marketers used AGNES—both within Mercedes cars and while playing games—they learned not only to respect the challenges their older customers unflinchingly faced every day but also to appreciate their own relative physiological functionality in a new way.

They each wore the suit, took it off, debriefed, handed it over to someone else, and the process repeated. As the day wore on, the companies' teams identified a number of friction points potentially standing between older consumers and the excitement and delight they were paying for. Perhaps more important, these engineers, designers, marketers—even executives—were finally seeing the customer's experience through the same set of eyes. By recognizing how they had been touching the same elephant all along, they were breaking through years, maybe decades, of institutional inertia—as a unified team.

That was just the first prototype of AGNES.

In the years that followed, we have continued to improve AGNES, broadening her potential applications and improving the accuracy with which she replicates physiological conditions. She now features a system of bungees that attach at key points on the wearer's limbs and connect them to a weighted vest and hip harness, which reduces flexibility and stride length and forces a forward slouch into the wearer's spinal posture. On the head, a helmet anchored to the body simulates cervical compression, a neck collar limits rotational mobility, and a variety of goggles reproduce specific ocular disorders, from diabetic retinopathy to glaucoma. Foam-padded shoes compromise balance by mimicking the loss of tactile feedback between the feet and the ground that can occur with age, and a variety of gloves replicate the diminishment of spatial acuity that takes place in the fingers.

In addition to engineers, designers, and marketers, later versions of AGNES have been worn by CEOs, CFOs, CMOs, heads of engineering, and "heads of innovation" (an increasingly popular corporate title in recent years), from companies including (but not limited to) New Balance, PepsiCo, United Healthcare, Cigna, Liberty Mutual, GlaxoSmithKline, General Mills, Hartford Funds, Raymond James, Toyota, Nissan, and others. A sitting governor has worn it. So has former Secretary of Transportation Anthony Foxx, back when he was mayor of Charlotte in 2013. And so, of course, have countless unwitting undergraduates and interns, who will probably go on to do more important things than all of the aforementioned combined.

In every case, the goal has always been to move beyond the simple transfer of information about old age: to deliver not merely cold facts but also a profound, emotional, "Aha!" moment. When people read about AGNES in the press, the focus is always on what she takes away in terms of the wearer's physiology, but in person, AGNES's secret weapon is the emotion she triggers in the wearer. It's one thing to understand on an academic level that it can be tough to grow old. It's quite another to grok deeply what it's like to try in vain to get something done, only to be thwarted by a world of products and policies built for people 50 years your junior.

One company that has made significant changes following an experience with AGNES is CVS. In 2011, CVS approached the AgeLab with an idea. The drugstore chain's customer base is older than most other top-10 retailers in the United States, and so they were (and remain) at the forefront of the aging-consumer trend.

Earlier that year, the news media, including NBC's *Today*, had realized that AGNES provided a good excuse to cover the physiological effects of aging, something that most of their audience was experiencing either first- or secondhand. Soon the idea of an age-simulation suit had become, if not a commonplace concept, at least less of a fringe academic notion. After AGNES's second appearance* on the *Today* show, CVS invited me to speak at an internal marketing and strategy meeting. Unbeknownst to me, the company, which remodels its stores on a regular basis, was planning for an upcoming round of renovations. What if, their chief marketing officer posed to me, they could incorporate AGNES into their design thinking?

---

*Natalie Morales, one of the show's anchors at the time, had the dubious pleasure of wearing the suit. Matt Lauer, the host of the segment, encouraged her to pour milk into a bowl of cereal. "I feel the friction," she said. "I feel like my joints are completely compressed."

"Clearly the vision is weird," Lauer joked, "because that's not cereal—that's potpourri!"

Early one morning in November 2012, key members of my team and CVS's marketing group put on AGNES suits and went on a shopping field trip at a couple of stores in New England. Later, we did the same at a facility in Woonsocket, Rhode Island, where CVS prototypes and tests new, sometimes radical, store designs.

In the actual stores, we received some funny looks from the handful of morning shoppers. There, a few design steps that the company had already taken seemed to have paid off. "I walked in constricted to look down," said one AGNES-clad CVS team member, "and I really did not want to look up." The linoleum pathway that wended its way through CVS's trademark grey carpeting, from the entryway in front to the pharmacy in back, helped him navigate, he said. The store's low shelving also meant that despite the anatomical limitations imposed on them, AGNES wearers were able to reach all the items on their shopping lists.

But AGNES soon began to point out problems. For one thing, CVS, like many retailers, tended to put heavy items on lower shelves. Such placement minimizes the chances of customers and employees bludgeoning themselves with falling objects, but regrettably, as the folks wearing AGNES quickly realized, places hard-to-lift items, such as Ensure nutritional shakes, in a hard-to-reach place. The problem isn't one that a store designer would necessarily recognize on his or her own, because a typical older adult capable of traveling to a CVS can lift a six-pack of Ensure unaided. She can also reach down to knee height—or up slightly above her head—no problem. The trouble arises when you ask her to do both at the same time—to lift something heavy *while* reaching at either extreme of her range of motion. Bending down or reaching high above puts her into a position of poor leverage, forcing her to fight against her own connective tissues and bodyweight while her muscles are extended or contracted in extreme configurations. In the midst of such contortions, grabbing, say, a two-liter drink becomes a Cirque du Soleil–worthy feat. Much better, the CVS team noted, to place heavy objects at hip height. The same issue came up when the team loaded and unloaded deep-bottomed shopping carts, into which our test shoppers found it hard to reach.

Other issues that arose included the fact that the stores' "lollipop signs"—circular product identifiers about the size of a DVD that stick out from store shelves into the aisles—tended to overlap visually when viewed from either end of the aisle, requiring our poor, mobility-impaired AGNES wearers to trudge halfway across the store to determine where things were. In another instance, a nurse practitioner at one store's walk-in MinuteClinic used a yellow highlighter to mark key information for her AGNES-wearing "patient," which was nearly impossible to see through AGNES's simulated yellow ocular lens.

But perhaps the most important (and underrecognized) aspect of the older shopping experience that AGNES drove home was how threatening a public, retail environment can be when you're coping with even minor sensory impairments. Although the shelves in the CVS stores we visited were relatively low, they were still organized into long canyons. It's hard to explain the feeling of claustrophobic panic that arises when you have balance issues, and a pair of people walking abreast comes barreling down one of these canyons at you. They don't know that you have equilibrium trouble or that you can't see very well or that there's nothing stable nearby to grab onto except shelves full of things that might fall over and break. The only thing to do in such a moment is to grit your teeth, think small, and hope nothing bad happens until they pass.

Unless, that is, there's a nearby escape hatch. Which is exactly what CVS ended up adding to its aisles.

To CVS, each store remodel represents a sizable investment in customer-friendly design. Following their AGNES experience, CVS's team made a number of recommendations for this renovation process. Given the stakes involved, no one could have faulted them for playing it safe and instituting just the bare minimum changes: higher-contrast signage with larger letters.

Worse, they might have done something overtly "senior-friendly," like installing grab bars throughout the store to give older adults something to hold onto for those moments when the canyon walls start to close in. In doing so, the team would have been following a long, time-honored trend of treating older adults as medical patients first, human beings second. It would have been, like Heinz's Senior Foods, a disaster.

Instead, they went another route. First, they changed those annoying "lollipop" signs to a street-sign design with larger, more readable text. More important, instead of using the signs to identify product categories—antacids here, proton-pump inhibitors here—they organized them by problem, such as heartburn remedies. Not only did this approach reduce the number of signs, preventing overlap, but it also more effectively served the underlying job of the consumer, which is always to address a given problem, not buy a given product. As a result of this new way of thinking, some items moved all the way across the store. Today at most CVS locations you can find compression socks, used by people with late-stage, Type-2 diabetes, next to glucose pills and insulin pumps. Once upon a time, these might have been found next to the other socks and tennis balls, which necessitated an undue amount of store-wandering from folks dealing with mobility impairments.

Other fixes CVS instituted included smaller, higher shopping carts that were easier to heft weighty objects into and out of and a broader entry space. One thing we observed older women do again and again upon first entering CVS stores was to grab a shopping cart for stability, put their bag in it, then stop and switch eyeglasses. It's not something a younger designer might necessarily consider, but having a space where older shoppers can stop and make that transition without feeling like a roadblock is critical.

CVS made a handful of other changes as well—they introduced backlit credit card machines, for instance, far better than the old black-on-grey—but the innovation that really struck me was their solution to the stuck-in-the-canyon problem. Instead of adding grab bars throughout, they broke up the long aisles into shorter ones and standalone, kiosk-type displays. As a result, at many CVS stores today, someone who's about to be bowled over by a group of bounding teenagers can execute a quick side step through a break in the aisle wall, a maneuver that is surely preferable to the old standby of hoping, praying, and bracing for impact.

Mental Models

In a certain sense, the opposite of a Mercedes-Benz is a BMW. They're both German luxury cars, of course, so perhaps they're only opposites in the regard that MIT is the opposite of Caltech, or Army is that of Navy. And yet, Mercedes is known for the luxury of the experience it provides its passengers and drivers. BMW, by contrast, though highly ergonomics conscious, is famous for prioritizing the precision of the driver's control over the surrounding machine. In a number of models, central dashboard elements are even tilted toward the driver and away from the passenger, a small gesture that speaks volumes. The company's engineers provide drivers with the opportunity to fine-tune their experience wherever possible. Treating the automobile not as a luxurious palanquin but rather as a "driving machine," as the company's marketing would have it, has served BMW well. Over the course of decades, however, its control-focused design ethos led to the dashboard equivalent of urban sprawl, as a miniature skyline of switches, knobs, and buttons took over ever-expanding swathes of the car interior's real estate. By 2000, the driver of one of BMW's top 7 Series cars had 117 of these interface devices to choose from, which made the interior feel disconcertingly similar to the cockpit of a Boeing 737.

　　In 2001, BMW took the dramatic step of folding almost all of those knobs and buttons into a single interface device known as the iDrive. From the start, the system worked amazingly well. It featured just a single LCD screen containing a number of menu items, which the user could navigate using a joystick-like input device found in the center console. In addition to moving in four directions,* the joystick could be twisted to scroll through a list of items and "clicked" toward the floor of the car to make a selection. All told, it was a singularly elegant way to clean up one of the most cluttered dashboards in the business. There was just one problem: everyone hated it.

"Your initial response to iDrive," read one blistering review at RAC (the United Kingdom's version of AAA), "will probably be, 'UDrive, I'm off to learn something easier like advanced Thai or particle theory.'" *Car and Driver* magazine described it as "a computer interface with the ease and clarity of James Joyce's *Ulysses.*" Tom and Ray Magliozzi, the legendary hosts of NPR's Car Talk, had the most scathing take: "We can only hope someone out there in Bavaria walks into the ergonomics department and fires a bunch of people before they move this disaster into other, heretofore untainted BMW models," they wrote on their website. Regarding the specific BMW line they were reviewing, they listed its good attributes as "superior handling, rich interior, many extras." The bad ones? "iDrive, iDrive, iDrive."

The reviews were troubling, to say the least, but there was an even deeper issue with iDrive that only BMW knew about. It wasn't just that people in general disliked it. It was that older drivers hated it the most. And because, like Mercedes-Benz, the market for BMWs is limited to people who can afford one—which is to say, mainly older people—that was very bad news, indeed.

The worst-case scenario had happened before. In 1986, General Motors had introduced a revolutionary touch-screen interface, the first of its kind, which it offered as standard in Buick's Riviera, and later Reatta, model sedans and as a $1,300 add-on in the Oldsmobile Toronado Trofeo. It was at that point the most cutting-edge dashboard interface ever sold. Drivers didn't like taking their eyes off the road to operate it, however, and found the menu system confusing. By the

---

*The very first iDrive system, which was available only in Germany, utilized an eight-way joystick and was quickly scrapped.

early 1990s, GM had ended the experiment and reverted to buttons, knobs, and switches. Somewhere, a design engineer cried out in pain, then was silent.

The question floating around BMW was whether they'd pushed their customers, heretofore always up to any challenge posed by BMW's engineers, too far, too soon. If so, it would have been an incredibly expensive, embarrassing mistake. Would BMW need to do what GM did in the early 1990s and revert to the old, impossibly crowded dashboard?

Over BMW's dead chassis. Throughout the mid-aughts, BMW clung to the iDrive with what was regarded in automotive circles as legendary tenacity, even obstinacy. Had they ditched it, however, they would have been committing the cardinal sin of design for older adults: denying them the best possible technology simply because "they don't get tech." That way, sadness lies: big, beige, boring products, built to solve the perceived limitations of older adults, not the actual job of the consumer.

The fact is, older adults *do* get technology, and by the time the baby boom fully enters its 60s and 70s, it will be the most tech-savvy group of elders ever to have existed. To the extent that older people have a reputation for fearing or failing to understand technology, there are two forces responsible. The first is the simple accident of timing I've already mentioned. For a roughly 20-year period starting in the 1980s, a divide emerged between people who used computers in the office (and later the home) and those who managed to retire without ever needing to bother with them. (There were shades of grey in between the two extremes: some older boomers, for instance, found themselves adapting computers to preordained work flows, while some younger boomers never worked a desk job that didn't have a computer on that desk.) The resulting drop-off in computer literacy by age happened to fit perfectly within preexisting, narrative-based ideas about the inability of old dogs to learn new technological tricks. Today, we're still stuck with the idea that older people fear technology, despite the fact that older age ranges are now rapidly filling with people who became quite comfortable using PCs in the office and later picked up tablets and smartphones with relative ease.

There is an additional reason why older people get a bum rap for tech acceptance, however. In many cases, because they've spent a long time doing something a certain way, their mental model for how a given problem should be solved becomes tightly tied to the method or tool they're most accustomed to. In terms of human energy, the real and sunk costs of switching to a new technology are greater for these potential users than young people. And so, when the value proposition of the new suggested way of doing things feels less than remarkable, they often simply shrug and say *no thanks, not worth it.* In my experience, when older adults reject a technology, it's not because they can't learn or are too stubborn. It's that the purveyor of said technology hasn't made a compelling enough case for them to care about it.

As a result, designing to excite and delight older adults doesn't stop at physiological factors. Before releasing a new product, it's vital to determine whether it flies in the face of the well-instantiated mental models that customers rely on to understand and move within the world. And if a product fails to connect because it doesn't take those mental models into account in its design and marketing, then that's on its producers, not the consumer. Our view at the AgeLab is that if older people don't like a technology, it's not because they're stupid. It's because *it's a bad technology.* That's not to say that this hypothetical bad piece of technology doesn't work, per se. It's just that the definition of a "good technology" needs to shift so that a piece of tech can't be considered "good" unless all its potential users, including older people, agree that they like it.

With iDrive, the question was how to make it "good" not just in the eyes of its engineers, who were justly convinced of its soundness, but also from the perspective of older drivers. First, BMW had to figure out what their customers didn't like about it. That was a tough question, because it appeared that there was nothing innately objectionable about the system beyond the fact that it wasn't what people were used to. And yet, although they had a hard time articulating why, something about it rubbed older drivers the wrong way.

In 2007, as part of a large effort to delve into the usability of its system, BMW had couriered to the AgeLab exactly one prototype iDrive interface, divorced from the car dashboard, in the kind of carrying case usually reserved for discrete diamond shipments or the US nuclear launch codes. We set it up in one of the Lab's test vehicles (which we'd named Miss Rosie) and studied how drivers of all ages interacted with it in real, on-road conditions. Then we had a lot of long discussions with those test drivers about what they liked and disliked about it.

We also happened to set the iDrive up at a desktop computer in the lab, where participants could use it while operating a small-scale driving simulator. That was where we had our breakthrough.

In the car, our participants found it difficult to describe exactly what the iDrive's input device most resembled. Was it a mutant joystick, modified for the automotive cockpit? Was it an iPod click wheel, fleshed out in three dimensions and designed to change more than just music? While driving, it was hard to say. At the computer desktop, however, it became obvious what the iDrive was. To older users in particular, it wasn't a revolutionary interface. Rather, it registered simply as a very bad computer mouse.

Of course, it wasn't a mouse—for one thing, there was no cursor onscreen. Rather, users encountered a series of menu items, one of which was highlighted with a selection field that could be moved using the directional input knob. An actual mouse would have been horribly difficult to use in a moving vehicle, at least while driving on anything other than an immaculate stretch of empty highway. But that didn't change the fact that when people approached the iDrive *expecting* a mouse, they found the lack of a pointer onscreen, combined with the joystick-like operation of the control knob, jarring. In terms of raw years, our oldest study participants had easily spent the most time using computer mice—in some cases going back to the early 1980s, when our youngest participants were still in diapers. Our younger participants, on the other hand, were of course familiar with computer mice but had put in fewer hours with them overall and relatively more time with joysticks, iPods, and laptop trackpads. Because of the breadth of their experience, the iDrive came across as simply one more in a long list of directional inputs. Meanwhile, the depth of older participants' experience meant they could only compare it to a computer mouse—and unfavorably, at that.

The idea that the older we get, the more we become used to doing things a certain way might sound like an old-style critique of the mental plasticity of aging adults. It's not—in fact, becoming "stuck in your ways" is often a profoundly rational thing to do. To stick to automotive examples, older adults are often slow to accept safety technologies, such as blind-spot warning systems, which is unfortunate because such systems can save lives. Older drivers can use blind-spot warning systems, for instance, to avoid turning their whole upper body to check behind themselves while changing lanes (thanks, reduced neck mobility). It's a great technology, but consider: if you've driven cars on the highway for 50 years and survived without a major accident, then your habits, as a driver, must seem pretty trustworthy. From that perspective, it would be highly illogical to suddenly go and "fix" your mental model for how changing lanes is done—especially when your life is on the line. It's the ongoing challenge of automakers, insurers, and governments to convince older drivers otherwise.

Ultimately, it would have been a bad idea to alter the iDrive system to better fit the mental models of older drivers—that is, to turn it into an actual mouse. But there was one change we could recommend. A major reason drivers gave for their frustration was the iDrive's menu system, which was fairly complicated, like a web of canals, creeks, and tributaries that you had to navigate if you wanted to turn on the air conditioning or change the radio station. Younger users were happy to acquaint themselves with these waterways through trial and error, but older users found themselves not only lost up a creek but also, since they were at odds with the mouselike control knob, lacking a suitable paddle. With its new prototype, however, BMW was testing a number of shortcut buttons positioned around the control knob. One of these would instantly bring users to the top-level menu, saving them the trouble or repeatedly finding the "back" option onscreen. Our older participants loved it, and it was easy to see why. Although it might not have been possible to build a better paddle, when the going got rough, at least this button could plop the user into friendlier waters.

BMW introduced this and a number of other changes to the iDrive's fourth generation, starting with 2009 model-year vehicles. Eventually the bad reviews stopped. The system is now standard in all BMWs, and the broader concept (which, to be fair, also arose independently at other luxury manufacturers) is easily the most-copied automotive cockpit feature since the cup holder.

If imitation is as flattering as everyone says, then the iDrive in general, together with its later improvements, must have been a pretty good idea. It bears emphasizing, however, that had the 2009-model modifications gained a reputation for existing primarily to help older drivers, consumers young and old alike would have rejected the system. The changes that ultimately made the iDrive age friendly only succeeded because they did so by way of making it better for drivers of every age.

Designing Transcendence

Beyond the importance of mental models, there's another lesson to be learned from BMW's experience with iDrive: it's possible to address accessibility or mental-model issues in such an intuitive, pleasing way that everyone benefits—even young, nondisabled people.

"Accessible design" is the term for building things so that people with disabilities can use them. A wheelchair ramp to one side of a stairway is an example of an accessible design feature. Design decisions that help everyone, meanwhile—both those with and without disabilities—are known as "universal design." (Variants of the term include "design for all" and "inclusive design.") A classic example is a lever-style door handle that can be operated with an elbow, prosthesis, residual limb, arthritic hand—even a knee. Accessible and universal design features are essential in any society that aspires to be both functional and humane.

But there's another, even higher level of accessibility that I believe has been mistakenly lumped in with universal design: transcendent design. It's essentially universal design that has been dialed up to 11 on a 10-point scale, with accessibility attributes so useful that they turn out to be highly desirable—even aspirational—for people with and without disabilities. If the defining, narrative-shaping forces in our older future will be those that make it easy for older adults to achieve their jobs as consumers, transcendent products and design features will be at the vanguard of this process.

A product can achieve transcendence in one of two ways. In the first, less common example, someone designs something explicitly for older people or for people with a specific disability, and it turns out to make life better for everyone.

One evening in 1988, Betsy Farber, an avid cook, was peeling potatoes.* She suffered from arthritis in her wrists, which didn't bother her too much—except, of course, whenever she needed to get something done with her hands, especially in the kitchen. As Stanford's Dev Patniak recounts in his book *Wired to Care,* the peeler in Farber's hand that night was endowed with a keen blade, but its narrow, slippery, cylindrical handle kept spinning in her compromised grasp. Noticing her frustration, Sam, her husband, came over and peeled the potato for her.

Pause this quiet domestic tableau and consider: all too often, insights gained in everyday moments of frustration like these float

---

*Some accounts maintain that the tuber being peeled that night was in fact no tuber at all but rather an apple. Food for thought, but the discrepancy doesn't affect the moral of the story.

away like dandelion seeds on the winds of everyday concerns and fatigue. Even if the frustrated party discovers a way to fix the issue, she hardly ever gets the opportunity to enact her solution on a wide scale—*especially* if the idea is a business innovation. We've discussed what happens in an economy structured to prioritize the ideas of young men: young people, mostly male, continue fixing the problems they see, and as a result, older people, mostly women, are forced to interact with the world (and compete in a harsh labor market) with only substandard tools to help them.

According to the conventional rules, what the Farbers, both retired at the time, were *supposed* to do when that potato peeler failed them was this: grimace. Worry about their continued ability to do things in their home. Eventually, give up cooking. Move someplace where meals are provided. Accept dependency well before it was strictly necessary.

But this moment of frustration was different, because the seed of insight happened to land on the most fertile soil imaginable. Sam Farber was retired, true, but what he was retired *from* happened to be COPCO, the celebrated cookware company, which he had founded in 1960. Cookware was in his blood; Farberware, one of the best-known brands in the business, bears his family's name.

The idea to create an arthritis-friendly, ergonomic line of cookware was the Farbers' first great idea. But the second, and perhaps more important, one was bringing in as coconspirator a designer named Patty Moore.

At the time, Moore was perhaps the world's foremost thinker when it came to designing things for older people, not that there was much competition. Starting a decade earlier, she had achieved a measure of fame by traveling to over 100 cities over the course of three years, which she explored while disguised in a white wig, old-age makeup, and a cane. Earplugs, a body brace that forced her to slouch forward, and vision-blurring, horn-rimmed glasses completed the ensemble. So equipped, she rode city buses, bought things in stores, hailed cabs, tried to use public phone booths, and more—always noting where the

built environment and the objects in it failed her and always observing when the people milling around her ignored her plight or, worse,
poked fun at her.

Needless to say, AGNES owes much to Moore's anthropological
research method. In fact, one thing Moore's undercover work did that
AGNES can't was to convey some of the social ramifications of aging.
It's one thing to worry about getting physically hurt as a result of falling
in a drugstore. What Moore uncovered in her disguise was another
layer of worry: fear of embarrassment after falling in public. Fear of
being deemed worthless or burdensome. Fear of being invisible. Fear
of being hated. When she recommended age-friendly changes to stores
and public infrastructure, the purpose wasn't just to make older people
safer. By fighting against places that threatened to physically compromise older adults, she sought to grant them freedom from fear.

Together with the Farbers, Moore and a crack team of product
designers conducted an exercise in which they put on gloves, wrapped
their finger joints tightly, and attempted to make dinner. It went badly,
and that was the goal. By the time they were done, they had identified
a number of pain points that weren't being addressed by existing cookware. Every one of them constituted an opportunity.

Of the utensils that the Farbers would go on to manufacture,
the defining feature was their oversized, oval-shaped handles, which
wouldn't spin around in even arthritis-afflicted hands. Today, no matter your age, there's a good chance you have a few of these utensils in
your home, because those handles turned out to be useful not just for
older adults but for everyone. The Farbers' company, OXO, went on to
become an unmitigated success, and its products have become synonymous with intuitive, user-oriented design across ability spectra.

Some in the design world might roll their eyes at my idea that
OXO utensils constitute transcendent design. The company's products are often used as quintessential examples of universal design—
that is, design that works for everyone. Why add another level above
"universal"?

First, I'm not here to denigrate universal design strategies, which do indeed make life better for everyone, including older people and folks with various disabilities. To return to the example of the lever door handle, almost without exception, wherever a doorknob can be found, a handle should be there instead, if not an electric opener. Even nondisabled people benefit: 364 days out of the year, they may not care whether a door has a knob or a handle, but on the one day when they're trying to carry a heavy box through, they'll appreciate a handle they can operate using only an elbow.

But here's where door handles and OXO utensils differ: unless it becomes absolutely necessary, switching doorknobs to handles isn't the kind of thing that gets people off the couch, into their car, and off to Home Depot. Door handles are great, work for almost everyone, and there's no real stigma attached to them. But no one covets them. And so, pragmatically speaking, when I think about products that will change the way everyone lives tomorrow, those that are helpful yet uninspiring don't top the list.

A product like OXO's potato peeler is different. When most people use the handle on their friends' front door, they don't even notice. But when someone accustomed to a slippery, wooden, cylindrical potato peeler tries their friend's ergonomic peeler, they stop and say to themselves, *I want that.* When I think about products that will change the way things are done as society grows older, this is the kind of thing that comes to mind. Today, in my experience, it's hard to find a peeler without a rubberized, oval handle. The way we peel potatoes may seem like a minor part of life, and yet it's hard to dismiss the fact that an activity humans have been doing for millennia has changed significantly over the course of the past couple decades.

When transcendent design occurs due to a concerted push for accessibility, as in OXO's case, the results can be breathtaking. There is another way it can happen, however: when innovators create something that simply makes life easier for everyone and, almost as a side effect, enables older people or people with disabilities to do things they couldn't do before. Often, such innovations prove so useful for such a wide swath of the population that they fail to even register as "accessible." Take the electric garage door opener. By 1921, the booming popularity of the Model T Ford had necessitated a new room for many a household: the garage. Often, these early garages had barn doors (many *were* barns), which blew around in the wind, took up space when open, and were less than secure—far from ideal, given that cars were, then as now, many families' most valuable possession. It was into such a world that one C. G. Johnson, a Detroit inventor, brought the first overhead, rolling garage door. These solved all of the problems of barn doors but were originally made out of heavy wood and didn't come with the spring-powered assist that today's do. As a result, not all of Johnson's customers could open them. Within five years, Johnson found it necessary to invent an ancillary product: the first electric garage door opener.

The company Johnson founded, the Overhead Door Corporation, persists today. So do his twin inventions, which became omnipresent following World War II as suburbs popped up and their inhabitants bought cars. The garage door opener didn't become an essential part of every garage, however, until it could be combined with a remote control. The first of these were hardwired and sat in a key-operated control post situated at the end of the driveway, which the driver could operate through the car's window. Suddenly, the garage door opener—once a technology that seemed like it was solely for the weak or feeble— became a technology for the merely lazy, and everybody wanted one. Thanks to the driveway control post, and later the radio-operated remote control, garage door openers became normalized in homes everywhere. Almost as an afterthought, they continued to make it possible for older people to get into and out of their garages. Today, they don't come across as "assistive," although they certainly are.

The story of the microwave oven is similar. Perhaps the greatest invention ever created for older people living alone, the microwave also happens to be one of the greatest things ever to happen to college students, busy moms and dads, and just about everyone else. Again, because it's perceived as the tool of lazy or busy people, not older people with disabilities, the microwave has avoided stigma.* Meanwhile, people with hand tremors, say, who might hurt themselves while taking something out of the oven, rely on it daily. It also has the side benefit of being far less likely to burn the house down than other kitchen heat sources. Perhaps most crucially, the microwave has led to the development of an entire industry of prepared meals, which can deliver a balanced dinner to someone who might otherwise eat grilled cheese sandwiches every night.

The most important example of transcendent design in recent years is the tiny, touch-screen supercomputer that is probably within arm's reach of you at this very moment. True, smartphones still have plenty of accessibility problems—and for many who see a steep learning curve ahead of them, the value proposition for buying into smartphone life simply isn't there. And yet, smartphones give people with vision issues the ability to zoom in on text online and illuminate restaurant menus offline. For people with hand tremors, today's models respond to voice commands almost as readily as touch inputs. For people with hearing issues, they can vibrate instead of ring and send texts instead of place calls. No recent technology has done more for deaf people than the text message.

Importantly, smartphones make possible all these things and more without alienating, separating, or infantilizing the older user. The transcendent design first made widely available in the original iPhone has proven to be one of the most life-changing technological forces of the past 20 years—for all consumer age groups. Meanwhile, the downstream industries that have sprung up to fulfill the new demands created by this device, and the ways that life has changed since smartphones became omnipresent, are too numerous to list.

---

* Imagine if the microwave were known as the "senior oven." I bet you'd think twice about buying one.

As the world ages, transcendent products will continue to shape the contours of our lives. They will also, on occasion, save those lives. About half of the AgeLab's team is devoted to the study of driver behavior, including how drivers of different ages interact with different technologies. We recently had a pair of studies published in the journal *Ergonomics* concerning typefaces in automobile displays. You might not think that the shape of the letter "e"—whether that empty space in the middle is round and capacious or small and boxy; whether its little horizontal line is truly horizontal or slants slightly—could save someone's life, but it can.

One thing I haven't mentioned thus far about dashboard interfaces is how little time, if designed correctly, the driver should spend looking at them. Drivers should be able to comprehend what's on a dashboard display in a fraction of a second because the longer it takes them to discern what's onscreen, the less time they spend looking at the road.

Working with Monotype, perhaps the world's best-known typeface design company, we plunked drivers of all ages down in our driving simulator and used eye-tracking equipment to determine exactly how long they looked at displays equipped with two different fonts. One was from the "humanist" class of typefaces, and one was considered a "square grotesque."

"The humanist and square grotesque typefaces we've tested represent two extremes in design philosophy," explained Jonathan Dobres, a research scientist at the AgeLab. "The square grotesque typeface is rigid and uniform. Many of its letters and numbers look highly similar to each other. It also has tight intra- and inter-character spacing"—that is, the voids inside letters like "o" and "e" and the spaces between letters. These design factors give it a technical, futuristic look that has made it a mainstay of science fiction movies and TV shows going back to the 1960s. By contrast, the humanist typeface we tested "has much more open spacing and varied letter shapes," Dobres said, "giving it a more organic feeling that most typographers feel should be highly legible."

"Most typographers" were right: it turned out that the curvy, humanist typeface shaved precious milliseconds off the time our test drivers spent looking away from the road. The results of that first study hinted that there might be differences in read time among different groups of people, and Dobres decided to dig in. He designed a new study wherein participants were flashed a group of six letters on a computer screen for very brief moments of time. All the participants had to do was say whether they were being flashed a real word—"garden"—or a fake one: "erdang." At first, everyone was able to read the letters they were shown. But as that window of time grew smaller, it became hard, then impossible, to tell exactly what they were seeing onscreen. Older participants, it turned out, found it especially difficult to decipher letters that were flashed very quickly. They had a much easier time, however, when those letters appeared in the humanist typeface, as opposed to the square grotesque.

In many car interfaces today, the grotesque class of typeface can still be found, mainly because it looks like it's straight out of *Blade Runner*. As safety data continue to come out regarding the risks involved, however, that's likely to change.

But, you might reasonably wonder, isn't there the risk that humanist typefaces will get a reputation for being "old-man's typefaces"—used strictly for the safety of older people? Wouldn't such an approach, like the "old-man's car," come across as undesirable to younger and older car buyers alike?

That might be an issue—except for the fact that the difference between the typefaces becomes statistically significant starting not at age 50 or 60, but 30. (In fact, it's reasonable to conjecture that people in their 20s are also affected, just not enough to register as significant in our sample.) Aging, especially in the eyes, starts far earlier than many think. Meanwhile, everyone wants to be safe. Already, one American and one European car company have implemented changes based on our research, and a Japanese company is soon to come on board as well.

In the years to come, design decisions and products that help everyone, including but not limited to older people, will take on outsize influence in the longevity economy. Transcendent products, in particular, are like the rising tide that lifts all ships, regardless of whether they're brand new or have braved decades of stormy seas. As you read on, keep in mind the potential for these sorts of broadly useful technological forces to raise young and old ships alike. These will likely include the autonomous vehicle; the Internet of Things, particularly as manifested in smart homes; and the on-demand and sharing economy. Though not traditionally included in the conversation about products for older people, such far-reaching forces have the potential to alter later life more profoundly than anything aimed explicitly at older adults. As they become available, expect older people to take full advantage of them. The young may have been the first to embrace advanced, connected consumer technologies, but it's older adults who now have the most to gain by incorporating such products into their lives. They will form the next major high-tech growth market—and companies who design their products empathetically will have the first crack at it.

6

Health, Safety, and the Triumph of Magical Thinking

"HURRY UP AND die."

It's the kind of line you'd expect a Bond villain to deliver to the hero, dangling above a pool roiling with sharks. Or perhaps an expectorating heavy-metal singer, to a thrashing crowd. Or a kid with a magnifying glass and too much time on his hands, to an ant on the sidewalk.

Or the finance minister of the oldest nation in the world, to a group of government officials meeting about social security reform. Actually, the title of finance minister doesn't even begin to describe the importance of Tarō Asō in Japanese politics. He's also, at the time of this writing, the deputy prime minister, State Minister for Financial Services, and Minister in charge of Overcoming Deflation—a keystone goal of Prime Minister Shinzō Abe's "Abenomics" economic plan. From 2008 to 2009, Asō served as prime minister. Where he goes, journalists follow, and when he speaks, they take notes.

When Asō declared in January 2013 that older, sick people should give up the ghost for the greater good, the news achieved escape velocity and blasted into the international press. "Heaven forbid if you are forced to live on when you want to die. I would wake up feeling increasingly bad knowing that [treatment] was all being paid for by the government," Asō was reported saying. "The problem won't be solved unless you let them hurry up and die."

Asō, who was 72 at the time, and who also managed to refer to those who can't feed themselves as "tube people" during his speech, has something of a reputation in Japan for issuing harsh, demographics-related pronouncements. He made similar complaints about Japan's record-sized older population during his earlier tenure as prime minister, saying, "I see people aged 67 or 68 at class reunions who dodder around and are constantly going to the doctor . . . Why should I have to pay for people who just eat and drink and make no effort?"*

His statements, regrettably, do not shock me. Across cultures, ideas of this sort, which take as given that a year of life in old age is worth far less than a year at age 20 or 40, are as common as they are wrong. Funnily enough, however, unlike older populations, whose life expectancies keep increasing, Asō's point of view may not be long for this world. In the longevity economy, particularly the part concerning fundamental health-and-safety needs, consumer demands are shifting, and new technologies are arising that stand to fulfill them in unexpected ways, often while cutting expenses. The net effect will be a later life whose value will rise faster than its cost: the sort of investment that wise nations won't be so eager to wish away and individuals will do everything in their power to be part of.

Companies in the business of later-life health and safety must ride this wave or risk drowning. Thus far, I've described how innovators stand to prosper by fulfilling older adults' wants and desires—the upper decks of Abraham Maslow's hierarchy of needs—mainly because our overly medicalized, problematized idea of old age has left those opportunities wide open. However, innovators facing the lower levels of the

---

* He's also managed to offend the young. "There are many people who are creating the image that [the growing number of] elderly people is bad, but more problematic is people who don't give birth," he said in a 2014 Sapporo speech.

hierarchy will also benefit from the same set of strategies: focusing on the job of the consumer, paying attention to lead users, and incorporating transcendent design. In the near future, the resulting products won't just prove Asō's viewpoint wrong; they will also form the very foundation for how we will live in old age.

Currently, population aging feels like a crisis. Asō's hostility toward older people, for instance, didn't arise in a vacuum: the cost that Japanese elders pose to his country is conventionally assumed to be astronomical. People aged 65 and up account for more than one-quarter of Japan's population, more than that of any other major economy. No other country in history has ever had a population so old. As a result, doomsayers there have long blamed aging for the archipelago nation's ongoing economic woes and have predicted that it will eventually lead to societal failure.

In reality, Japan has done reasonably well in coping with rising, age-associated expenses. Its healthcare costs come to roughly 10 percent of GDP, slightly less than average for advanced economies and well below the United States' 17 percent, and its social security program is relatively frugal. Meanwhile, although its dependency ratio is high as traditionally calculated (dividing the raw population below 15 years of age and above 64 by the raw working-age population), if you look a little deeper into Japan's workforce numbers, the situation becomes less alarming. Thanks to its high level of older workforce participation, decreasing birth rates, and the continued introduction of women into the workforce, Japan's ratio of nonworkers to workers is projected to *improve* by 2032.

But don't tell that to people of Asō's mindset, who are by no means limited to Japan. In a 2014 cover story for *The Atlantic*, Ezekiel Emanuel, a respected American oncologist and bioethicist who was a key architect of the Affordable Care Act, likewise wished for death in old age—his own. In the article, titled "Why I Hope to Die at 75," he presents a thorough case that on both a personal level and in terms of public spending, life beyond three-quarters of a century isn't worth much. (The title is misleading—his idea is not to actively seek eutha-nasia at 75, just to refuse nonpalliative medical treatment.)

Although life expectancies are extending, he explains, the average time spent coping with one or more functional physical limitations—health issues that might prevent you from climbing a set of stairs or standing up without special equipment—is outpacing longevity advances. (Broadly, this is true, although the average figure he men-tions obscures a highly bifurcated population. The wealthier and more educated you are, the longer your healthy life expectancy.) A long, slow decay is not what anyone wants. Most hope for what's known as a "compression of morbidity," the term for longer life with as short a period of terminal sickness as is possible. Health officials around the world who write their nations' healthcare checks also pray fervently for such an outcome. But, as Emanuel notes, the compression of morbidity is not in the cards for everyone—or even most people.

Even more concerning is the always-looming threat of dementia, including Alzheimer's, which isn't likely to be solved anytime soon. "Instead of predicting a cure in the foreseeable future, many are warn-ing of a tsunami of dementia"—it's always a tsunami—"a nearly 300 percent increase in the number of older Americans with dementia by 2050," Emanuel writes. Again, this is a fair concern, although any increase in dementia diagnoses in the United States will occur only as a result of the growth of the older population. In fact, the dementia rate relative to population aging appears to be decreasing, however slightly.

But even in the absence of a dementia diagnosis, our mental pro-cessing speed slows slightly over time. Emanuel also says that creativity takes a nosedive with age, the flimsiest part of his argument.* What it

---

* "Currently, the average age at which Nobel Prize-winning physicists make their discovery—not get the prize—is 48," he writes, as evidence that youth is more creative than age. To the authors of the study responsible for that figure, however, an average age of 48 proves how *late* profound creativity now comes to our foremost scientists: "Although the iconic image of the young, great mind making critical breakthroughs was a good description of physics at that time [the 1920s and 1930s], it turns out to be

all adds up to, he argues, is a dull, frustrating, small life: "Aware of our diminishing capacities, we choose ever more restricted activities and projects . . . bird watching, bicycle riding, pottery, and the like. And then, as walking becomes harder and the pain of arthritis limits the fingers' mobility, life comes to center around sitting in the den reading or listening to books on tape and doing crossword puzzles." Emanuel goes on to acknowledge the important roles older adults can fill as mentors and grandparents, before arguing that life stretching out into one's 80s and beyond gets in the way of the lives of one's children, who wind up tasked with an undue caregiving burden.

In short, old age constitutes a problem—for the people experiencing it, for their families, for entire nations, for the world. If this idea sounds familiar, it should: it's a line of thought that can be followed straight back to the moment at the beginning of the 20th century, when society collectively decided that "the aged" were something that required solving. Declaring something a problem is another way of saying that it's of *negative value*: that the world would be better off without it. With this perspective in place as a norm, calls for death over later life shouldn't come as a surprise—if anything, they're the natural result of our going narrative of aging. Even as early as 1905, when the problem of "the aged" was still a young notion, William Osler, an influential turn-of-the-century physician whom Emanuel references in his essay, joked that men older than 60 should be given a period of quiet contemplation and then death by chloroform. However, as easy as it is for younger folks to look at a struggling 90-year-old and glibly say that such a life is not worth living, when it comes down to it, we almost always opt to prolong life. To borrow terms coined by famed MIT economist Paul Samuelson, although the *stated* preference of many is to die rather than suffer through life with multiple morbidities, our *revealed* preference—what we actually choose to do for ourselves and

a poor descriptor of age–creativity patterns more generally or even of physics today." The mean age of Nobel-worthy discovery, meanwhile, is rising.

our loved ones—is almost always to cling to life at all costs. And those costs, in the form of time, energy, and health and caregiving bills, can run very high.

Because there's a vast discrepancy between what we think later life is worth (little, possibly less than nothing) and what we're willing to pay to preserve it (everything we own, sometimes more), measures commonly employed to keep older people alive often feel like they're not worth the expense. To be blunt, when we spend on products for older adults' base-level, health-and-caregiving needs, what we get in return feels like a rip-off. It's for this reason that the challenge of supporting the world's aging population is routinely termed a crisis and never an opportunity. We're not getting a result that seems worth what we're paying, and yet we have no choice but to pay because the alternative is debility or death.

Caring for an older world is a real challenge we face, and I don't have all, or even most, of the answers. I don't, for instance, know of any technological advance that will bring down the costs of the final month of an older person's medical care, which account for a third of the expenses of the last year of life, as Emanuel and other researchers have determined. I don't know how to cure Alzheimer's or slow down the aging process. I don't know how to attenuate the loss of mental processing speed that occurs with age (and neither does anyone who's trying to sell you "brain-training" exercises).

But still, as health-and-safety products become automated and commoditized, many of the costs posed by older populations will fall. More important, products that don't yet exist or seem helpful yet nonessential today stand to improve how we live in old age, even despite chronic health issues. Such products, which are likely to experience great demand in the years to come, will raise our stated valuation of old age closer to the level of our revealed valuation. And the general sense of crisis will lessen as that awful "ripped-off" feeling eases.

Today, pessimists look to the future and see an enormous, once-proud generation ravaged by age, no longer able to undertake meaningful pursuits. Frankly, there's an extent to which this vision is accurate: the breakdown of our bodily systems is biological destiny. But such an outlook ignores the shades of grey separating the bloom of youth from utter dependency. In these in-between stages, artificial narrative forces play just as important a role as biology in determining what we're allowed to do—shaping even our very ability to *imagine* an unfettered old age. For every grandmother stuck at home doing crosswords (a fun pastime Emanuel unfairly bemoans), how many are really incapable of more meaningful activities, and how many are *actually* being held back by the fact that everything—from technological systems to transportation to the workplace to cultural expectations—is stacked against the full participation of elders in society? As health-and-safety products become better and in some cases cheaper, however, the odds will shift in favor of a more engaged and empowered old age. Even younger people may register that the value of a year of old age is on the rise. And the longevity economy will continue to grow, inspiring even more investment from the business community.

Enchanted Machines

When I talk to people in the gerontology world about what might increase the value of healthcare and caregiving for older adults without breaking the bank, most agree that technology is a strong candidate. However, when I ask *which* technologies, most people immediately jump to one of two ideas: eldercare robots and medication-reminder systems. As I explore ahead, the field is actually far larger than these two categories. But because eldercare bots and med reminders are flashy and jibe well with our going narrative, they tend to come to mind first.

That's not intended as a smear against the gifted technologists working on these issues, however, some of whom are making astounding progress. Among the ingenious systems that may help forgetful people—a group by no means limited to older adults—track their medications, perhaps the most intuitive example is the Vitality GlowCap, invented by my friend and MIT colleague David Rose. He is famous in tech-design circles for his "Enchanted Objects": single-purpose, connected devices that include an umbrella whose handle glows when it's supposed to rain and a crystal ball that tells you when the stock market is doing something of personal interest. The GlowCap is similarly straightforward (even if the underlying technology is quite involved): it simply glows when you need to take your meds. Another medication solution that seems low tech on a surface level but relies on highly sophisticated back-end processes is PillPack, an online pharmacy that organizes pills in small plastic envelopes by time of consumption, as opposed to type of med. The approach has drawbacks—it's difficult to adjust prescriptions when they're apportioned out in advance—but it's still a great remedy for forgetfulness and convenient for travelers.

Across the board, if innovations like the GlowCap and PillPack can improve medication adherence, that will be a very, very good thing. It will save lives. It will also happen to save insurers money while helping pharma companies get more business out of their current patients, something both industries are well aware of. But still, let's not kid ourselves: any improvement to life engendered by such systems will be one of degree, not kind.

Meanwhile, robotic caregivers that could help with activities of daily living—that is, feeding oneself, bathing, dressing, toileting, moving from place to place, and continence—could utterly upend the way care is done, potentially ending the so-called "caregiving crisis." Unfortunately, I have serious doubts about whether such robots will become commercially viable in the next 10–15 years. Although robots are getting better at performing delicate tasks like folding laundry, executing such motions in concert with the frailest people alive will constitute one of the highest possible bars of human-robot interaction, second only to infant care. I expect that any device capable of safely identifying when and how to bathe someone or to assist her with going to the bathroom will emerge only after other types of household robots prove themselves safe in everyday use.

That's not to say that companies and governments aren't trying extremely hard to make it happen sooner than later, however. If caregiving robots do become a normal part of aging, it will probably take place in Japan first. Japan faces a shortfall of 300,000 professional caregivers by 2025, and so, in 2015, on top of the country's social security and medical insurance systems, the Japanese government earmarked ¥72.4 billion ($720 million, as of 2016) in extra funds to build up the caregiving sector. That same year, the Japanese ministries for industry and health announced that 5.3 billion yen ($53 million), a full third of its budget for robotics research and development, would be dedicated to robots for the nursing and medicine sector. Today, both Toyota and Honda have prototype humanoid robots that can do impressive feats like playing the violin and swerving safely through a crowd of people. Perhaps the most intriguing Japanese, caregiving-specific bot is RoBear, developed by the research institute Riken, which can gently lift someone out of bed and deposit her in a wheelchair and vice versa. None of these robots are currently for sale, unfortunately; they're more proof-of-concept than product-on-the-shelf.

In the fairly unlikely event that that will change in the near future, assuming the technology is truly safe, I will be in full support of robot-assisted caregiving. The standard worry about care bots is that when they do become available, they will lead to a dystopian future full of nursing homes where elderly, frail people are woken, toileted, dressed, fed, and medicated by machines—and so on, until the day is done, and they've encountered nary another human being. We must be vigilant against any development that even begins to resemble such a possibility. But there's another dystopian scene in the making, and although there's nothing science-fictional about it, it's still quite alarming. The vast majority of eldercare provided in most major economies, including the United States, European Union, and Japan, is done in informal settings. It's impossible to overstate the toll such caregiving duties take on the people involved, from young professionals to work-ing parents to caregivers who are north of 65 themselves. Economists have attempted to quantify what this care is worth, and the number is big: $522 billion per year in the United States alone, according to the Rand Corporation, based on data compiled by the Bureau of Labor Statistics. That number accounts for the present-day opportunity costs of eldercare, but it doesn't describe the long-term career toll it takes or the fact that women shoulder a disproportionate share of the burden. It also doesn't account for caregiving's effects on businesses. Worker fatigue and caregiving-related scheduling issues cause both absenteeism and, worse, "presenteeism"—that is, when employees find themselves anxiously and surreptitiously scheduling doctors' appoint-ments and checking senior transportation timetables from their work desktops. One estimate suggests that the business cost of eldercare-related presenteeism, though difficult to quantify, may come to as much as 10 times that of absenteeism, totaling hundreds of billions of dol-lars per year in the United States alone. And these are just the costs of informal care—now add $220 billion per year in the United States for formal, professional caregiving services, whether they take place in homes or in dedicated facilities.

Caregiving is, it should be said, a beautiful thing. It's the definition of a labor of love, and so when the subject of automating it comes up, many balk. As celebrated MIT researcher Sherry Turkle wonders in her best-selling book *Alone Together,* "In the long term, do we really want to make it easier for children to leave their parents?" Although her critique is mainly aimed at companionship bots (more on them in a bit), the same concern applies to robots that could help elderly peo-ple with their bodily issues. Ideally, if such caregiving robots could be invoked in a way that would only add to the efforts of human caregiv-ers, not replace them, then it would be hard to argue with their moral value. But in practice, the availability of caregiving bots could very well lead to a dearth of human interaction in at least some cases. The frame of thought we've built around eldercare, Turkle argues, makes this result all but unavoidable. It assumes "that it has already been decided, irrevocably, that we have few resources to offer the elderly. With this framing, the robots are inevitable."

However, while giving Turkle the tremendous respect that is her due, I worry that in our current, negative narrative of old age, the choice we face may not be between robots and universal, loving, human caregivers. Rather, it may be between either a society that provides a good deal of care, made as effective as possible thanks to the technological tools at hand, and a nightmare scenario in which we effectively give up on our oldest and frailest. To judge by public intellectuals like Asō and Emanuel, life in old age already is of such low perceived value that it's not worth paying for at all. Emanuel treats older adults' needs as a societal millstone: "the very real and oppressive financial and caregiving burdens that many, if not most, adults in the so-called sandwich generation are now experiencing, caught between the care of children and parents." He's not wrong: eldercare is already taking a huge toll on the time, money, and energy of individuals and nations, an effect that will only grow. It's easy to imagine that even those who would readily mortgage their house to obtain the best medical treatment for their loved ones might blanch when it comes to supporting older adults on a national scale.

It seems we're caught between hard alternatives. On the one side is the justifiable desire of younger generations to live full lives (and run functional economies) without being yoked to the greatest set of eldercare responsibilities in the history of the world. On the other is the fact that we all hope to be treated humanely when we eventually need care. The influx of automation into care could improve the situation—diminishing the stress incumbent on informal caregivers while serving as a force multiplier for the army of care professionals. But it could also create opportunities for rationalized neglect: *Oh, Grandma likes her robot better than people. That's why we don't visit her much.*

It's a good thing, then, that the technology that will upend the way care takes place in the near term is nowhere near as flashy, nor as ethically troubling, as robotics.

Invisible Technology and Underground Engineers

The main problem with robots as a caregiving technology is their coldness. Even the most lovingly designed caregiving bot would still replace the human touch with the chilly precision of actuators, the human mind with the mathematical intransigence of an algorithm. But the term "technology" encompasses far more than doodads filled with wires and circuit boards, and nowhere is it written that tech must remove humans from the caregiving equation.

Virtually every part of today's increasingly tech-centric life relies not just upon the Internet and devices that access it but also staggeringly sophisticated back-end processes, from the proprietary workings of Google's vaunted search algorithm to the supply chains that keep Amazon and Walmart running. From the consumer's perspective, these kinds of tech innovations are largely invisible, and yet they have utterly changed the day-to-day lives of people around the world. When it comes to the health and safety of older adults, it should come as no surprise that the same kinds of hidden, tech-enabled services stand to utterly upend the traditional way of doing things, defanging at least some of the financial threat posed by the "caregiving crisis" in the bargain—all without removing the human touch from professional caregiving.

Near the offices of Stitch.net in San Francisco's Potrero Hill neighborhood—so close, in fact, that someone with a decent arm could hit it with a baseball—is a nondescript door in a row of nondescript doors, sunk into the side of a converted warehouse. There is no name anywhere on the entrance. Although the company within isn't exactly running in stealth mode, it keeps many of its cards close to the vest. Named Honor, it's been described as an Uber for home care.

Just inside the door, a narrow entryway, tastefully appointed with miniature, potted palms, opened into a cavernous, shared office filled with rows of oversized computer monitors. Despite the scale of the space, the noise level was low. Conversations passed in whispers, and even Jessie, the gregarious office dog, managed not to bark when she came over to say hello. At the far end of the room, natural light filtered in through frosted windows, and the ceiling overhead, made of what looked like grey, wooden two-by-fours, sat on narrow pillars of the same color. The disconcerting effect was akin to wandering under a busy pier at low tide, only to find a nest of tech workers hidden beneath, quietly and inscrutably pecking away.

Honor's cofounder and chief executive, Seth Sternberg, is a wiry cyclist in his late 30s. By local standards, he has a long history in Silicon Valley. In 2005, together with current business partner Sandy Jen and another cofounder, he launched Meebo, whose major offering was a browser-based service that aggregated a variety of instant-messaging applications, including AOL Instant Messenger, MSN Messenger, Facebook Chat, and Google Talk. In 2012, Google bought Meebo for $100 million. Soon, Sternberg and Jen were casting about—not just for a new problem to solve but a new *kind* of problem.

Sternberg led the way to Honor's lunch table: a solid plank of dark wood with, in that part of town, enough square footage to draw rent.

"A lot of things that start in Silicon Valley," he said, come from "building something that's easy to build, and you don't know if people will want it." In such a technology-first approach, it's all too easy to find oneself selling solutions that no one is willing to buy to problems that don't exist. Meanwhile, the most successful consumer products to emerge from this ethos tend to correspond to the deepest of human desires: the Seven Deadly Sins. For lust, see: Tinder. Sloth: TaskRabbit. Pride: Twitter. All of the above plus wrath and envy: Facebook.

I was familiar with what can happen when you take a technology and go searching for a nonsinful problem to solve. That was how we'd ended up touring Procter & Gamble's prototype store in Ohio, foisting diabetes-fighting barcode scanners on people who wanted nothing to do with them because they didn't address the problem the consumer cared about: price.

In their search for a new project, Sternberg and Jen decided to try a different approach: find the right problem, *then* figure out how to solve it. "We wanted a problem to solve that fit some very key criteria. Basically, it had to be something where we could look a human in the eye and know that we were making their life fundamentally better."

The insight they were waiting for came in 2013, when Sternberg flew to his parents' home in West Hartford, Connecticut. His mother picked him up at the nearest airport, Bradley International. "We used to frequently get caught by speed traps as kids, with her driving," said Sternberg—even on trips to Montana, where the speed limit reached 80 miles per hour. She was "a total lead-foot."

But when she picked him up in Connecticut, he noticed that she seemed to be driving more cautiously than usual. "It was just like, 'Why are you driving so slow?'" he recalled. "And she said, 'Driving's harder than it used to be.'"

The episode caused Sternberg to picture life 5 or 10 years hence. Caregiving would ultimately be a concern. "If I don't want to be the kid who says, 'Mom, you've got to leave your home'—how would I fix that?" he said. He began to look into the home care industry. And then he got excited.

The world of professional home care, he discovered, consisted mainly of small firms and individuals, with some larger franchises thrown in. There was no one major player, and as a result, the industry benefited from none of the advantages of scale. Typically, if you needed a care professional for, say, an hour, you had to pay for three hours' worth of care, minimum, to cover travel and overhead expenses. To make matters worse, because even the largest companies had only a small pool of professional caregivers on staff, scheduling problems arose frequently, as did difficulties connecting the right providers to care recipients with specific needs. Language barriers proved problematic. Personalities clashed.

If anything, Sternberg's account felt like understatement. I have personally heard so many war stories from stressed-out, adult children about the travails involved in finding care professionals that they've begun to blend together. Usually, if the account ends on a happy note, it's because the right caregiver finally arrived. *Oh, thank goodness for Mary. We went through three companies before someone recommended her to us. I honestly don't know what we'd do without her.*

At first, Sternberg focused on just a small part of the care equation: hospital discharge. When a patient is released following a hospital stay, it can happen very suddenly, and all too often, there's not a caregiver at the ready to pick that person up and take her home. Sometimes, older adults discharged in the morning end up waiting all day to be picked up by an adult child on her way home from work. Sternberg, who lives in California, realized that if his mother were hospitalized in Connecticut, he wouldn't be able to do even that. With more and more geographic distance separating family members around the world, he was far from the only one with that problem. And so he began to think of ways to provide professional caregivers to discharged patients at a moment's notice.

"The transportation is an issue, preparing the home for their arrival is an issue, making sure the meds are there, making sure they can get up the stairs. Like, it's not smooth," he said. Twenty percent of Medicare patients return to the hospital within 30 days of discharge, a problem that often starts with poorly managed transitions from hospital to home.

With a large enough pool of care providers and robust enough technological infrastructure, he and Jen reasoned, it would be feasible to create a care service that could respond quickly and reliably to hospital discharges. That idea opened other possibilities, however. There wasn't much difference, after all, between sending a professional caregiver to a hospital, as opposed to anywhere else nearby. What if they could create an online, one-stop shop for home care? As Sternberg mulled the idea over, he realized that hiring a long-term caregiver for his mother was yet another problem he wouldn't be able to solve from California. He would have to fly to Connecticut, interview a large number of providers, and then fly home, trusting a stranger with his mother's well-being.

Honor, the company Sternberg, Jen, and two other cofounders went on to create, is now operating in the San Francisco Bay Area and Los Angeles metro area. It's raised a remarkable $62 million in two funding rounds and counts among its investors some of the most influential venture capitalists in Silicon Valley. Sternberg wouldn't say exactly how many clients or care professionals the company has—these are some of the details Honor keeps close to the vest—but both appear to be streaming in. He claimed that the company turns away 95 percent of caregiver applicants, a degree of selectivity it's able to achieve only because large numbers apply. That the company has a reputation for being generous to its workers, who are all actual employees, not independent contractors, is in no small part responsible. At the same time, Honor allows clients to obtain care in one-hour increments, a remarkable improvement over the industry's standard three-hour minimum. Sternberg attributed Honor's ability to have its cake and eat it—to pay more for labor while shrinking the caregiving time window—to efficiencies the company has gained as a result of its scale and powerful data-crunching capacity. For instance, when you have plenty of care professionals on the ground and detailed information about their present and planned whereabouts, it's possible to use algorithms to calculate how to minimize costly expenses like travel time. That's a novel approach in the care space, even if it's old hat for the Ubers and FedExes of the world, and it has the potential to reduce some of the sizable overhead costs that currently go into professional care. What's more unprecedented is how Honor matches its "care pros," as Sternberg calls them, to clients. When your mother needs a professional caregiver, for instance, but she only speaks Mandarin and has multiple cats, then that caregiver must speak the language and not be allergic. Otherwise, "the care pro's just going to be sniffling the whole time, and that would be terrible for your mom." Sternberg said. "And," he added: "that would be terrible for the care pro."

In fact, owing to its size and data-analysis capacity, Honor can do better than merely matching its clients and care pros according to factors like languages and shared interests. After all, those are the sorts of things any old company could figure out, given enough time and spreadsheets. There are harder questions to be answered, Sternberg said. "If you're getting home care for your mom, do you prefer someone who has high skill or high customer service?" It sounded like the kind of decision one hopes not to have to make—Couldn't you hope for both?—but he had an answer. If your mom "just needs a little bit of help, you don't care much about skill. You care a lot about customer service. But if your mom's in advanced dementia, and it is hard to get her to even want to go out for a walk"—well, then the equation changes. "You just care if the care pro is so skilled that she knows how to get your mom with advanced dementia to go for a walk. You optimize on skill, not customer service."

Most new eldercare consumers, if asked to make such a decision, wouldn't know how to answer. "But we're able to take these massive streams of data, analyze them, and find insights," he said. And, because Honor scores each of its care professionals according to such criteria, it's able to provide them to the clients who will best benefit from their respective skill sets.

Perhaps what's most remarkable about the technology separating Honor from its predecessors in the homecare field is how unremarkable it seems. It's nowhere near as flashy as, say, RoBear, or any other potential robotic solution for the looming caregiving shortage. Honor does offer a mobile app, of course, although customers can just as easily schedule a care pro over a landline phone. But the real reason for the company's status as a *tech* start-up is the deep data analytics responsible for its efficient routing and matchmaking procedures. And that—invisible to clients and care pros alike—is what's being quietly built and maintained by the engineers hidden away under the pier-like ceiling of Honor's office.

Slaying the Healthcare Dragon

When I think of ways that products for elder health and safety are poised to become cheaper and more effective in the near future, Honor's example comes readily to mind. The company is now moving so fast that much of the above information about its size, funding, and reach may well become outdated by the time of this book's publication. Frankly, I hope that happens. And I hope its success bolsters the case, made by canny entrepreneurs and intrapreneurs in boardrooms and venture capital offices everywhere, that older consumers are worth serious investment.

Nowhere is this sort of efficiency-minded tech innovation more needed than in the healthcare sector, whose rising costs, please recall, inspired Tarō Asō to urge people to "hurry up and die." The healthcare industry has not succumbed to the kinds of Silicon Valley broadsides that have rattled other industries—from music to mattresses to meals. Tech founders have historically steered clear of health because of its high level of regulation. Honor gives the sector a narrow berth by providing only nonclinical home care, which is not subject to close regulation by the US Food and Drug Administration (FDA) or HIPAA, the act of Congress that guards the movement of patient data. Doppler Labs, manufacturer of the Hear One earbuds that can play music, make phone calls, and also amplify natural sounds, operates in a similarly easygoing, nonmedical regulatory zone. "If you're in real need of a medical device, you need to go buy a hearing aid," the company's CEO told *Fast Company*'s Harry McCracken in September 2016. "That's the fact of the situation, and it's a regulatory decision about who needs a medical device and who doesn't." And yet, McCracken pointed out, "For a startup that emphasizes that it isn't building a product to compete with hearing aids, Doppler spends a lot of time thinking about what its technology could do for people with hearing loss." Sure enough, by early 2017, rather than fight its way into the traditional assistive-hearing market, Doppler had begun working with a bipartisan congressional group to push for a new, deregulated category of hearing aids.

Of the relatively few tech start-ups daring enough to work within healthcare's entrenched regulatory and institutional structures, the tale most often told is a cautionary one, complete with a moral warning against hubris. In this story, adventurers armed with newfangled information technologies approach the sector assuming it will be an easy dragon to slay—it's an industry where fax machines are still in heavy use, for heaven's sake—but never stop to ask why, if killing the beast seems so straightforward, no one's done it yet. Today, anyone attempting such a quest would see quite a few charred skeletons along the route, many of recent extraction, most of whom had enjoyed loud, early fanfare when they first embarked on their missions. In 2013, the FDA ordered DNA analysis company 23andMe to pull its main offering because, the agency claimed, 23andMe had become uncommunicative and hadn't provided sufficient proof of the accuracy of its tests. It would take two years for the company to bounce back with a less comprehensive, more expensive product, then two more years for it to resume genetic testing for disease risks, finally with the FDA's seal of approval. In 2016 the founder of Theranos, a company that promised to perform dozens of diagnostic tests using just a drop of blood but whose findings were deemed by regulators to be of poor reliability, was ordered to refrain from owning or operating medical labs. Within a few months of the order, the company shuttered its labs and laid off nearly half its workforce. That same year, the CEO of Zenefits, an enterprise-facing company that offers free administrative software as a loss leader for its corporate health insurance brokerage service, resigned after it was revealed that he'd helped employees bypass a required, 52-hour training course. As a result of these and other regulatory disasters, it's become nearly axiomatic in the tech industry that the healthcare sector is uniquely resistant to the sorts of innovators who like to "move fast and break things," as Mark Zuckerberg once put it. Tellingly, following the ouster of Zenefits' CEO, the company changed its motto from "Ready. Fire. Aim." to "Operate with Integrity."

Healthcare innovations that avoid being blasted outright by regulators can still easily run afoul of a force of equal importance, if not greater: physicians. Doctors rightfully fear technologies that could saddle them with undue data management responsibilities or sacrifice their effectiveness in order to prioritize hospitals' and insurers' bottom lines—or, worst of all, sever communication between physicians and patients. In his address at the 2016 annual meeting of the American Medical Association, James Madara, the Association's CEO, questioned the value of many healthcare tech products—"from ineffective electronic health records, to an explosion of direct-to-consumer digital health products, to apps of mixed quality." Hidden among genuinely useful advances, such as robotic surgery and advanced radiation treatments, "are other, digital, so-called advancements that don't have an appropriate evidence base, or that just don't work that well—or that actually impede care, confuse patients and waste our time,"* he said. "This is the digital snake oil of the early twenty-first century."

Picture the apotheosis of Madara's worries: a world of connected devices talking to each other, quantifying all sorts of health data about the humans in their midst, with no one around to extract meaning from all the statistical noise except fickle algorithms and overburdened physicians. Already, doctors and nurses experience so many visible and audible alerts emanating from the technology surrounding them that critical information sometimes fades into the background, which

---

* It's been calculated that 50 percent of the average physician's day is now spent entering data in the multitudinous fields of electronic health records systems. "American physicians have become the most expensive data entry workforce on the face of the planet," Madara said in his address. "What a waste."

can cause lethal oversights. Today's intensive care units, Madara said, "sound like primitive swamps abuzz with a cacophony of bells, alarms, and whistles"; electronic health records add their own contribution in the form of constant reminders. Imagine, adding to the din, information emanating from everything from Fitbits to connected homes.

The only thing that might be worse, from the perspective of both physicians and regulators, would be for these newfangled streams of data to cut doctors out of the loop entirely. Frank Moss, former director of the MIT Media Lab and founder of the New Media Medicine group within it, summed up the idea up in a 2011 *New York Times* op-ed:

> It would begin with a "digital nervous system": inconspicuous wireless sensors worn on your body and placed in your home would continuously monitor your vital signs and track the daily activities that affect your health, counting the number of steps you take and the quantity and quality of food you eat. Wristbands would measure your levels of arousal, attention and anxiety. Bandages would monitor cuts for infection. Your bathroom mirror would calculate your heart rate, blood pressure and oxygen level.
>
> Then you'd get automated advice. Software that could analyze and visually represent this data would enable you to truly understand the impact of your behavior on your health and suggest changes to help prevent illness—by far the most effective way to cut health care costs.

In the years since the publication of this vision, mounting evidence has emerged to suggest that cutting the doctor out of the loop won't work. We've seen the FDA reprimand 23andMe for providing direct-to-consumer DNA tests whose results could have easily been mistaken for medical advice. The most concerning of these, a test for breast cancer risk that might have sent patients in search of unnecessary prophylactic surgery, has not been reinstated in 23andMe's FDA-approved 2017 testing kit. Before it ran into its own regulatory troubles, Theranos attempted something similar, and even managed to get an Arizona law changed that allowed it to provide the results of some blood tests directly to consumers. (To be fair, in addition to the fallout from Theranos's direct-to-consumer gamble, the bigger factor in the company's 2016 collapse was the fact that its blood tests were simply inaccurate.)

Madara's opinion aligns with that of the regulatory bodies. "Direct-to-consumer digital health devices—which only in the fine print say 'for entertainment purposes only,'" combined with "our clunky electronic records," and the aforementioned cacophony of alarum in hospitals, add up to "something I'd call our digital dystopia." Contributing energy to the crush of companies pushing new and, to Madara, troubling, products, are hordes of technologists like Moss, "predicting a future of digital healthcare that, in the near future, will bypass physicians altogether—where patients can largely look after themselves . . . then follow algorithms to essentially self-treat." "Anyone," Madara wondered, "been reading the papers of late? Been following the many evolving investigations and apparent fraud of such touted new pathways? That hallucination didn't turn out so well, did it?"

*　*　*

HUBRIS, IN THE tale of the healthcare dragon slayers, claims knight after knight, and sends any survivors scuttling back to the consumer tech sector. In a work of fiction, that result might convey a sense of poetic justice. But in the real world, the dragon of healthcare inefficiency is still burning people. No matter how obnoxious some of its would-be slayers might seem, it still needs to die, or at least have its wings clipped.

Perhaps what's needed is a new kind of technology entrant who's willing to show a little more respect for healthcare's many entrenched interests. At the deepest level, the problem with the kinds of tech companies that have promised for decades to "fix healthcare" is that they have never fully taken into consideration the jobs of all the consumers involved. And I do mean *all* the consumers: not just patients but also doctors, hospital administrators, insurers, the FDA—you name it. In far too many cases, these changes have prioritized the demands of hospitals and insurance companies, often by adding to the work expected of physicians or else by reducing the role of physicians in ways that send regulators scrambling for their red pens.

Five years later, Frank Moss's tune has changed somewhat. Compared with other industries that have weathered a tech takeover, he's written, "Healthcare is a different beast." In fact, even in the absence of the obstacles unique to healthcare, health tech products may simply not be able to accomplish everything that their apostles have promised. According to a 2016 study undertaken by Scripps Health, wearables and health-related phone apps don't seem to affect overall healthcare costs. Moss now advocates for—and founded the company Twine Health in order to provide—"health coaches." These intercessors track patients' technologically derived health data, parsing these numbers for primary care doctors and intervening when patients seem to be backsliding from a treatment plan.

Zealous techies may not want to hear this, but at least in the near term, a model along these lines may be the only way to fully leverage the power of information technology in the health sector. For the time being, a human must be included in any healthcare decision-making feedback loop, if only as a failsafe. The fact is, as newfangled wearable and smart-home technologies mature, they will make it easier than ever for older adults to live on their own. Over time, as people grow to rely on them, these measures will begin to feel less like optional, life-improving purchases, and more like comprehensive life-support systems.

As a thought experiment, imagine an older adult in the near future, whose life runs seamlessly on a framework of interconnected gadgets and apps. She's got a home computer that coordinates most of her household, doing everything from managing food inventory and delivery to summoning car rides to issuing emergency alerts. Her Social Security check is autodeposited into her bank account, and her expenses automatically come out of it. A medication management system tells her when to take her meds, refills her prescriptions automatically, and even adjusts dosages, within limits, based on readings from her wearable blood-pressure-and-glucose meter, her smart toilet,* and other devices. A smart scale tracks her weight in the morning and night, watching for any fluctuations.

Let's zoom in on the smart scale, which, of the above technologies, is one of the least science fictional. As long ago as the early aughts, the AgeLab was working with a major medical device manufacturer to field-test a smart scale that would alert a call center if its user experienced any alarming weight fluctuations. For some patients, such as those on loop diuretic medications for congestive heart failure, maintaining steady weight is of critical importance. In congestive heart failure, the heart isn't able to move blood around the body as efficiently as needed, and as a result, fluid accumulates in the lungs, liver, and elsewhere. Diuretic drugs help prevent this effect by causing the kidneys to excrete more water than usual, reducing the total amount of water in the body. When congestive heart failure patients take their diuretics religiously, their weight stays fairly even. But when they miss a dose, they can gain weight very quickly as they fail to excrete water and it fills in around their vital organs.

The manufacturer was confident that their scale worked—in the lab. As any applied scientist knows, however, in the wild, unexpected variables tend to creep in. To see how the scales fared in real-world use, a graduate student of mine helped the company set up scales in the

---

* Smart toilets are more common in Japan than anywhere else but are growing in popularity around the world. At the time of this writing, there are models on the market that can analyze urine flow rate, among other metrics. One unsung attribute of many models is the built-in bidet, which can be utterly liberating for people with Parkinson's disease or other conditions that impair coordination.

houses of roughly a dozen patients with congestive heart failure. They all took their diuretic meds every morning and weighed themselves every morning and evening. We expected that, if one of them missed a day's dose, it would begin to show up on the scale starting that evening, and the weight gain would be unmistakable by the next morning.

What no one expected was the friendly, older woman who kept gaining weight in the evening—a lot of it—only to lose what she'd gained by the time she awoke. It made absolutely no sense: more than 10 pounds were vanishing into thin air nightly, only to return doggedly by the end of the next day. My student dutifully went to see what was up. There was nothing wrong with the scale, he determined, and she was both healthy and taking her meds right on schedule. She wasn't wetting the bed. So he asked her about her nighttime routine.

"Oh, I do the same thing every single night," she said. "I make dinner, eat, feed my cat and weigh myself."

Wait, what was that last part again?

"I feed my cat and weigh myself."

It turned out that those two activities were closely linked. Once Fifi was done with his Fancy Feast, she would scoop him up and walk resolutely over to the scale, onto which she would step *with the cat still in her arms.* During her morning routine, on the other hand, she would weigh herself without any furry companions to keep her company. The difference in weight was causing the scale to go haywire. It was exactly the sort of malfunction that the manufacturer was worried about—the kind that doesn't occur in the lab, where there are generally no pets.

Now let's return to our hypothetical, hyperconnected grandmother with the smart scale, smart toilet, and other smart-home doodads. Just for argument's sake, imagine she makes the same cat-related mistake. What's the worst that could happen?

Let's give her home tech the benefit of the doubt and assume that any future medication management system reliable enough to get past the FDA would be designed not to do something rash like quintuple her dosage. Instead, when she starts carrying the cat onto the scale, it sets off messages throughout her smart home—telling her to get to a doctor and offering to summon an Uber to convey her there. She doesn't; instead, she turns off the loud, bothersome notifications. At the same time, messages in her kitchen tell her to reduce her sodium intake immediately because salt will cause her to retain water. Her home computer instructs her meal delivery service to bring her a sodium-free lunch, which is so bland that she picks up the phone and, in a break from routine, orders fast food for dinner. By evening, she's eating large quantities of salty food while questioning whether to take her next dose of diuretic meds, because she knows something is wrong with that medication, even if she's not sure what. Suddenly, her health is at real risk. All because there was no one around to ask her about her evening routine—or inquire about her cat.

In this example, danger arises as a result of simple poor planning and bad luck. Now imagine if a nefarious actor were involved. The more parts involved in a computerized system, the more potential entry points there are for malevolent, uninvited guests. Already, in 2013, to the amusement of many a tech blogger, it was revealed that the "My Satis," a $4,000 smart toilet with a number of smartphone-controlled features, could be made to open, shut, and spray water into the air by anyone within Bluetooth range. There's no denying that, on its face, that's pretty funny. It would be less so, however, if a device connected not to a water pipe but, say, one's bank account were caused to discharge freely. At least in the early stages of the care-enhancing smart home, a human on the watch for these kinds of problems could go a long way toward catching issues that simply don't occur in the sterile world of research-and-development facilities. Yes, an algorithm could recognize situations that are far out of the ordinary—like when your credit card company wonders if that's really you buying 10,000 rubber ducks from a warehouse in Malta—but once the smart home takes on a life-support role, shutting down operations until a problem gets resolved won't be a viable course of action. Such a system would call for the kind of judgment that is still, for now, best left to human beings, whether they're family members, friends, or caregiving professionals.

Even in the world of electronic health records, there have been calls for the reintroduction of a human touch. Automated systems are great at drawing attention to problems like dangerous drug interactions, but, because their input is limited to medical records data, they can make suboptimal or insufficient treatment recommendations. Such a system, for instance, might correctly recommend medications for a child with asthma symptoms. But only a human can pick up on things that never enter into health records, such as whether that child's parent's clothes smell like cigarettes, and tell the smoker to cut it out or at least take it outside. Such observations "change the diagnostic algorithm and are easy to miss when work revolves around the computer and not the patient," writes a team from the Stanford University School of Medicine in the *Journal of the American Medical Association*.

Garry Kasparov, the chess grandmaster many consider the greatest of all time, came up with a term for when humans and computers form a team that outperforms either acting alone: the centaur. In this metaphor, humans make high-level, creative decisions, while machines support that process with computational horsepower. When it comes to care, combining high-tech and high-touch approaches has the potential to create a combination more potent than either component part. Honor applies such an approach to caregiving, and the time is now ripe for the same to happen in healthcare. It remains to be seen whether such a line of attack will reduce healthcare costs, but it is likely to improve healthy life expectancy, and in so doing, enable older people to live the way they want for longer than ever.

Harry Potter and the Emerald City

Still, if you didn't know about the promise that the centaurs and other technological fixes hold for health and caregiving, you could be forgiven for siding with Emanuel and Asō about the future of old age. From the outside looking in, it can seem like there's no way technology will ever elevate our low stated valuation of old age to match our high revealed valuation. The flashiest technologies, such as caregiving robots, feel science fictional at best. Whenever companies apply tried-and-true information technologies to healthcare, they seem to strike out. And the technologies that *do* seem to work, like the ones that make Honor's efficiencies possible, remain largely hidden from sight—at least for now.

But in the meantime, scientists and engineers pursuing basic, elemental research continue to push forward every technical field, a process that inevitably (albeit unpredictably) leads to happy surprises. Some of these may well change how we live and age, and sooner than one might think. It was one such discovery, and the promise of a related, nascent smart-home technology, that made me walk across MIT's campus on a humid summer's day to meet with Dina Katabi, a professor of electrical engineering and computer science. We sat down in her office on the ninth floor of MIT's Ray and Marie Stata Center. On my way in, she had to warn me to not trip over a piece of Plexiglas wedged into the bottom of the doorframe. She'd had it specially cut at the machine shop downstairs for use as a barrier: easy to step over, yet high enough to keep her impossibly small Yorkshire terrier, Mika, from running amok. Some labs, it turns out, do allow pets.

Katabi is one of the world's foremost experts on how radio waves interact with each other and the world around them. Once, at the White House, she told President Obama that "radio waves are amazing creatures if you understand them enough," and back in her office, as she did her best to explain their behavior, it became clear that they were as tangible to her as dogs and cats are to you or me. Mika, meanwhile, curled up in a corner. She'd heard it all before.

We were discussing smart-home systems with the potential for cross-generational appeal—that is, the sort of transcendent products that might "accidentally" help older adults en route to making life better for all age groups. The leading prototype in my mind for the kind of central interface that might eventually command connected devices throughout the home was Amazon's Echo, a voice-operated computer whose intelligent personal assistant, Alexa, can already do a variety of tasks, such as play music, read out Wikipedia articles, predict commute times, and control lighting and heating. Perhaps most important, the number of things Alexa can do is constantly increasing. Other contenders with similar functionality include Cortana, Siri, and the Google Assistant, intelligent personal assistants available in Microsoft, Apple, and Google products, respectively.

Katabi let me unspool my disorganized thoughts, then cut through with a soft smile. Sure, she told me, you could set tell Alexa to do all sorts of things—more and more every day. Still, there are some seemingly simple feats it can't pull off. Say, for instance, you set a wake-up alarm: it knows when to go off but not where. "If you tell Alexa, 'Wake me up at eight AM,' then Alexa will ring the alarm at eight AM," she said. "But it wouldn't know whether you left the bed or are still in the bed." I was flabbergasted by the notion, because I'd never thought of the alarm clock as a technology that is missing a dimension. But, I reflected, of course it is: it interacts with time, people, and in Alexa's case, the Internet, but it doesn't know where in your house it is, or where you are. Whenever the truly seamless smart home reaches maturity, it will need to be able to identify the locations of objects and people within it.

On the subject of location, it would have been hard to find a more striking one at MIT than where we were speaking. Arthur C. Clarke once said that any sufficiently advanced technology is indistinguishable from magic, and so is whatever's holding together the Stata Center. The building, which was designed by the Pritzker Prize-winning architect Frank Gehry and which houses MIT's famed Computer Science and Artificial Intelligence Laboratory (CSAIL), is the most eccentric—some might even call it shambolic—structure on campus. Were it built of timbers and thatch instead of concrete and chrome, it would call to mind an oversized version of The Burrow, the magical family home of Harry Potter's best friend, Ron Weasley. Both are leaning conglomerations of rooms stacked haphazardly on top of each other; both are lent stability only by unseen forces.

It was fitting, then, that the Stata Center was home to a technology that Katabi had initially named after a magical artifact from Harry Potter. In J. K. Rowling's books, the enchanted Marauder's Map allowed Harry to sneak around school at night by miraculously revealing the location of hall-prowling professors. Katabi's version was similar: a tracker capable of detecting people in complex spatial environments—even through walls—without issuing a single X-ray.

Born in Damascus, Syria, into a family of doctors, Katabi wasn't supposed to become a wizard of radio waves. She was expected to pursue the profession of her father, grandfather, aunts, and uncles. When she aced her mandatory examinations at the end of high school, scoring sixth in all of Syria, she signed up to study medicine at the University of Damascus, a coveted academic specialization reserved for the best and brightest. There, she quickly rose to the top of her class, which was why it was so unexpected when she suddenly switched from medicine to electrical engineering. She said she'd needed more math in her life. I asked if her parents were surprised.

"They were furious," she said, in part because the Syrian government monitored engineering jobs far more closely than medical ones. "Basically the only profession where you can control your life is the medical profession."

She chose a third path. Upon graduation, she came to MIT to pursue a master's, then a PhD, in computer science. Her dissertation applied control theory, which is used in the efficient design of power plants, to computer networking problems, and introduced a new theoretical way for information to flow more efficiently through the Internet. Her advisor, a senior scientist at CSAIL, told *MIT Technology Review* that the work "shifted the standard for what it takes to publish in this space." Soon, Katabi was an MIT professor herself, working on new ways to move information through wired and wireless networks.

One aspect of information transfer that she would put her personal stamp on was something called the Fourier Transform, a mathematical tool essential to the functioning of modern electronics. The Fourier Transform is used to isolate the individual, constituent wave patterns that add up to form a complex signal. It could be invoked, for instance, to figure out which distinct tones contribute to the unique fingerprint of someone's voice. It's an incredibly versatile tool, with applications ranging from communications signal processing to the pricing of stock options to magnetic resonance imaging, but it can be computationally intensive. Together with a group of colleagues from MIT's computer science department, Katabi found a way to make the Transform less computationally unwieldy under certain conditions— the first such improvement since 1965. She soon began wondering what else could be done with the troves of data hidden within complex radio signals. What if, she wondered, she could use the technique to locate someone within a home?

Determining distance by bouncing a wave off an object has, of course, been possible for decades. However, whether an observer hopes to detect an object using radar or its cousin, sonar, it must be relatively alone in an expanse: an airplane in a big blue sky, a submarine in the deep blue sea. Ground-penetrating radar became commercially available starting in the mid-1980s. Crowded-apartment-penetrating radar, however, seemed unlikely to ever come about—at least until Katabi came along.

Her plan called for sending Wi-Fi–esque signals—that is, ones belonging to the same frequency bands as Wi-Fi but structured differently and of far less power—into a home. The ones that bounced back off people's bodies but not nearby tables, chairs, and walls could then be timed and the location of those people determined. That posed a new challenge, however: although people are mostly made of water, which does reflect radio waves, hard surfaces like tables make much better reflectors.

But one thing that tables and walls don't do is move around. Do you recall that old myth about *Tyrannosaurus rex,* which held that the dinosaur's vision relied on motion? ("Don't move! He can't see us if we don't move," Sam Neill's character warns his young companions in the film *Jurassic Park.*) Katabi's system, as planned, would be something like that. When it sent out Wi-Fi–frequency radio signals into a room, its sensors would detect a cacophonous hodgepodge of reflections returning from a variety of surfaces. But when someone walked in front of the sensors, the system could theoretically hone in on only those reflections bouncing off her body, because, unlike those returning from tables and chairs, the body-reflected signals would change over time. Such a system should, Katabi reasoned, be able to measure the direction and distance of a person in motion. At the very least, it could locate people when they walked around the house, if not when they sat watching TV.

When she and her students began testing the system, however, something unexpected happened. They set it up to visualize location data in a variety of ways, some of which appeared in the form of a line graph. Lines representing distance, position, or altitude would climb and drop as she and her grad students walked in front of the sensor. That was to be expected. What came as a surprise was the way the lines behaved when the human test subjects stood still. They took on a wavelike pattern, with peaks repeating every five seconds or so. Katabi told her student standing in front of the sensor to hold his breath. The mysterious peaks leveled out, which could only mean one thing: the system, more accurate than she had imagined, was detecting the subtle abdominal motion involved in breathing. Then the team noticed something else, which the breathing motion had heretofore obscured. While the tester, eyes now bulging, continued to hold his breath, a series of smaller, more frequent waves pulsed down the line. There was only one thing it could be: a heart rate. Katabi's team had built a device that could detect far more than the location of someone at rest or in motion from across a room and even through walls. It could *monitor her vital signs.*

The question was what to do with it.

The system's military applications were obvious, as was its potential as an interface mechanism for smart-home devices. Katabi's team quickly demonstrated ways to control a room's lighting with a gesture. It could be used to cut a home's energy consumption by turning off lights not in use and determining when the occupant was away. She even began thinking about video games that could be played throughout one's house—an augmented-reality version of Call of Duty, perhaps, where you ran around defending your own home from evildoers. It was around this time that she considered "Marauder's Map" as a potential name for the technology, before deciding that it was too fantastical.

In 2013, she received news that she'd been awarded a John D. and Catherine T. MacArthur Foundation "Genius Grant," which confers large, no-strings-attached lumps of cash on people who, according to the Foundation, demonstrate "extraordinary originality and dedication in their creative pursuits." The award, in addition to amounting to a goodly sum, tends to push scientists, artists, and others into the public eye. In the ensuing flurry of press attention, Katabi mentioned her intention to apply her work not only to the smart home but also to hospitals.

Then, as it so often does, life intervened. Katabi received word that her grandfather had suffered a serious fall. Within the same month, the same thing happened to the grandmother of one of her graduate students. Luckily, both grandparents were quickly discovered by a family member and survived. But visions of worst-case scenarios in the home remained lodged in Katabi's mind. And so when she went on to spin a company out of her Wi-Fi tracking work, its mission, from the start, was to watch for and prevent falls in the home. She named her company Emerald.

In 2015, at the first-ever White House Demo Day focused on "inclusive entrepreneurship"—that is, businesses formed by those other than young, white men—she had the opportunity to demonstrate Emerald's technology to President Obama. From my perspective, with the benefit of full knowledge of the Emerald system's capabilities, footage of the event was amusing to watch. The president walked over from a previous demonstrator's table and, surrounded by members of the press, shook hands with Katabi and her grad students, Zach Kabelac and Fadel Adib. "We are presenting Emerald, the health companion for older people," she said. "It helps people stay safe and healthy in their homes."

It's impossible to know exactly what President Obama was thinking at that moment, but if he were like most people familiar with old-age-safety tech, he would have been mentally checking his watch. The world is full of prototype sensor systems designed to detect falls, often consisting of pressure-sensitive floor pads or accelerometers worn on one's person, and these hardly ever go into production, let alone achieve any measure of market success. They just never seem to work very well, don't jibe with the user or caregiver's wants, are too expensive, or come across as too invasive or infantilizing. If the president had any of these thoughts, however, he kept them to himself. Katabi was a guest in his home, after all. Then she demonstrated how the device could detect a fall—Adib, serving as guinea pig, tipped over on command—and told him how it could see through walls. His interest appeared to grow.

Then Katabi revealed that Emerald had been tracking Adib's vital signs the entire time. She showed Obama the graph representing Adib's breathing motion, and then, after instructing him to hold his breath, the curve describing his heart rate. The president paused. "Wow," he said.

Katabi took her time explaining the heart-rate feature, and Kabelac had to remind her that Adib was still holding his breath, which got a laugh out of Obama: "Poor guy . . . he was really starting to turn blue!"

He went on: "The part about the falling I understand, because those are sort of big motor movements taking place." But, "I'm surprised that you've got a sensor that is that sensitive from that distance."

Actually, the system is both highly sensitive and reassuringly vague. Although Emerald's ability to convey subtle motion in a complex environment is far greater than that of video, its ability to form pictures is next to nonexistent—and that's a feature, not a bug. Beyond rough measurements like whether someone is tall or short, sitting or standing, it can't create an image of a face or body. These limitations cut down on potential privacy invasions, although Emerald can still detect plenty of things that older people might not want shared with anyone, such as what's happening in the bedroom on a Saturday night.

That's just one of the potential faults that users might find with Emerald. The greater issue is the same as with PERS like Life Alert: No one wants "old people's" technology. As Katabi told President Obama, "I'm sure you've seen commercials where, 'I've fallen . . .'"

"Where you're wearing a necklace," Obama chimed in. "Right. My grandmother lived by herself, so this was always something we were worried about."

"For older people," said Katabi, "we know that it's very hard to remember to put the pendant on themselves, and even when they have it on themselves, they don't remember to push the button."

"Right, or they're just cranky about it," said Obama. "They're like, 'I don't want to wear this thing.'" He made the noise of a dismissive, grumpy person: "Agh."

It was meant as a joke, and it was a penetrating one—the only thing I would have added is that it's anyone's right to be cranky about a technology that violates one's sense of self. Emerald, by eschewing doodads worn on the body, does away with one of Life Alert's major failure points: the fact that owners must decide whether to put it on in the morning, if at all. But the potential for Emerald to carry the stigma of an "old man's device" is still a threat to its future marketing success.

Since our meeting, Katabi and I have been talking about how to change that: how a system like hers could be made to come across as ageless while oh-so-conveniently happening to save the lives of older adults. Regardless of the path she chooses to take with her remarkable invention, it's worth thinking about how such a system might, in theory, cross the age barrier and become a normal piece of household tech.

There are a few ways it could happen. The system could be integrated into the smart home to give residents some combination of gestural and voice control over their connected appliances. Such redundancy can be useful when people are learning to use a brand-new interface on the fly: it gives them (and the system) two chances to get a command right. For instance, if you were to point at a light bulb and say, "light bulb, on," your smart-home computer would know (1) which bulb you wanted illuminated and (2) not to turn on the television directly behind it.

Or, at some point in the future, it could well become unthinkable to exist in your home without being able to summon a Marauder's Map of the people and select things inside it, all of which could be located using a combination of Emerald and small, RFID-enabled tracking tags. Already, the days of puzzling out one's location on paper road atlases are fading into memory, thanks to the advent of GPS-enabled maps, which we now take for granted. Could the same thing happen in the home? All at once, gone would be the days of hunting for your keys, worrying where your teenage kids are, and obtaining expensive, single-purpose intruder alarms. Katabi's grad students have been testing a handful of Emerald prototypes in their own homes, and Kabelac told me he's already started using it as a burglar alarm when he travels.

In addition to these sorts of ageless functions, the system would still fulfill its original purpose: keeping older adults safe in their homes, in many cases by communicating important information about them to their caregivers. Some of the inevitable privacy concerns could be addressed by having the care recipient, not her caregiver, set the amount of information to be shared. In the least private, most data-intensive example, an adult child could see where his or her parents are at any given moment, whether they've eaten, whether their gait is normal, and whether they've deviated from normal habits. At the other end of the invasiveness spectrum, the system could be made to resemble yet another magical technology from Harry Potter, this one found in the Weasleys' Burrow. Mrs. Weasley, Ron's mother, owns a clock with a hand for every member of her family—nine in all—and positions on the clock face for where each family member can be found, including "work," "home," "school," "travelling," "lost," "prison," and "mortal peril." For the most privacy-conscious users, a Wi-Fi tracking system could deliver an even more reduced output: only "mortal peril" or "all's well." Many sandwich-generation caregivers would welcome the option to be warned if any family member, of any age, is in mortal peril (i.e., lying immobile on the ground), and invoking this measure for the whole family would add an element of agelessness to the technology. After all, young and middle-aged people, too, can fall and hit their head when home alone. Or choke on an olive. Or eat something they're allergic to. Or . . . you get the picture. The point is, even when dealing with weighty concerns such as health and safety, cutting-edge tech products can sidestep stigmatizing older people. Quite the contrary: they can and should be fun and perhaps even "indistinguishable from magic," as Arthur C. Clarke put it. The advent of such transcendent technologies will, yet again, add to older adults' independence while improving health outcomes—both improving later life and moving another pebble from the "crisis" side of the longevity scales to the "opportunity" side.

Still, you might reasonably point out, a technology like Emerald, even if it were set up to be as stingy as possible with the data it provides about older adults, would inevitably compromise privacy to a degree. Might those hoping to maintain their independence consider this a disqualifying factor?

In fact, older adults are less likely than you might think to bristle at the privacy imposition posed by Emerald or a system like it. For a 2011 study conducted with the help of Nippon Telephone and Telegraph, Japan's largest telecom, the AgeLab built a pill-reminder system that could determine the identity of a pill bottle and, by weight, whether the right number of pills had been removed at the right time. The device, known as "e-Home," could be used by itself, or it could be included as part of a highly intuitive, two-way video-chat-and-text-messaging system connecting an older adult's home with that of an adult child. This combined option alerted those adult children if their parents missed a dose, and it also created a mode of easy communication between two geographically separated households. Overall, the older adults in our study rated the system as very satisfactory, and more important, the ones who used it in shared mode liked it more than those who used it by themselves. They simply didn't mind that their kids knew whether they'd missed their meds.

Even if you're an older person who finds caregiving technologies intrusive, you still might find yourself desiring them, strangely enough, for reasons of privacy. In the future, the choice many of us will face won't be whether to obtain a technological support system or go without. Rather, it will be between the system and moving—in with one's kids, into an assisted living facility, into a nursing home. Compared to the total surveillance of many an institutional setting, a relatively impersonal electronic system that keeps tabs on your health can feel significantly less intrusive. The same, looking farther into the future, could be said for caregiving robotics. Given the choice between a robot that helps out with intimate, potentially embarrassing care, or a human provider with the capacity to cast judgment and make gossip, many will choose the machine every time. Even today, you might even find yourself making such a decision without even realizing it. Imagine buying something potentially embarrassing at a CVS. Do you choose the checkout counter with the human behind it or the automated one? I know I tend to go with the robot.

Meanwhile, well before machines take over home care, technology will provide ways to reverse the direction of surveillance and protect recipients of human care. Katabi suggested that an Emerald user would be able, for instance, to make sure that a babysitter is doing his job. "You want to check that, if they came to take care of your baby, they didn't leave the baby in his room and they were watching TV the whole time." The same might apply for a plumber coming by while you're at work, she said: you might want to make sure he sticks to the kitchen and doesn't wander into your bedroom. "You don't want to have a camera—that's invasive," and many governments require you to inform someone if you're filming him or her. But other technologies can do the trick more effectively—and (at least somewhat) less creepily. Seth Sternberg provided one example of how his company flips caregiving's normal surveillance relationship on its head. "We knew when we were starting Honor that there was, like, an unbelievable amount of fraud in this space." I wish I could say I found that surprising. Anecdotal stories about caregiving gone wrong in homes and institutional settings alike abound. Fraud is one of the least alarming things that can happen.

Honor's applicants all go through multiple security screenings and are even fingerprinted, Sternberg said. Nevertheless, once, early in the company's history, a care pro drove up to a care recipient's home, checked in on Honor's app, and then drove away. The client, who had severe dementia, would never have been able to report that no one had provided care for her. But GPS-enabled tracking measures identified the malfeasance instantly. "We can reliably catch it one hundred percent of the time, and then take that person out of the system immediately," Sternberg said. At the same time, the system protects care pros from their clients. "It's much more common that we get calls from family members saying, 'My mom said no one showed up.' And we're able to go in and see the GPS logs and say, 'You know, someone actually did show up. They were there from this time to that time. Your mom just doesn't remember.'"

Any company thinking about engaging with older adults online should recognize that security and fraud-detection measures are non-negotiable. One recent report estimated that older Americans lose $36.5 billion every year to scammers, a total that would come to about $750 per head if it were distributed evenly—which it isn't. Seven percent of victims lose $10,000 or more. Most of these scams take place over the phone, but like everything else that once happened over land-lines, scamming is shifting to the Internet.

Around the corner from Honor at Stitch's headquarters, Marcie Rogo said that fraud plagues the online dating world. In the experience of her customers, other dating services—including some supposedly devoted solely to older users—can be full of scam artists, a charge that several attendees at the Stitch event on San Francisco Bay later corroborated. One source of frustration was explicit messaging from what appeared to be young, attractive people of the opposite sex. One Stitch user, Rogo said, described her experience with a rival site as "like she was in the red-light district." The young men expressing interest weren't who they said they were. "She's not 30. She's 60. People that are messaging her are scammers."

At Stitch, Rogo instituted a multitiered verification procedure for its users, similar to what Airbnb uses for its hosts. It couldn't keep out every scammer, but it could make sure people weren't lying about their identity, and that went a long way toward making users feel at ease on the platform. In fact, Rogo said, users became far more comfortable talking to each other on her site than she had ever anticipated. She hadn't planned on including community forums, but one day, on the spur of the moment, she decided to include a comments section as part of a notice for one of Stitch's periodic meet-ups. Members, it quickly became clear, relished the opportunity to converse freely in a forum that, though public and full of strangers, brooked no anonymity, thanks to the verification measures Stitch had put in place. As a result, conversation stayed relatively civil. Encouraged, Rogo added freeform chat forums to the site, and they proved a hit. She pulled one up on her computer screen, on the subject of Vegemite, the polarizing, yeast-extract-derived Australian food. "Oh my god, this has been the most popular discussion," she said. Was it a condiment or not? Was it edible or not? Both were debatable. And because Rogo had instituted relatively strict safety measures, her members, many of whom hailed from Australia, found themselves free to hash it out with each other, with something approaching wild abandon.

Fun Is Magic, Fear Is Tragic

Fun, not fear; aspiration, not apprehension—these are the factors that motivate consumers, even when it comes to high-tech products focused solely on basic bodily needs and personal safety. The multi-trillion-dollar question we're now facing is how to address these base-level concerns while increasing, not sacrificing, older adults' ability to do what they want, achieve their goals, and have fun. Heightened online security, for instance, shouldn't feel like a gulag—it should create a safe place where the merits of Vegemite can be discussed. (It's more of a spread than a condiment, in case anyone's wondering). A fall-detection system should be such a joy to use that people of all ages go out of their way to get one. A homecare company should deliver caregivers that somehow speak your language and have the skills you need, without your ever having to articulate those issues. And so on.

Products that prioritize fun, a delightful user experience, and the aspirations of the older consumer are in no way limited to the futuristic or high-tech. The shift of many healthcare services from hospitals to retail settings, for instance, makes it easier for patients not to feel like patienthood is their primary purpose in life. It's far more appealing to be, say, the kind of person who meets a friend at Starbucks on her way to dialysis than the kind of person whose only item on her day's agenda is treatment in a hard-to-reach part of town.* Another

---

*This idea reaches a logical extreme in MinuteClinic, the walk-in medical clinic originally conceived by a father who wondered why his son needed to wait for two hours in urgent care to be given a simple strep test. CVS's 2006 acquisition of Minute-Clinic is a great example of how large incumbents can approach small, potentially disruptive upstarts built by lead users. Not only did CVS eliminate a potential competitor, but in so doing it also created a highly profitable synergy between the two companies.

way to support customers' positive self-image in health products may be to market them with an emphasis on performance, as opposed to disease mitigation. There are differences between Soylent, the meal-replacement shake intended for dot-com workers who are too busy to eat, and Ensure, a supplemental shake intended for older people who need the nutrition. But the biggest difference is marketing.

It's even possible to focus on what older people want, not just need, at the highest levels of eldercare, such as assisted living and nursing homes. Such institutions have a reputation for prioritizing health statistics over happiness. As Atul Gawande writes in his magisterial meditation on the end of life, *Being Mortal,* "We have no good metrics for a place's success in assisting people to live. By contrast, we have very precise ratings for health and safety. So you can guess what gets the attention from the people who run places for the elderly: whether Dad loses weight, skips his medications, or has a fall, not whether he's lonely." There are places that do make the desires of older adults a main concern, however. The Beacon Hill Village is a shining, if unorthodox, example, and if you know where to look, there are also enlightened, traditional institutions to be found that are not, as Gawande writes, "designed to be safe but empty of anything [older people] care about."

At places with such a reputation, long waiting lists are common. It's the sort of thing the free market should sort out: the short supply should, in theory, rise to meet demand. The main reason it hasn't yet done so is the continued influence of the going narrative of old age. Viewing older people merely as problems to be solved leads to products that attempt to eliminate negatives from life but fail to provide positives like fun, delight, and magic. The best thing older adults can hope to achieve using such products is to climb up from a bad quality of life to a middling one. There's no hope to rise higher: to claim

---

The walk-in approach has its drawbacks, but if imitation is the sincerest form of flattery, then let testify the fact that walk-in clinics have since popped up at Walgreens, Walmart, Kroger, and elsewhere.

meaning, excitement, and satisfaction in one's later years. Based on such testimony, if you didn't know better, it would be easy to assume that old age isn't worth living.

As the baby boomers make their demands heard, however, a new groundswell of products will actively add value to later life. Although it will have a salutary effect on life in old age, the economics surrounding this trend are not yet clear. In terms of personal finance, when I talk to financial advisors about the unforeseen costs of aging, even the most forward-looking among them tell me that very little has been done in their industry to prepare for a more active, technologically ena- bled old age. Yes, care-cutting—when you replace traditional modes of care with online, à la carte services—can save you money. But no one's created, for instance, a high-liquidity savings product designed for a heavy-use care-cutter. Once upon a time, perhaps Mom needed a lift once or twice a week to the grocery store and the doctor's office. Now she can summon an Uber to her doorstep—soon, a self-driving Uber—and take it to the bowling alley every day. That might amount to a wonderful quality-of-life improvement for her, but it's also an expense that no one ever planned for, because when she started saving, Uber and Lyft were science fiction.

A related, and seriously underappreciated, financial effect of innovation in elder health and caregiving will be the creation of premium products. I'm talking not only about sleeker or motorized wheelchairs—improved versions of a product that already exists—but also brand-new product categories. One example connected to the AgeLab is Paro, a robotic seal created by Takanori Shibata, a Lab fel- low. It's roughly the size of a big baby or small toddler and can move its head and flippers, make noise, and blink its eyes at you. It's equipped with sensors that can detect touch, light, voices, temperature, and its own posture. When you pet it and deliver praise, it remembers what it was doing at that time and repeats those behaviors. On a darker note, if you hit it, it remembers associated behaviors and avoids them. In effect, you can train it—and if you don't give it enough attention, it becomes really annoying. We have two Paros at the AgeLab, and we have to keep them turned off, because no one's bothered to teach them not to mewl all day. The reason Paro is a seal and not a dog or cat is that we all understand at a deep level how dogs and cats move and act. For most of us, the same can't be said for seals, and so Paro has an easier time passing as the real deal. Its effect on people with dementia is often profound. Among other outcomes, it diminishes agitation, and, anecdotally, it's been shown to reduce sundowning, a period of late-in-the-day irritability common among Alzheimer's patients. Like many prototype robots, Paro has been around for more than a decade now; unlike Toyota and Honda's humanoid creations, it is available for purchase. It's in use at a number of institutions and private homes in Japan, the United States, and European countries, including Italy and France. It costs several thousand dollars, however; the few private individuals who have one usually rent it.

As next-generation Paros and other companionship robots become available, the price point will come down, although the latest and best ones will probably remain costly. Regardless, they constitute an unplanned-for expense. Until very recently, companionship bots had never been part of anyone's healthcare cost equation. Now they exist, and although they're not vital to keeping someone alive, if they demonstrably bring joy to your mother's life, you may find it hard to deny her one.* If they are eventually shown to add years to her life, or

---

*Serious ethical questions have been raised about companionship robots, most notably by Sherry Turkle in *Alone Together*. Chief among these are the ideas that companionship bots exist, in effect, to confuse people with dementia. As Turkle describes, even those who know that a given bot is a machine, not a baby or a seal, often end up giving it a name and talking to it. Shouldn't this level of intimacy be saved for real people—grandchildren, for instance? And doesn't a companionship bot alleviate the guilt of absent adult children? Who is it really serving—the adult child or the parent? The dilemma of whether to provide someone with a companionship bot (or, perhaps, a disembodied voice, as in the movie *Her*) in many ways mirrors the decision families face when they consider invoking paid care or a nursing facility. Frankly, companionship bots may not be appropriate for everyone. But they add to the number of options at a family's disposal, which is a good thing. And ultimately, if an adult child provides

quantifiably improve quality of life in other ways, governments and insurers, too, may find it hard to deny her. Paro and its ilk are far from the only products that fit this description. Soon, there will be an entire new class of products, nonessential or nonexistent today, that will prove so useful and become so deeply ingrained in the fabric of our later lives that it will feel strange or cruel to make someone do without them. A similar process is already taking place outside healthcare: the United Nations Human Rights Council, for instance, now condemns when countries block Internet access. This step arguably classifies the Internet, once a technology not considered essential to everyday life, as a de facto human right.

This trend may contain within it some of the seeds of its own financing. We don't know what older adults will do with themselves once technology grants them more years of safety and autonomy. But one thing a lot of them will want to do is work.

Soon, older people constrained by an outdated narrative will find their horizons opening. Better, empathetically designed products, many of which may seem like magical technologies straight from the pages of Harry Potter, will support their explorations. These products won't just keep them healthy and safe but will do so in a way that enhances independence, happiness, and the pursuit of meaning. As that happens, the idea of "hurrying up and dying" will begin to seem ridiculous. There will simply be too much for us to experience in old age and so much more time in which to do it.

In such a future, the several-trillion-dollar question becomes not "how" but "what." Given all that extra time and freedom, what exactly will we choose to do?

---

his parent with an object that brings a measure of joy into her life, perhaps he deserves at least some freedom from guilt.

7

The Pursuit of Happiness

THE COMING WAVE of improved health and safety products promise a longer, more independent old age. Unfortunately, it won't arrive with instructions; we'll still have to figure out what to do during those extra years. As our narrative of aging currently stands, healthy older adults have but a few socially sanctioned pastimes to pursue, including leisure, consumerism, volunteerism, and spending time with family. Soon, however, led by the baby boomers, they will demand additional outlets. They will fight to work, pursue romance and social ambition, contribute works of culture—and that's just the beginning. As the world of later-life possibilities expands, successful longevity-economy companies will find themselves running ahead to anticipate what older consumers will want to do with themselves and the tools they'll need to do it.

In so doing, they will be helping older adults ascend Abraham Maslow's hierarchy of needs. One appealing way to think of Maslow's hierarchy is to break it down into those three fundamental rights enshrined in the United States Declaration of Independence: life, liberty, and the pursuit of happiness. The needs found at the bottom of the hierarchy (such as food, shelter, healthcare, and safety), which dominate much of contemporary innovation for older adults, can be said to correspond to "life." Many of us discover that our rights in old age, for all practical purposes, begin and end here. Improved healthcare prod-ucts, however, that provide for health and safety *without* sacrificing older consumers' sense of self and aspirations, will soon help us climb from the level of life up to that of liberty. As a result, as you age, you won't just find yourself still up and kicking—you'll also be able to do many of the things you want to do, even despite chronic health condi-tions like diabetes and congestive heart failure. For the sake of argu-ment, let's assume you've also saved up some money (a big assumption, admittedly). The question then becomes: how will you approach that third unalienable right? How will you use your newfound liberty to pursue happiness? Or legacy? Or meaning?

Retirement financial advisors pose this question to their clients all the time, though not in so many words. They always ask, "What are your goals in retirement?"

"Well, not to be destitute."
"Mm-hmm."
"And to stay healthy for as long as possible."
"Okay."
*"And . . . I want to relax."**
"You can afford to relax."
"And . . . I don't know."

Don't worry; none of us do.

I like to think of life in 8,000-day chunks. From birth to college, there are 8,000 days, give or take. Eight thousand days separate college and the midlife-crisis years, and then it's another 8,000 until retirement.

Then you have one more set of 8,000 days. It might even last as long as 12,000 or 16,000 days, if you live to age 90 or 100, as is becoming increasingly likely. This last set is different from the days that preceded

---

* "Relax" was the word brought up most often in our study of the language people use to describe "life after career."

it. For instance, unlike the first three chunks of life, people who haven't yet reached it simply can't picture what motivates those who are in the thick of it. Often, people will go to bed the night before this encore stretch begins without knowing what will inspire them, or what they will aspire to, when the sun rises. Sure, they'll start by unpacking the boxes from the office, maybe taking a vacation. But when the honeymoon's over—what then?

The reasons for this collective case of blindness include the narrative factors I've already discussed at length. Importantly, work—the animating force behind our education and primary-career years—was taken from older people through the normalization of retirement, and no substantive replacement has ever come along to fill in the void. Part of the problem is that, although retirement in its original sense is now well over a century old, longer, healthy lives are relatively new. Women have benefited the most in length of life and overall health in old age. In 1990, only women in Japan and Andorra had a healthy life expectancy of more than 70 years; today, women in 40 countries have achieved this once-remarkable measure. (So have men in Japan and Singapore.)

This new expanse of healthier years is an open frontier that utterly lacks the sorts of cultural signposts that tell younger people how to navigate their lives. When we're young, we're always looking forward to the next thing: a graduation, a wedding, maybe having kids, maybe a new job or a raise. Later life, however, beyond walking your daughter down the aisle, say, or maybe showing up at your grandchildren's christenings, is devoid of such landmarks. The last ceremony that older people celebrate that is focused on them, not their offspring, is the funereal office retirement party. There's no ritual that says, "Hey, this guy is really nailing the whole later life thing—let's hear it for him!"

In fact, to the limited extent that the younger crowd interacts with older people other than immediate family, it's usually at events like weddings, baptisms, and, yes, funerals. Younger people experience later life mainly in settings where the purpose of older people seems to be to applaud the young, or else on television, where the purpose of older people is usually to amuse the young. Nowhere do younger people see older people setting personal goals and achieving them. It's not because they don't have goals. It's because older people are tucked away, out of sight. They are displaced geographically from the young because they stop coming in to work and because some live in special, no-youngsters-allowed housing situations. And since they're not at work, they get to shop and dine during the workday, which displaces them temporally as well. The disappearance of religious and civic institutions, where different ages once commingled, has only added to the dislocation of generations.

In the big, wet, chemical experiment that is modern life, older people now fall out of solution and settle on the bottom of the test tube—even as dazzling reactions continue overhead, unabated. When you're in the midst of these reactions and a financial advisor asks you to hazard a guess as to what you'll do when you fall out of the solution, if you're like most people, you can't. Frankly, it's telling that financial advisors even ask this question. In any other industry, dealing with any other 8,000-day period of life, companies would *tell* you what your goals should be. I'm not saying this is always a good thing, but when you buy a car, you're buying what that model says about its owner— and if the auto company's marketing department has done its job, that something is exactly what you aspire to be. The same goes for housing, soft drinks, clothing, even careers. Part of why I came to MIT in the first place, if we're being honest, is that I wanted to be the kind of person who conducts research and teaches at MIT. So it goes.

The fact that neither financial advisors nor anyone else in the so-called retirement industry can tell you what to aspire to in old age speaks to the fact that we've been hardwired to believe that older people *have no real aspirations*. No one's been able to erect landmarks that signify success in old age because no one even knows what late-life achievement might look like. And as a result, the remarkable freedom we've been granted in our extra years is arriving with a sort of unsettling, unmoored sensation. That's a problem: after all, no one moves more freely than an astronaut on a spacewalk, but if the tether connecting her to the space station has been cut, a fat lot of good that liberty will do her.

In February 2014, I found myself among the freest people who have ever lived: a group of retired CEOs. Although former Masters of the Universe aren't representative of most older people, they do provide a sort of natural experiment. There's no better group to observe if you want to know how older humans act when they're free of constraints— when they have a great education, are utterly without want, receive the best medical care money can buy, and have no work obligations.

I was at a congregation of the species called the Imagine Solutions Conference, which is held every year in Naples, Florida, a city that claims to have the country's highest concentration of retired CEOs. Former chief executives "sit on numerous non-profit and for-profit boards; they know senators and congressmen; are well-suited to solving problems and they are used to getting things done," one of the conference cofounders has said. And so, instead of bringing these former titans to places like Aspen and Davos, the conference founders decided to bring the innovation show to them.

I was slated to speak on a Saturday afternoon and found myself with a few hours to kill in the morning. I was in the midst of a delusional phase that had me thinking I could enjoy golf if I gave it a chance, so I got up early and headed over to a driving range near my hotel. I pulled into the lot in my rental—a cherry red Impala convertible; it was America on four wheels—and parked in a row filled with expensive German and Italian cars. I grabbed a bucket of balls and something to hit them with and wandered over to the range. There I saw, and please believe that I am not exaggerating, a row of about 20 guys who looked, to a man, exactly like the judge in *Caddyshack,* played by Ted Knight. They were all in their late 60s or early 70s—think silver hair, polo shirt, a white golf glove, and khakis. The only way they could have looked more like clones would have been if they were all swinging their clubs in unison. But what really struck me was their sun-visor-clad wives, who were sitting on a lawn chair behind *each and every* golfer. Most were 10 years younger than their husbands, all were reading, most on Amazon Kindles.

It was clear from the hardware in the parking lot that these were people of some means, and so, after clobbering the contents of my bucket half the distance of everyone else, I sat down, picked up my paper cup of coffee, and struck up a conversation with one of the reclining wives. She told me that her husband—still applying club to ball in front of us—was a retired CEO. *Thwack!* In fact, almost all of the guys at the range were retired execs of one stripe or another. *Thwack!* Was this a club? I asked. Did they meet here once a week? Nope, she said. They came here and did this every day.

Thwack.

That's right: the freest human beings on the face of the Earth—healthy, educated people with the time and money to go almost anywhere and do almost anything—pass their days hitting stupid white balls in the general direction of nothing. Worse, their wives, all doubtless highly educated, effective people, got dragged to the range with them daily. What a waste of potential. And it wasn't because older people lack imagination or the will to grow. In fact, the Imagine Solutions Conference—the whole reason I was in Naples—was founded by former execs who wanted to remain engaged and to continue to learn. As the conference's cofounder has said, "There's only so much golf you can play and so much wine you can drink before you begin searching for ways to give back." But the very fact that he and his cofounder found it necessary to build such an institution testifies to the paucity of options that were available to them. Unfortunately, the overwhelming expectation for what even the wealthiest older people should do with themselves is to precipitate out of life and settle down in Florida, the tip of America's test tube. And if the super rich can't figure out anything better to do with their time, what hope have the rest of us?

Researchers have been striving for decades to explain why our worlds seem to shrink with age. For instance, across a wide variety of cultures, older people's social networks (in real life, not just online) are smaller than those of younger people. In the same vein, over time we weed out the nonessential activities that we decide are less than meaningful. The most important research regarding these trends has been produced by my friend Laura Carstensen, a geriatric psychologist (and rock star in gerontology research circles) who runs the Stanford Center on Longevity. Her best-known work, called *socioemotional selectivity theory*, attempts to reconcile our shrinking worlds with what's known as the "positivity effect": the tendency of older adults, relative to the young, to pay more attention to positive information than negative and recall it more easily. This fact of old age, supported by more than 100 peer-reviewed studies, is commonly cited as a mechanism for why most people report feeling happier and more satisfied with life as they grow older—one of the most underrated benefits of a highly underrated process.

Boiled down, socioemotional selectivity theory suggests that both the positivity effect and our scaled-down interactions with the world occur for one underlying reason: as we grow older, we want—above almost all else—to experience and do meaningful things. Earlier in life, when we're young and assume we have a hazy three-quarters of a century ahead of us, we prioritize the future over the present and cast a wide net in an attempt to gain knowledge about the world. "What we see in younger people is a motivational set where you're collecting," Carstensen told me. "You're collecting experiences, you're collecting knowledge, you're expanding your horizons, and you've got all this stuff that you're sort of putting in a bucket because you've got lots of years ahead, and you never know what might be important."

When we have less time remaining, however, our goals change. We start to focus less on seeking out new things and double down instead on tried-and-true sources: the people we love, the activities we find satisfying. "You've got your bucket full of stuff," Carstensen said. "It's time to take advantage of the good stuff that you've collected."

The phenomenon has less to do with age than the time remaining in one's life. As Gawande has pointed out in *Being Mortal*, even young people with potentially terminal illnesses, including a cohort of young men who had HIV/AIDS in the 1990s, report this social winnowing. So did people of all ages in New York City following September 11 and in Hong Kong during the SARS epidemic. At times when a long future doesn't feel guaranteed, we don't venture forth on voyages of discovery—we focus in on what we know to be meaningful.

Among other theories that attempt to explain our shrinking social circles, the most persuasive one argues that we become more selective because everything in late old age simply takes more effort and energy. We reduce the size of our aspirations down to what we can achieve and the people in our lives down to those whose society feels meaningful. In both this and Carstensen's theory, which are not mutually exclusive, there is a predictable result of spending more time with proven bringers of good feelings: we become generally happier.

To listen to some, however, focusing on the here-and-now comes at a cost. One common interpretation of socioemotional selectivity theory holds that old age claims one's willingness and ability to go out and get things done in the wide world. As Gawande writes, in youth, "When horizons are measured in decades, which might as well be infinity to human beings, you most desire all that stuff at the top of Maslow's pyramid—achievement, creativity, and other attributes of 'self-actualization.' But as your horizons contract—when you see the future ahead of you as finite and uncertain—your focus shifts to the here and now, to everyday pleasures and the people closest to you." In this mode of thinking, those high-level Maslovian needs—for example, for the esteem and respect of oneself and others—become less important with age and less desirable. It calls to mind Thomas Midgley's poem, which he recited as his death drew near: "My eyes are growing dimmer and my hair is turning white, / And I lack the old ambitions when I wander out at night."

Critical to this interpretation is the idea that when we grow older and begin to prioritize emotionally meaningful activities, those activities will always be minor, "everyday pleasures" that never further large, ambitious goals. However, there's no rule decreeing that something has to be small in scale in order to be meaningful. In fact, it doesn't even have to be pleasant. In one study of the positivity effect among Chinese residents of Hong Kong, researchers showed study participants pictures of faces displaying various emotions and then, using eye-tracking equipment, determined how much visual attention participants lavished on each photo. In similar studies, older, Western adults tend to spend more time looking at happy faces—they "show attentional preference to positive stimuli," as researchers would have it, which is a way of suggesting that happiness is most interesting to them. But the opposite was true among older Chinese people in Hong Kong, who fixated on faces expressing negative emotions. The authors write: "Fear and anger, being socially disruptive when expressed, may be particularly attention grabbing to people from interdependent cultures who define good feelings and success in terms of being able to fit in to a group and to avoid being a burden to others."

The search for meaning, then, is universal, but culture helps determine what older people find meaningful. And that raises a question: can the definition of meaning change? Or, just as important, can new, socially permissible routes to meaning open up?

Picture a serial entrepreneur in her 70s, say, who loves spending time with her immediate family very much and also has a great idea for a business, which she wants to launch as a start-up. If you asked her which of those goals she finds meaningful, she'd say both. But which is more doable? Today, the answer is hanging out with her family, by a factor of about a million.

For many of us, this state of affairs is perfectly adequate. There are many who, beyond base-level needs, have few upper-level desires beyond having family and friends close at hand; for whom "meaning" is measured in meals eaten together, memories shared, stories told, meatballs rolled. These are the lucky ones: the going narrative is up to the task of fulfilling their drive for meaning. Assuming the presence of an amenable family that will hang out with each other (an increasingly big "if," but that's a different story), this route to meaning is achievable and socially condoned.

But there are legions of others who find their close familial relationships meaningful—*but would also* find meaning in other activities, relationships, and achievements, if given the chance.

Right now, that chance is not forthcoming.

For this group, having close, loving relationships is still utterly essential—isolation is hellish and will literally take years off your life—but they may not be enough. Meanwhile, other potential routes to happiness and meaning, including work, professional ambition, climbing the social ladder, education, athletic achievement, leaving a legacy—even sex—are closed off. They're seen as strange or comical pursuits when older people are involved. Other than the desire for perhaps a better golf handicap, the only sphere in which we see late-life ambition as normal is politics. On Election Day in 2016, Hillary Clinton was 69 years old, and Donald Trump was 70. It's unremarkable for a septuagenarian to want to run a country, but should he or she, say, apply for a PhD in entomology—well, that would be bizarre, or at least fodder for a human-interest piece in the local paper. It's this lack of socially permissible options that sends older people with all the time and money in the world to the driving range, where they can hit golf balls toward the horizon in lieu of banging their heads against a wall.

It would be a mistake, however, to assume that alternate routes to meaning and happiness will always be closed off. The narrative is already shifting, and older adults are starting to demonstrate what they can achieve when the full power of business, science, and technology are aligned toward their goals. As that process gets rolling, the products that serve those aspirations will add up to an explosive growth industry. Soon, it won't be enough for companies to provide merely for the socially acceptable version of happiness that older people have been permitted in the past several decades. To remain competitive, they will need to offer a vision of later life replete with new routes to meaning. And as these new avenues are cleared, I expect to see older adults streaming onto them like it's Black Friday and their future is on sale.

Working Tomorrow

Of the aspirations that older adults will tackle head-on in the near future, the one that will affect all business sectors, not just older-consumer-facing companies, is the widespread desire for meaningful work in one's "retirement years."

To hear many fiscally minded folks talk about older people, the main problem is that they *don't* work enough, and the solution inevitably floated involves raising the eligibility age for Social Security or its local equivalent. It makes intuitive sense: when the Social Security Act was passed in 1935, the 65-plus proportion of the US population was half what it is now. The national pensions of many countries, especially in Europe, were founded even earlier, and reflect an even more outdated demographic reality.

When you squint at the retirement-age bogeyman, however, it begins to resemble a red herring. For one thing, fiscally speaking, raising the age of Social Security eligibility in the United States is much less of a priority than lowering medical spending. More important, as a way of putting older adults to work, it's backward. There's a better way than to cut off a paycheck that is critical for millions in their mid-60s (the elimination of which would, by the way, disproportionately affect populations with lower life expectancies, especially African and Native Americans and whites with lower income and education levels, compounding an already unfolding disaster). Before resorting to such extreme measures, why not try to find employment for those in their 50s, 60s, 70s, and even 80s who already desperately want to work? In no way do these people need the nudge of a cut-off Social Security check to strong-arm them into the job market. The fact is, willingness isn't what's lacking. The right jobs are.

Older jobseekers are forced to spend significantly more time looking for work than their juniors, and of the quarter of US adults aged
50-plus who sought employment between 2011 and 2016, a third said
that the job market had proved so difficult to break into that they had
simply given up looking. Often, especially in the 60-plus set, older
people who want to work but can't find any simply say they're retired.
Traditional employment metrics fail to account for this population of
would-be workers, which should technically be categorized as unemployed, not retired. And that population is sizable: In one major survey, *40 percent* of people who described themselves as retired said they
would have preferred to keep on working, and 30 percent said they
would jump back into the workforce if the right job opened up.

The plight of older, under- or unemployed workers is act one in a
two-act tragedy. The second act concerns the mushrooming number
of industries that are in a mode of quiet crisis because they're losing
their best workers every day to retirement, a trend especially vexing
to businesses in Japan and older, Western European countries such as
Germany, Italy, Finland, and Denmark. As to the United States, here
is a short, nonexhaustive list of industries threatened by retirement:
the electrical, petrochemical, defense, healthcare, concrete, agricul-
ture, financial advisory, commercial manufacturing, and railroad
industries, not to mention state workers—a group of important func-
tionaries that includes (in case your eyes were glazing over) air traffic
controllers. There is even, and I am not making this up, a national
clown shortage. The *New York Daily News* reports: "Membership at
the World Clown Association, the country's largest trade group for
clowns, has dropped from about 3,500 to 2,500 since 2004. 'The challenge is getting younger people involved in clowning,' said Association
President Deanna (Dee Dee) Hartmier, who said most of her members
are over 40."

I find clowns creepy and would be willing to live in a world with
fewer of them. But the rest of those workplace shortages present a
real problem to industries and to economies at large—a problem that,

though visible from a great distance, only became apparent in scope in late 2016.

For a long time, economists thought that population aging would affect per capita economic production simply by shrinking the workforce relative to the size of the overall population. That's true, it turns out, but it's not even half of the story. A landmark 2016 study published by the National Bureau of Economic Research upended these prior assumptions by suggesting that only one-third of aging's toll on GDP is due to its effect on the size of the labor force. A whopping two-thirds is due to the fact that as populations age, overall productivity—of younger and older workers alike—seems to drop. Crucially, unlike earlier studies, this report achieved its result not by predicting the future but rather by looking at what's already taken place, leveraging variations in how US states have aged since 1980. After controlling for factors like migration between states, the authors concluded that every 10 percent increase in the size of the 60-plus population comes at the eye-popping cost of 5.5 percent of annual GDP growth per capita. By that reckoning, between 1980 and 2010, when US per capita GDP was growing at an average of 1.8 percent, it would have grown at 2.1 percent if not for the aging population.

Today, aging is happening far more rapidly. The authors estimate that by 2020, GDP growth during the 2010s will have been just over *one-third* what it would have been without population aging. Between 2020 and 2030, the effect will weaken somewhat, but population aging is still projected to limit GDP growth to two-thirds of its potential. And that's just in the United States: in the many countries that are aging even faster, production will likely be affected far more severely.

In the media, there have been two interpretations for why a larger older population might lead to a less productive workforce. One is as lamentable as it is predictable: blame older workers. As economics writer Matt Yglesias said on the popular podcast Vox's *The Weeds,* "If you just think really in like lazy, like, non-expert terms, just like a country full of old people is gonna be, like, maybe not that dynamic, not that creative—it's gonna be full of, like, cranky people who are set in their ways . . . You're not as good at working; you're not learning new stuff; you're not as healthy, maybe." The "topline conclusion" of the NBER report, he says, is that "we are taking into account the fact that our labor force will be getting slower, but we're not taking into account the fact that it will be, like, older and worse."*

But there is also a more considered possible interpretation of the study's results: not that older people are impeding progress at companies because they're "not as good at working" but rather, because their ranks include some of the very best workers out there, older workers' *retirement* is what actually hurts industry when populations age.

Nicole Maestas, the study's lead author, said that although the study wasn't designed to differentiate between the two competing explanations, both could in fact be true. "What I suspect is overall there's probably both effects at work. I can't tell you that it's one or the other."

My distaste for Yglesias's phrasing aside, in some industries and for some workers, age can hurt productivity. Certainly, in physically intensive work such as the trades and some manufacturing jobs, age can take a toll. However, regarding older workers' ability to think and solve problems on the job, emerging research is dismantling the once-accepted wisdom that serious cognitive decline is an inevitable part of growing older. Once upon a time, by surveying groups of people at different ages, researchers had determined that some aspects of cognitive ability seemed to naturally diminish with age, even in older adults who appeared not to have dementia. However, in 2011, a large, groundbreaking longitudinal study was published that didn't just sample cross-sections of the population but instead tracked over 2,000 people over the course of 16 years as they grew older. Those who

---

*Steam was rising from my ears by the end of Yglesias's monologue, but perhaps what bothered me most was the fact that he is extremely fair minded about most other topics. Old age, however, apparently fell into its own special category. If anything, the opinion of older workers he espoused on his podcast just goes to show how deeply indoctrinated even open-minded people are by the prevailing narrative of old age.

experienced cognitive losses in early old age, it turned out, were often the same people who were later diagnosed with dementia. The cognitive function of many others, meanwhile, remained essentially full-fledged from early old age into late. The implications were profound: for decades, researchers hoping to understand cognition in healthy older adults had accidentally been including those with early-stage dementia in their studies. That meant that the cognitive toll of normal, dementia-free aging was likely far smaller than previously thought.

If age-related cognitive losses may not account for much of the productivity cost of population aging, there's no doubt about the effects of retirement, which culls the best workers from the workforce as surely as a lawnmower cuts down the fastest-growing blades of grass. Older workers with high levels of education—who are some of the most economically productive workers—claim that they want to continue to work beyond the age of retirement. And yet, Maestas and her colleagues found that highly productive workers are more likely to retire than their less productive contemporaries. The best workers, it seems, are voting with their voices in favor of late-life work, even while they're marching with their feet away from it as fast as they can. What gives?

Well, the human body, for one thing. If you have a job that is pleasant yet physically demanding, you might want to work forever, but your aching knees wield ultimate veto power. In such cases, people "who have earned more all the way along and are in a better position to retire," said Maestas, "retire as soon as they can." Others, meanwhile, who may have less stashed away in their 401(k)s, find themselves working through pain, becoming less effective in the process. Even for those with desk jobs, physiological factors can have this weeding-out effect. We've all been admonished not to sit all day, and yet many workplaces fail to provide ergonomic alternatives to old-fashioned desks. When we're young, a seated posture that may ultimately lead to spinal curvature, poor circulation, muscle atrophy, herniated disks, a diminished insulin response, and more may not seem like a big deal, but when we're older and several of those things are happening at once, it can feel like a deal breaker. Those who can afford to retire do so (and in many cases head straight for the golf course or hiking trail, because the first thing they want to do is stand up and move around). Others, however, suffer through workplace discomfort because they have no alternative.

The same effect happens in environments where it's a pain to work in a figurative, if not physiological, sense. "If your job is really unpleasant, or let's say there's just a lot of politics and interpersonal tension in that workplace, then you're less likely to want to stay in that environment," said Maestas. Ditto for jobs that can't make scheduling allowances for caregivers or for people with "a health problem where they need just a little additional daily flexibility in their daily schedule to manage it," said Maestas. For older adults in unpleasant jobs who don't, financially speaking, need to work, "it may be worth it to them to stop working."

When an unpleasant job or workplace drives wealthier, often-more-productive workers to retire, less-productive older workers are left behind. Perhaps their productivity has taken a hit because they're working through pain or multiple health conditions, or perhaps they're secretly providing care while on the clock. Just as likely, they could be part of the 50 percent of workers who are, by definition, less effective than average—who are unable to afford to retire in their 60s because they've earned less throughout their careers. Either way, when the most productive members of a workforce exit, overall productivity suffers and GDP growth slows. Additionally, older workers left in the workforce, who find themselves hampered by physical and social structures designed for youthful bodies, fail to perform optimally, giving all of older workerdom a bad reputation in the process. For that reason, combined with good-old-fashioned ageism, the legions of older adults who would be highly productive at work can find it difficult to convince anyone to hire them for anything resembling an impactful role.

Although retirement seems to select against economic productivity in older workers, the good news is that there is a one-size-fits-most solution: keep your best older workers by keeping them happy. "My opinion is that it is a net win to try and retain older workers," Maestas said, stipulating that some companies and industries might benefit more than others. Solving points of workplace pain, from bad backs to overburdened schedules, would not only allow great workers to retain their roles longer but could also boost their productivity—and that of less-productive older workers too.

Now, you may be thinking, making work pain free in old age might sound easy on paper, but in the real world, where different job-related challenges constantly fly at people coping with a wide variety of age-related issues, such a task sounds possibly unmanageable and certainly uneconomical. The corporeal challenges faced by older people in hard, physical jobs, for instance, have existed for millennia. Surely, that's not the sort of issue a manager or CEO can just go ahead and solve with the stroke of a pen.

Or is it?

New Knees

German automakers have a problem. Just as they need older drivers to buy their most expensive cars, they rely on a rapidly aging group of experienced factory workers to manufacture them. Manufacturing is often much more skill- and knowledge-intensive than many presume, especially when it comes to complex or precision-engineered products. In certain automotive factory roles, workers rely on so much specialized knowledge that they might as well have PhDs. In many cases, this knowledge is of the sort that can't be taught, only experienced—such as how to avoid mistakes that can shut down a production line or what a certain component feels like when installed perfectly. It can take decades to achieve the proficiency needed to work on certain parts of, say, a BMW i8, and so replacing veteran factory hands at one of BMW's German plants poses a riddle that can't be solved by simply hiring inexperienced kids from Spain. Meanwhile, there is no productivity loss associated with age for even the most repetitive assembly-line roles, although they are often physically demanding and require relatively little training. In fact, one large study of Daimler assembly lines revealed that while older workers are slightly more likely to make mistakes than their younger colleagues, they make significantly fewer errors of the major, show-stopping variety. The upshot is simple: BMW, Volkswagen, Daimler, and others (not to mention companies that produce auto components, such as Siemens and Bosch) need to do whatever they can to keep older workers working.

The plight of the German auto industry resembles that of the country as a whole, whose economy is built in great part on advanced manufacturing. Germany's workforce is shrinking rapidly and is projected to dwindle faster than that of Japan by the early 2020s. Part of the issue is the country's high-and-climbing life expectancy and its anemic birth rate, the lowest in Europe. Meanwhile, because its powerful post–World War II baby boom began a decade later than that of the United States, as of 2017, Germany is only at the leading edge of its significantly older future. Compounding the issue, those German baby boomers had relatively few children. The most significant effects of that lurch from baby boom to bust are only now taking place. "Because Germany's birth rate has been falling for decades, those who would now perhaps be thinking about having children were never actually born," said the president of the German Federal Bank at a 2014 economic forum in Frankfurt. He quoted German demographer Herwig Birg: "Our country is like a rowing boat. The number of rowers is falling, while the number of older passengers will increase for a number of decades."

In an attempt to keep the boat seaworthy, German automakers have begun trying out new, sometimes unconventional, measures to retain older workers. In 2007, for instance, when its average plant worker was 39 years old, BMW experimented with a futuristic factory line in its Dingolfing plant, which was designed to mimic the workforce of 10 years hence—2017, the year of this book's publication. They assembled a group of workers whose average age was 47, and, after surveying them extensively about what they would change about their work environment, made a total of 70 small changes to the production line. They added low-impact wooden flooring in lieu of concrete, instituted rotating work assignments designed to minimize sources of repetitive stress, provided ergonomic benches and chairs, promoted regular exercise routines, and more. The experiment, which cost BMW a total of €40,000 in capital investment and wages spent on workers' workshops, improved productivity by 7 percent, reduced absences below the plant's average, and saw the defect rate of the line drop to zero. Most tellingly, once the experimental line began hitting its productivity targets, none of the workers—even initial skeptics—said they wanted to leave. Soon, BMW instituted similar projects in other German and Austrian plants. By 2011, it had applied the approach to a large, new facility in its Dingolfing plant, run entirely by workers aged 50 and over. The facility, affectionately nicknamed "Altstadt," or Old Town, boasts over an acre and a half of floor space and represents a €20 million investment.

BMW's devotion to its older workers is more than mere lip service— but it's also becoming clear that a productive, grey future won't come for free. In the realm of exciting-yet-expensive workforce solutions, none seem more tantalizing than powered exoskeletons of the sort worn by the Marvel superhero Iron Man. These wearable robots can, in theory, boost your strength multiple times while taking a load off your tired joints. Developments in this field, which would find eager users not only in manufacturing and construction but also in medical and military settings, have enjoyed breathless media coverage since at least the mid-aughts. If that sounds similar to the hype surrounding the never-quite-there-yet category of domestic robotic assistants, it should. A mixture of high cost; functional, technological limitations; and a steep learning curve for the user is keeping these technologies out of everyday workplace usage. To be fair, there are hints that things are starting to change: for instance, at least one Japanese construction firm has begun experimenting with such devices. For now, however, most workers will have to wait for their Iron Man suits—and in the meantime, younger workers will be wearing out their joints without realizing it, and older workers will be considering retirement as they find themselves working through pain.

However, there is one low-cost technology that has supported the bodies of older workers for millennia: the chair. What if, instead of fixing those older bodies—designing high-tech solutions straight out of Marvel Comics to make old joints perform like they're young again—engineers tried hacking *the chair*?

Keith Gunura was born in Zimbabwe and moved to London in his late teens, where he found a job with a manufacturing staffing company. He spent his first day on the job stuffing envelopes. His second day found him on an assembly line at a different factory, packaging Hugo Boss fragrance products—"deodorant, aftershave, and some other weird spray," he said, sounding as though he'd seen so many of the boxes that they had etched themselves onto his retinas. His assignment was only temporary, but he found himself working shoulder-to-shoulder with people who'd been packaging things at that line for years. Two things about his older coworkers stuck with him. The more obvious one was how much it literally hurt them to work. Although he started off at the most physically demanding spot on the line—the end, where he stacked the professionally wrapped fragrance boxes onto wooden pallets—he was soon asked to move to the middle of the line, where he had to put the boxes' lids on. "We were standing the whole time," he said, and "there were a couple of older ladies who worked next to me." They had been at it a long time. At lunch break, "They were just saying, 'Oh, it's just difficult. When I get home my feet are hurting, my legs, my knees'—you know, we heard that every day."

"The question I asked myself is, 'Why are there no chairs here?'"

He went on to pursue an undergraduate degree at the United Kingdom's Lancaster University, where he posed this question to one of his professors. The answer was simple, the professor said: factory floors are so highly optimized for space that if every worker had a chair, it would be a major waste of real estate. Gunura went on to pursue a robotics PhD at the Swiss Federal Institute of Technology in Zurich with the vague idea of solving the no-chairs-in-the-workplace issue, as well as many other problems, with a "full-body exoskeleton that any-body and everybody would be able to use." He found, however, that the lab he'd joined was, like many, still working on the minutiae of pow-ered exoskeleton development—how the leg swings in the hip joint, for instance—and that it would be a long time before the field would be ready to produce his dreamt-of Iron Man suit.

There was another problem, too, which went back to his days on the Hugo Boss line. The reason he'd been asked to switch from the rel-atively arduous task of unloading boxes at the end of the line was that another, more senior worker wanted the exercise involved in stacking the boxes. The need for constant exercise to remain healthy is some-thing that sometimes gets overlooked in the conversation surrounding exoskeletons in the workforce. It's one thing to wear something that augments your strength on occasion but quite another to replace eight hours you'd normally spend supporting your own weight with time strapped into a device that does it for you—every day. "If you use an exoskeleton for eight hours, you're basically not using your muscles anymore," Gunura said. "You sort of neglect the muscle function and you become dependent on the system."

His answer, which he dropped out of his PhD program to produce, is called the Chairless Chair. The idea—a nonpowered, lower-body exoskeletal frame—was, as lead-user innovations so often are, finely attuned to the actual needs of the user, as opposed to what ivory-tower eggheads like me assume those needs to be. It also disposed of all the components that make powered exoskeleton prototypes so expensive, a move that positioned Gunura as a potential low-end disruptor of powered exoskeletons *before they even hit the market.* Although the Chairless Chair would bear between 60 and 80 percent of its users' weight, its primary purpose was not to aid the wearer's muscles but rather to allow her to sit anywhere, at any time, thanks to a knee joint that could be programmed to stop bending at a given angle. Then, once the user wanted to stand, the spring-loaded knee joint would help her back up. It was exactly the sort of invention I've found myself longing for while standing in a long line at a concert or amusement park, with my lower back and feet aching. "Instead of adding on super-expensive sensors and actuators," Gunura said, necessary for augmented strength, he and his Zurich team stripped the idea of the exoskeleton "to its bare minimum, that would allow us to achieve this one simple task, which was just sitting."

The company behind the product, of which Gunura is cofounder and CEO, is called Noonee. I wondered if it had some meaning for someone who spoke German or perhaps Shona, a principal language of Zimbabwe, but Gunura laughed. "Actually, it's a play on words. 'Noonee,'—like 'new knee'—you know, like you've got a new knee. And then, you also have no knee problems."

As I write this, Noonee has beta-version prototypes in five BMW, three Audi, and two Volkswagen factories. All told, when the product launches officially in 2017, a company buying in bulk will be able to obtain Chairless Chairs at a unit price of about $3,000—a pittance compared to even the least expensive powered exoskeletons on the cusp of the market, which are generally intended for medical use, clunky to operate, and carry prices in the mid-to-high tens of thousands of dollars. BMW is now experimenting with a nonpowered upper-body exoskeleton as well.

Gunura was quick to explain that the Chairless Chair isn't just for older adults and that companies could give "it to not just the elder workers, actually, but everybody." The idea, he said, is to start early with the Chairless Chair, long before your knees start to hurt, so that you maintain healthy joints later into your career. That such an approach also helps Noonee avoid the dreaded "old-man's product" stigma is, of course, an added benefit.

Still, he said, "All our clients are focusing on the elderly workers." Should they succeed in retaining them, the effect, as Maestas said, will be a "net win": companies will hold on to some of their most productive employees while jettisoning much of the productivity toll of pain and discomfort. In the process, they get to preserve something else as well: social capital, human capital, and institutional knowledge.

Social and Human Capital

Occasionally, to shake them out of their slumber, I'll ask my graduate-level management and planning students a deliberately obtuse question: *What is General Motors?* It's a company, sure, worth about $50 billion, give or take. But where exactly does that value come from? Certainly, the company owns a lot of manufacturing plants and high-tech machinery and wrenches and oil rags. But that's not even the half of it. One 2015 study determined that 87 percent of S&P 500 companies' value is attributable to intangible assets such as intellectual property, brand recognition, goodwill, and human and social capital—which is to say the skills, experience, and knowledge stored in employees' heads, and the relationships and personal networks those employees form within a company and without. More than anything else, *that* is what companies should worry about losing when retirement is in the wind. If GM or Ford fired all of their workers and hired all new ones with the same level of training, the company would find itself in utter chaos—to the extent that it could even be considered the same company. As Jerry Seinfeld once observed regarding professional football, "I love the Giants, but when you think about it, who *are* the Giants? You know what I mean?" The squad, he pointed out, is made up of different people every year, and teams routinely move from city to city. Even the management gets fired every now and then. Given all that personnel turnover, what exactly are fans left rooting for? "You're rooting for clothes when you get right down to it," he said—the team's uniform. When workers retire, it similarly eats away at what really makes a company what it is: the people who compose it, the way it solves problems, how it interacts with the world. Some of the most costly retirement-related losses are the least tangible. Someone who knows what to do when a given situation arises, or who has a uniquely good relationship with clients, or knows how to find her way across the company to another branch when teamwork is called for, is the kind of person who greases the wheels when she's there but is inconspicuous in her absence. When she's gone, things simply don't work as well, and no one can say exactly why. As Terry Milholland, who has served as the top technical officer at Visa, Electronic Data Systems, Boeing, and the Internal Revenue Service once told me at a London forum on older workforces, "We don't know what we don't know."

The retirement crisis isn't limited to the private sector. Twenty-five percent of career federal employees were eligible for retirement in 2015, a proportion that is projected to have risen to nearly a third of federal employees as of September 2017. "Their retirement could produce mission critical skills gaps if left unaddressed," reported the Government Accountability Office in 2014. At first blush, this might sound like the sort of thing the market could sort out—workers flow to where they're needed—but when you're talking about jobs that require years or even decades of experience, such as air-traffic controllers or department administrators, it's not always possible to pull in someone off the street to fill in gaps. In an effort to preserve the kind of institutional knowledge that lubricates the gears of government administration, Congress passed a law in 2012 allowing retirement-eligible federal civilian employees to enter "phased retirement," which allows semiretired employees to work for 20 hours per week for half pay plus half their retirement pension. As of early 2016, the program hadn't seen much use at all—*Government Executive* discovered that a grand total of 31 people had signed up for it across the federal government— although, to be fair, some agencies hadn't yet set up their phased retirement plans. The Smithsonian Institution led the pack of phased retirees with 11 people who had signed up. Just one person had signed on to preserve the institutional knowledge of the Nuclear Regulatory Commission.

The subsections of the private sector that have bothered to deal with the brain drain of retirement have, in some instances, seen more success. YourEncore, for instance, a venture launched by Eli Lilly and Procter & Gamble in 2003, is a sort of high-level employment agency for semiretired consultants, serving more than 120 companies in consumer products, foods, life science industries—even aviation. Over 1,000 of the company's 9,500 experts are former P&G execs.

But the real challenge posed by the aging workforce isn't the question of whether we can connect highly desirable workers who are sick of their workplaces and schedules (if not work itself) with employers who are all but begging to have them back. The real issue is all the out-of-work older adults languishing without meaningful employment, despite the fact that entire industries are threatened by waves of retirements. How can companies be persuaded to hire these workers, and how can workers throughout their lives learn the skills needed to compete in a rapidly changing labor market? Underlying both of these issues is the one ur-problem that will be hardest of all to fix: the long-standing, unmovable rules of work.

Changing the Rules

When people talk about what must be changed in the workplace for companies to retain older adults, a few solutions inevitably come up, including reduced hours, more flexibility, more sick time, greater ability to work from home, and better office ergonomics. When the will is present to instate such fixes, doing so is a relatively easy process, accomplished with little more than a few emails from Human Resources. There is another group of issues, however, that is harder to fix because there is no simple corporate lever to be pulled to influence them. These include ideas such as: the older you are, the higher your salary; young people can't be the boss of older people; and, most importantly, you only ever go to school once, when you're young. Such ideas are utterly pervasive and, unlike other, more blatant examples of workplace ageism, they're not even morally reprehensible. They're just simply the way work works. That they rob older adults of the opportunity to pursue meaning, get paid, and lend a shoulder to the economy-at-large, however, often gets overlooked.

And at the same time, forces that have nothing to do with age amplify the lamentable effects of these taken-for-granted workplace rules. The most important of these is the accelerating march of technology, which makes middle-aged-and-older workers feel like they're in the land of the Red Queen from Lewis Carroll's *Through the Looking-Glass*. The Red Queen said, "It takes all the running you can do, to keep in the same place. If you want to get somewhere else, you must run at least twice as fast as that!" In the workforce, whether you're running to stay in one place—retaining up-to-date knowledge and skills in your current career—or running twice as fast to learn cutting-edge skills for a new job, chances are what you're doing is not really part of your job. You're doing it in your free time, if you're doing it all. Perhaps your company offers continuing education opportunities, but even then, it's usually hard to find the time to take advantage of them. And anyway, even if you do gain new skills—even if you earn a certification of some kind to signify your intellectual growth—it still doesn't always translate to a promotion or a thumbs-up from a hiring manager. The issue goes back to the starkness of the frontier of old age: even as early as one's 30s, there are no professional signposts as significant as, say, college graduation, that shout, *Hey! I'm here, I'm qualified, and I'm ready to work.* Instead, most of us in positions to hire and promote people rely on our gut: *Does this feel like the sort of person who should be in this position?*

And, just as important, *Does this person expect to be paid more than this position is worth?* All too often, if it's an entry-level job or one that would put an older person under the authority of a younger one, managers take the easy route and hire someone who feels right—that is to say, someone younger. I don't even blame them for their reticence to break with the norm. Once, in my first managerial role, I found myself with someone 25 years my senior answering to me. It felt weird at first—and I bet it did for him, too! But we both dealt with it, and we were both better off as a result. The question is: how can we change the sorts of cultural expectations that made it feel so strange?

One major issue is the expectation that age should be tied to salary, which perhaps made sense at a time when workers could plan to stick with a single company for their entire career. No longer: the US Bureau of Labor Statistics reported in 2015 that the average young boomer held 12 jobs between the ages of 18 and 48—a new job every two-and-a-half years. Now that we're switching jobs so rapidly and often changing *careers* as well, the common idea that someone in her 40s or 50s doesn't belong in an entry-level job because the salary is beneath her has become a problem. Almost anyone in need of for a late-career switch or a new job in retirement will tell you that he or she would happily take a lower salary to start—but there's no way to say that in an interview without sounding desperate, and so it goes unsaid, and valuable older workers go unhired.

Underlying hiring breakdowns of this sort is a still more significant fact: the skills of many of the people who need jobs don't align with the skills required by the jobs that need people. This is a complicated problem, but one major culprit is the mistaken idea that education is the sole province of the young, which goes hand in hand with the stereotype that old people can't learn new tricks. As a result of both, there are no cultural expectations around late-life learning and no rituals to celebrate it. Yes, night schools and working master's programs can be found, but these are the exceptions, not the norm. It's become quite common to talk about how we're living longer than we did when Social Security was first instated. But no one talks about how we're living just as long past the age when formal education ceases.

Where there are unmet needs, however, technology and the market often find a way of filling in the gap. In the case of the widespread need for cultural signposts that signify readiness to try something new throughout one's working life—including, but not limited to, old age—an answer may finally be forthcoming.

In Sanjay Sarma's office at MIT, models of internal combustion engines sit on various shelves, and the glass surface of his coffee table is held up by a six-cylinder engine, painted black, that his students salvaged from a junkyard Buick. He is an engineer's engineer. It is not an exaggeration to say that he is one of the co-inventors of the Internet of Things, and his work in RFID technologies has, among many effects, revolutionized the way companies track their inventories. But he is also something else—something perhaps more important. He is an educator. "Professors are always wearing two hats," Sarma said. "One is research; one is education. And the vitality of the research shows up in the vitality of education, right? That's the MIT formula."

In 2000, L. Rafael Reif, the then-provost, now-president of MIT, asked Sarma to help the Institute found a new university in Singapore, known as the Singapore-MIT Alliance for Research and Technology, or SMART. There, Sarma and his team tried some new tactics to shake up the way learning was done. "We decided that we would focus the curriculum as much as possible on design—where you learn things, and you almost immediately figure out how to use them," he said. For instance, "If you learn some abstract concept like entropy, right, wouldn't it be great if you applied it in an engine or something?" It went well. SMART is now burgeoning, and MIT professors vie to go there on sabbatical. While that was happening, a series of online learning efforts took off at MIT, including the pioneering OpenCourseWare, which, starting in 2002, has offered materials from over 2,200 MIT courses to learners and educators around the world; and MITx, the online-first education platform, which later expanded to provide the technological backbone (and a great deal of content) for edX, the world's premier purveyor of online education. In 2012, Reif tapped Sarma to be MIT's first director of digital learning, a position that allows him to oversee all of MIT's digital education endeavors. From that vantage point, he's had the ability to see who's signing up for online learning and why. "First of all, the median age of an MITx class is 27," he said. "Median, right? That means half the population is older than 27."

I asked him, who's taking the courses?

"One category is folks who want to go to Greece on vacation because they're retired, and want to learn about Greece so they can enjoy their vacation. So it's enrichment.

"The second is what I call mild professional—folks who learned computer science in the '70s, and want to see the most recent pedagogy and the recent concepts.

"The third is deep professional. What I mean by that is folks who want to learn programming for the first time because it's going to be useful in their jobs.

"And the fourth is—and I need a better term for this because it has a negative connotation, but actually has a very positive spin on it—is utilitarian."

It's the story of people like Matt Reimer, a Manitoba farmer who, using free MIT courses, taught himself how to code. He then modified an eight-year-old John Deere tractor into a robotic, self-driving farm vehicle, using a tablet computer, open-source software, and aerial drone components.

For categories one and four, accreditation isn't overly important—the goal is more about gaining and using knowledge than signifying it. For numbers two and three, however, where jobs are on the line, tokens of accomplishment are essential. Online courses have spawned a wide variety of accreditations, from nondegree certificates of completion, provided by organizations like edX and other purveyors of Massive Open Online Courses (MOOCs), to online master's programs offered by various universities. Some of these, when they signify vocational skills such as proficiency in a certain coding language, have the potentially to be highly valued by industry.

But still missing are the narrative signposts that signify, in a way that anyone can understand, a general sense of accomplishment and readiness for new challenges. At MIT, which doesn't offer online master's degrees, a new potential answer is emerging. Sarma and his team—including Chris Caplice, my colleague at MIT's Center for Transportation and Logistics who occupies the office next to mine— have come up with a new sort of online credential: the MicroMasters. In the program, which is currently available in the field of supply chain management and will soon to be applied to other courses of study, students can earn their MicroMasters by completing a semester's worth of online courses. That's analogous to a few other online accreditations. What's new, however, is that the students who do particularly well in that online program are then given the opportunity to come in to MIT in person for a semester, to earn a full master's degree from MIT. (Soon, Sarma said, partner universities around the world will accept these students as well, a nod to those who might, for instance, live in Australia and not want to leave their families behind for a semester.) This approach to admissions is a very hopeful sign. In many competitive master's programs, one or two token older adults might be typically admitted in an attempt to round out a large group of 20- and 30-somethings. The MicroMasters route, however, is more meritocratic. If you demonstrate excellence, you're in—no matter your age.

Most people signing up for the inaugural MicroMasters course are working professionals. Those who continue on to earn a full master's at MIT will enjoy all the benefits of an internationally renowned credential—all thanks to a program uniquely structured for midlife learners. Should such markers of educational achievement become commonplace, even expected, throughout one's working life, the stereotype of the older worker with outdated skills will fall away. That optimistic future won't necessarily come easily—someone will need to pay for constant midlife education, for one thing—but it *will* be in high demand as more and more people fill the once-stark frontier of the new old age.

WomensForum

Beyond pursuing work, beyond seeking out new knowledge, there is one other important thing that older people chasing wild new sources of meaning are likely to do: buy stuff—and a lot of it. And yet, companies are only lately coming around to the idea of supporting a wide variety of aspirations for the older, usually female consumer.

It's hardly a new problem. Jodie Luber knows something about convincing reticent companies to court an undervalued group of supposedly tech-phobic consumers. In 1996, she and a cofounder launched WomensForum.com. Together with Women.com and iVillage.com, it was one of a trio of women's lifestyle sites that ruled the first dot-com era. More than 20 years later, it is the sole survivor. In the first half of the 2010s, it brought in roughly 45 million unique visitors per month, Luber said, a very respectable rate. It's one of the most venerable sites on the web, period, and is without question the grandame of the "women's lifestyle" category.

Since WomensForum first blinked into existence, Luber has seen marketing trends come and go. "I ran the business by myself from conception until funding," she said, the first round of which occurred in 1999. During that time, she was the only full-time employee: editor-in-chief, writer of the popular blog "Girl Talk" (which became "Mom Talk" after the birth of her son), chief press officer, face of the company, sole advertising salesperson, and roper-in of partner websites. "I literally look back now, and you think, 'What the hell?'" she said. She worked so hard that "it was stupidity."

Throughout its history, WomensForum has not relied on cost-per-click advertising partners like Google Adwords (in fact, it predates Adwords's 2000 launch) and has gone instead straight after advertisers themselves. "We've had a lot. We've had most of the pharmaceuticals, all of the automakers, Chrysler, Macy's, Dove, Sears, Purina, Kraft—all the major companies that you would expect to see," she said. "StarKist," she added, with a nod of recollection. "We always called on brands directly, and we always called on their agencies directly. And we said, 'What's the dialogue that you're having with women?'"

The response was cold at first. "In '96, '97, no one wanted to talk to us. I was told by many sponsors that women would never go online," she said. "That this was not a place for women. This was a male environment, and women had no place on the Internet. It's laughable when you think about it now. And we just kept at it, because if you just looked at the population numbers, you knew it's inconceivable that this would not be a place for women."

Around that time, she had an advertising sales meeting in Detroit with the marketing head of one of the Big Three automakers, who fully understood the importance of female auto consumers. "He told me that most of the autos that were purchased in the showroom, the person who made the impact behind that decision was a woman. Even if it was a car for her husband." Nevertheless, "they would not commit to dollars online to target women."

A shift took place in the late 1990s starting with Procter & Gamble, which, Luber recalled, was the first major packaged-goods retailer to go after women online with an approach specifically intended for the medium, just like on television, radio, and in print. "Once they went online, all the other packaged good companies, pharmaceutical companies—all the brands targeting women and families—went online, and everything changed," she said. It was a welcome development, and yet the shocking idea that women used the Internet didn't always equate to an enlightened marketing approach. The same automaker that had initially refused Luber came back with an offer. "We had a very large campaign for minivans. And they conceded at minivans because minivans screamed 'female.' It was just laughable," she said. "Absolutely laughable. There's still a double standard."

As WomensForum matured, so did its visitors. "The audience got a little older. And I was happy to see that. I was happy to see that we attracted an audience of older women, more mature women who were able to contribute to the dialogue and bring their experience online."

Just as in the case of young women online, companies took a long time to wrap their heads around the existence of tech-literate, middle-aged-and-older women. "It used to be thought that older women were only going online," she said, "for email."

"I mean this is actually laughable, I feel like I'm telling you a story from the Dark Ages. For email. Then, they were just sending pictures to family."

As marketers gradually realized that older women—and their money—could be reached online, however, dollar signs began to appear in their eyes. Now, "every advertiser from AARP to financial services, credit cards, insurance, health, pharmaceutical—they're all there," Luber said. Some are even going so far as to appreciate that older women might want to do more than email photos of their grandkids all day. She rattled off a list of companies she thought were doing a good job of portraying older women in nonstereotypical ways in their marketing: some financial services companies, which show customers achieving goals in retirement beyond golf courses and cruise ships. American Express, which asks older women to consider, "How are you going to fund your business?" Microsoft, which asks them, "How are you going to run your home office?"

"They speak to women like people," she said.

The biggest standout at aligning itself with a fuller vision of later life, she said, is the clothing brand and retailer Chico's. She pulled up their website on her office computer.

The women's fashion industry is uniquely loath to sell its version of the "old man's car"—that is, to rely on marketing that, by focusing on older women, might scare off younger buyers and thus, paradoxically, older ones as well. If she were, say, a typical makeup retailer, Luber said, then she would value the older female customer highly, because "she's the recurring revenue customer I can count on. Not the babysitter with the occasional $20 on the weekend." And yet, such companies' marketing efforts consistently feature 18- to 25-year-olds because no fashion brand wants the stigma of age. Companies may refer to older women as "a secondary audience," she said, "but it's a prime revenue generator."

Chico's, however, isn't trying to indirectly reach the older market by blasting younger women with marketing and hoping the message trickles up. Rather, it's going straight for the revenue jugular. Luber pointed at her computer screen, which was populated with images of beaming women. "Chico's is a very interesting line. The models are older. They're beautiful. They're in their fifties or plus." She scrolled down, and one graceful model after another flew past. "They're wearing. They're *being*." Luber stopped at one particularly striking urban scene. "She looks like she could either be going to dinner, or going to a meeting." Possibly both: "One weekend in New York City, one bag," read the photo's caption. "They're all traveling. They're on the go."

A few years ago, said Luber, who is 51, the brand didn't give off the same urbane vibe. It would have been "a little more kaftan-y, and a little more loose blouse-y . . . over the stretchy pants, maybe. And it's become much more chic." Older women have always been able to obtain modern fashions for a price, of course, but the conspicuous absence of these items at major, off-the-rack retailers has had an effect, as has the lack of older women in large-scale marketing efforts. It has meant that the idea of later-life elegance has long been the exception, not the norm, in the eyes those who have grown up, as Luber said, "like I have, looking at all these magazines." On the rare occasions when older women did appear in marketing campaigns, it was hardly ever to confer a sense of elegance or sophistication onto a product. Rather, older models have historically been used to represent exactly one thing: oldness, with all its negative, narrative-derived associations.

One important thing this longstanding marketing approach didn't do, Luber said, is "bring sexuality into it, or sexiness into it." The idea that sexuality in older people, women in particular, is somehow aberrant, even abhorrent, has limited happiness in old age *for centuries*. In fashion marketing, where sex appeal is a prerequisite for virtually every grownup model, the default, unsexy treatment of older models is conspicuous and distressing. That's not to say that older adults or anyone else one should feel compelled to act or dress in any particular way. Any true vision of liberty in old age would include the freedom to appear however one wants, no matter what anyone says, and I would never presume to suggest otherwise (and neither would Luber). But brands have been limiting that freedom by refusing to treat older adults like everyone else. In the process, they have framed sex, an essential part of life for many, as weird, funny, and unusual in old age. It's unbelievable when you stop and think about it: older people don't, as a rule, hate sex. In fact, they've seen far more of it than young people. But the idea that consenting older adults might find some life-affirming meaning in sexual intimacy is nearly always treated as unthinkable. In fact, there's a good chance you're chuckling to yourself as you read this! Ask yourself why. There's no biological reason for it; the real culprit is our long history of cultural indoctrination. By breaking with that received narrative and using older models to represent a new, aspirational, expansive—and yes, sexy—way of life, Chico's is in fact doing something quietly revolutionary. It's rejecting the idea that older women should narrow their horizons.

Still, I wondered if Chico's focus on appearance might represent a source of unwanted stress. As Luber had said, the pressure to look beautiful "starts when you are about ten years old." In marketing and entertainment, companies tell women: "You are not enough. You're not thin enough, you're not pretty enough, someone is better . . . you're doing it all wrong." Chico's is in the business of selling nice clothes; it's never going to eject the idea that its customers should spend money to look a certain way. However, Luber said, the brand is making one important gesture toward acceptance by using its own sizing system, which theoretically carries fewer judgmental connotations than does traditional, 0–22 sizing. "I don't think this is, 'You're doing it all wrong,'" she said. "I think this is really pretty fashion for multiple sizes."

Making Old Age Look Good

Chico's, BMW, and the rest are just the beginning. In the coming years, as more avenues to late-life meaning unfurl, all anyone will want to talk about regarding age will be all the astounding, even scandalous, new things that older people are up to. Critics with no grasp of economics will inevitably accuse older workers of robbing the young of jobs. Others will be shocked—shocked!—by the burgeoning business of elder pornography, already booming in Japan. Many others will wonder why Grandma, who doesn't seem to be dressing like Grandma anymore, has become so outspoken, both online and off.

Likely to get lost in this swirl of amazement and scandal will be the question of how young people will respond to a vision of their future that looks, for the first time, appealing. As it stands today, they are far from convinced that a good old age is not only possible but worth working for. In the narrative-constrained vision of late life they encounter in person and in the media, the only socially condoned route to meaning is through close family and friends, and even that small-yet-legitimate source of succor may feel insufficient. Students of socioemotional selectivity theory aside, no one younger than middle age understands that someday her goals will flip; someday, a small circle of friends might be just the right size. Combine that misapprehension with the narrative-derived idea that to be old is to be a taker, never a producer of work or culture, and you've got a recipe for a dismal-looking future.

One sign of how wanting young people find the going idea of old age is how little they're willing to save for it. Although young adults are stashing away more than is commonly believed—the savings rate of 20-year-olds rose from 5.8 percent of income in 2013 to 7.5 in 2016—they are still woefully underprepared for the future according to most conventional measures, which recommend a 15 percent savings rate. In fairness, this risk may be slightly overblown. If life in the year 2062 turns out to be as different from 2017 as life today is from 1972, the "retirement" that 20-year-olds will someday face may turn out to bear little resemblance to our current version and may be financed differently as well. However, the best way to prepare for an uncertain future is to, well, prepare, and so it is still concerning that young people aren't doing much saving. Serious factors outside of their control, such as crippling student-loan debt, high housing costs, and a recession recovery that has been less than forgiving for young job seekers are all partly responsible. But so is the fact that the future feels far away, and the ins and outs of older life can seem inscrutable or worse. As Laura Carstensen said to me, "We tell people you've really got to save more money, save more money, save more money—so you can pay your nursing home costs." She laughed: "Wow. Somehow people aren't inspired." That negative, hazy take on the future has profound effects in the present. For instance, employers have become less likely with each passing year to offer retirement plans (only 43 percent of millennials without such plans report saving consistently), and the reason why retirement plans are often first on the chopping block is that saving for the long term is simply a lower priority for younger workers than more immediate concerns like salary, sick pay, and health insurance.

Meanwhile, young adults are choosing experiences in the here and now over the nebulous future. It's hard to even blame them. Although their elders give them grief for spending on things like video games, flat-screen TVs, and restaurants—millennials spend more on dining out than any other generation—it should come as no surprise that they're choosing, say, brunch this upcoming Saturday over a hypothetical one 40 years hence. Compared to saving for a future meal that seems like it may never come or will only be enjoyed by a future self who seems not wholly familiar, those warm Belgian waffles seem like a solid return on investment.

Unfortunately, should we continue to favor our present over our future, the consequences will be neither warm nor pleasant. If everyone—from teenagers on up to public intellectuals who hope to die at 75—thinks that old age isn't worth the short-term deprivations involved in preparing for it, the result will be catastrophic: a whole lot of unhealthy, older people, totally reliant on public support.

As new routes to meaning in late life open up, however, expectations about the future will change. Younger people may see their parents and grandparents working and volunteering at meaningful jobs.

They may see them expressing themselves though fashion, expanding their minds through education, experiencing new forms of entertainment, and taking a powerful interest in civic life. And they may realize they have more in common with their future selves than they'd thought.

In the process, younger people will pierce the barrier to understanding the final 8,000-day chunk of life. Cracking the once-unknowable mystery of *what makes older people tick* will diminish alienation between generations and may well inspire younger people to invest in their future selves financially, emotionally, and through the adoption of healthier lifestyles. Should saving and taking proactive care of one's body in youth and middle age start to feel less like homework and more immediately important, the public at large may ultimately bear less of the cost of the aging population than today's doomsayers estimate.

But enough about young people. The most important thing about an improved old age will be the simple fact that it will be good to be old. Given life, liberty, and a variety of clear paths to happiness, late life will be fuller than ever before. It will not feel like a diminished version of middle age or a second childhood but rather a standalone, worthwhile state of being. And the frontier of longevity—the greatest achievement human ingenuity has ever given us—will blossom with the sort of cultural signposts that we use to mark meaningful moments, achievements, and new directions. As we find ourselves chasing our goals and aspirations in old age, will we also find ourselves attending downsizing parties, empty-nest celebrations, MicroMaster's graduations—even divorce parties? Funerals are often called "celebrations of life." Now, I submit that we are on the cusp of learning to celebrate life in old age—while we're still alive.

Starting in the 1950s and 1960s, as a consolation prize for the loss of status and opportunity that came with retirement and age, older people were offered the idea of the Golden Years. In the decades that followed, we clamored for the relaxation and leisure promised in this vision of life not because it coincided with oldness but despite it. The better old age we're now facing might seem similar—it certainly sounds golden—but it couldn't be more different. Thanks to advances in technology; the willingness of businesses to recognize the importance of, and accurately target, older adults' wants and needs; and, above all else, the size, attitude, and tech-savvy of the baby boom generation, old age itself is about to transform. No longer will you need a consolation prize for oldness. Far from it: you'll want to be old.

8

Meaning and Legacy in the Longevity Economy

FOR COMPANIES IN the longevity economy, there is opportunity to be found at every level of Abraham Maslow's hierarchy of needs—from meds that lower one's blood pressure on up to the heights of technology and fashion. Regardless of the type of need being served, these business openings owe their existence to the same process: the widening gap between what older adults should *theoretically* need, according to the traditional narrative of age, and their *actual* demands as consumers. So far, I've described these opportunities at the levels of both physiological needs and higher-level desires. Companies addressing the former must reject the idea that older people are little more than a bundle of medical problems to be solved and instead prioritize their goals and aspirations. Meanwhile, businesses addressing higher-level wants can create new, fertile relationships with older adults by offering them unexpected routes to meaning.

At the very apex of Maslow's pyramid, similar opportunities await, although they're even easier to miss if your mind is stuck in the going narrative of age. When consumers manage to satisfy most of their needs and wants, they don't stop living—and they don't stop consuming either. A deep drive still prevails, even among those who are lucky and competent enough to find themselves safe and healthy, in loving relationships, and held in general high esteem. Maslow believed that as a matter of course, such fortunate, high-functioning people strive to achieve something he called "self-actualization": a sort of secular enlightenment wherein one achieves one's full human potential. "In one individual it may take the form of the desire to be an ideal mother, in another it may be expressed athletically, and in still another it may be expressed in painting pictures or in inventions," he wrote in 1943. "This tendency might be phrased as the desire to become more and more what one is, to become everything that one is capable of becoming."

In the decades since Maslow came out with this idea, the business community has done its best to put it to work through both management and marketing. Only in the light of Maslovian self-actualization, for instance, does the genius become apparent in "Be All You Can Be," the longstanding recruiting slogan that ad agency N. W. Ayer created for the US Army. In its outreach to young people, some of whom presumably desired direction in their lives, the Army was offering a ticket straight to the top of the pyramid. However, at least as Maslow originally envisioned it, self-actualization was actually reserved not for every member of the rank and file but rather just the fortunate few. He reckoned that only a very small percentage of a given population ever achieve this rarefied state: perhaps as few as one in a thousand, none younger than middle age. So uncommon were true self-actualizers, he reasoned, and so aloof were they from "ordinary conventions and from the ordinarily accepted hypocrisies, lies, and inconsistencies of social life," that "they sometimes feel like spies or aliens in a foreign land and sometimes behave so."

And that raises a troubling question. To be one of the handful of self-actualizers walking the earth in a state of sublime perception and self-mastery certainly sounds enviable, but what about the rest of us? As we grow older, must we suffer agonizing pangs of disappointment for not becoming all we can supposedly be? This dismal prospect isn't just depressing on a personal level—it also limits the incentive for businesses to help consumers approaching the tip of Maslow's pyramid, since so few of them will presumably succeed.

Happily, there's another way to look at the highest level of motivation, particularly as age enters into the equation. Laura Carstensen's research suggests that even if we don't all manage to squeeze maximal accomplishment out of every ounce of our human potential, we can and do still pursue meaning as we individually define it—through our goals, activities, and relationships. That's encouraging for two reasons. First, even if self-actualization isn't in the cards for most of us, many may still find significance in life. And second, more relevant to business: there's a poorly understood market out there, filled with people who seemingly have little in the way of needs as they're traditionally conceived, and yet simply *must have* meaning in their lives—and will pay for products that deliver it.

This drive—and the closely related desire to leave behind a positive legacy—constitutes perhaps the single greatest unexplored area on the frontier of the longevity economy. It won't stay uncharted for long, however. Already, pioneers are beginning to dot the landscape: looking around, staking a claim, and calling a once-stark country home.

One of these trailblazers is Jodi Luber, the cofounder of WomensForum, who also teaches budding entrepreneurs at Boston University. The first night of December 2016 found her presiding on a panel of judges at BU's Latkepalooza, an annual Hanukkah celebration held at the university's Hillel House. The third floor of the building, a cafeteria space directly across the soon-to-be-frozen Charles River from MIT's West Campus, was packed with festively clad undergrads downing potato pancakes with cream cheese and applesauce. One faculty member roamed the room in a boxy, sky-blue dreidel costume; students, their paper plates laden, swerved to avoid his corners.

In addition to the latkes available for general consumption, three student-submitted recipes were up for the panel's appraisal: one that was gluten free, another made with bits of apples, and a third that was

more fritter than pancake. The recipes weren't the only things facing scrutiny that night. Just an hour earlier, Luber had initiated a soft
launch of her new web venture, TheJewishKitchen.com.

Luber grew up in a culinary household. Her father owned a kosher
bagel bakery in an Orthodox neighborhood of Borough Park, Brook-
lyn, and she spent many a weekend there, helping out. "He knew his
customers; he made an amazing product; the line was out the door,"
she said. "He had nicknames for all of his customers, like the guy with
the garlic seeds in his beard who had the bad breath . . . When he'd
come in the bakery, my dad would say, 'Hold your breath—ten o'clock,
north wind.'" She paused and gazed around the room. "I loved just the
ethnic crazy feel of all of this."

After college, when Luber first struck out to live on her own, she
realized that she needed to learn to cook for herself, which should
have been a cinch, except no one in her family had ever written down
a recipe. She would call her relatives—her grandmother in Florida,
for instance, who knew how to make her favorite sweet-and-sour
meatballs—but the instructions she received were never exactly
straightforward. Luber later recalled on The Jewish Kitchen's site,
"Getting her to tell me exactly how to make meatballs was like having
someone tell me by speakerphone how to take out someone's appendix
while they were on the eighteenth hole at Pebble Beach and I was in
the operating room, having never gone to medical school." In addition
to her relatives' hard-to-follow instructions—"*How do I know when
the onions are done?*" "*Oh, you'll just know!*"—every recipe came with
a backstory about prior generations: the people who had prepared and
enjoyed the same food Luber was learning how to make.

Time passed, and Luber founded WomensForum. When it received
its first major round of funding she couldn't wait to tell her father, so
she called him up and told him to turn on his fax machine. "When I
faxed him the receipt from the wire transfer, you know, seven with all
the zeroes, he was like, 'Hold on.' And I hear this in the background,

'seven million.' I go, 'What are you doing?' He's like, 'I'm trying to figure out how many bagels I'd have to sell!'"

Four years ago, her father passed away. "My heart was broken, so I just had to do something that kind of captured everything I grew up with, with my crazy family and his recipes." She didn't know what that something would be, however, until the summer of 2016, when she took a trip to the Jacob K. Javits Convention Center in Manhattan's Far West Side. She'd been planning to find some items to feature on WomensForum and wandered over to the booth of an exhibitor selling a variety of Judaica products, including beautiful linens and napkin rings. Luber struck up a conversation about some of the Rosh Hashanah table settings she'd seen, and suddenly, a third woman was standing at her elbow, eager to join in. The conversation grew, and more women appeared—five in total. Soon they had produced their smartphones, which were filled with images of holiday foods and tables. "You wanna see table settings? Look at this!" "No, look at this!" "That's not Rosh Hashanah—wait, *I'll give you Rosh Hashanah.*" One of the gang, Luber recalled, had dozens of photos of one table that looked like it was decked out for a state dinner. They discussed their special recipes for challah bread and kugel and pomegranate tarts and how their mothers and grandmothers had prepared them. At a certain point, Luber realized that no one was trying to sell anyone anything. They were all simply, warmly—and yes, with hints of competition— hoping to share *how my family does it; how we've always done it.*

"It was clear it was about so much more than food," Luber said. The people she met that day wanted to share more than recipes and table-setting tips. They wanted to share *stories.*

And in order to do so, they had, without even noticing that it was remarkable, begun using their smartphone screens in an unexpected way: not to convey information so much as to serve as a backdrop for family lore, traditions, and the tales behind the cuisine. It was a subtle instance of lead-user innovation—all too easy to miss, if you weren't in tune with the desires of women aged 50 and up. And yet, Luber said, "I got that feeling that I got when I started talking about WomensForum 20 years ago—that little chill up the back of my spine." As far as she knew, there was no online service in the world set up to facilitate the kind of communication she was witnessing.

So she built one: The Jewish Kitchen. The site is set up explicitly with stories in mind: Users can submit recipes, but far more space in a typical recipe's webpage is devoted to backstory than instructions. More important, users can submit *videos* of themselves or loved ones cooking—and, as the garlic sautés, talking to the camera.

"Here I am making latkes for Hanukah," said Luber, imitating a hypothetical Jewish Kitchen contributor. "Here I am with my daughter making jelly donuts. Here we are making a noodle kugel. Oh, you don't know from noodle kugel. Here's how you make a real one."

Talking family traditions and recipes with the others at the Javits Center, she said, "I knew that I hit something because people want to record these things, and they never wrote them down. They didn't ask their mothers, and their bubbes, and their aunts. They just—they call when they need a recipe, and eventually they write it on a piece of paper and they stick it in a folder. But they don't have it from their relatives, and many of them are gone."

The Jewish Kitchen gives this inextricable tangle of recipe, folkway, anecdote, and family history a permanent home online: a one-stop lending library of culinary memories. In so doing, the website, which is now bursting with so much mouth-watering imagery that I can't spend too much time looking at it, has jumped to the forefront of the market for meaning in the longevity economy. Companies I discussed earlier, like BMW and Chico's, are opening new *pathways* to meaning in old age. Even the very phones and computers used by The Jewish Kitchen's contributors can be considered avenues of this sort: technologies that are not innately meaningful but allow the consumer to get at something that is. Running a business on this sort of model is akin to setting up a tollbooth on an alluring, expansive highway that promises great things at its end. As more of these highways open up, however, another class of products will emerge. The Jewish Kitchen is just one early example of a product offering not a road to meaning but the meaningful experience itself.

Or rather, one version of it. Luber's company, though forward-looking, still has a foot planted firmly within the domestic sphere—the rare area of life where, under the going narrative, older adults are permitted to exercise their innate desire to chase meaning. (Another, better-known company that sells meaning within this scope is Ancestry.com, which allows subscribers to learn about their family history, stitch together a family tree, and submit DNA samples for genealogical testing.)

For the most part, meaningful end-products outside the domestic sphere will become available only after new avenues to meaning are created. However, there is one glaring exception. Legacy has preoccupied the thoughts of older people since the dawn of time, and products offering to preserve one's name and deeds for posterity already abound. For instance, the self-publishing book industry, which has been on a tear in recent years thanks to tools and distribution platforms introduced by tech giants like Amazon, has also benefited enormously from older adults' desire to write down their thoughts and recollections. Seventeen percent of customers at Lulu.com, a major print-on-demand website, are said to be older adults, a figure that rises to an estimated 50 percent at AuthorSolutions, the largest self-publishing house in the United States. There are also more expensive products to be had, which all but guarantee to preserve one's name in living memory. Universities are particularly adept at selling this sort of legacy, for instance, in the form of named professorships, monuments, and buildings.

But the desire to leave behind something concrete, be it a book or a building, is just one way the legacy drive exerts itself. More commonly, people simply decide to give back to a community that once helped them and let whatever improvements they make stand as their legacy. It's an idea that dovetails nicely with Laura Carstensen's socioemotional selectivity theory. Carstensen suggests that in the first half of our lives, we experience the drive to fill our brains and pocketbooks with the knowledge, skills, and resources that society makes available. "You withdraw from the bank of culture—and that's medicine and education and everything that's been learned and stored and built before we were ever born." Then in the second half of life, we get a chance to reinvest those things. "The second 50 years are where you pay it back; you invest in the bank for future generations . . . You change the culture, you make contributions that make the world a better place."

Making those reinvestments can feel meaningful in the extreme. And crucially, unlike most other nondomestic routes to meaning, philanthropy and volunteerism present immediate, socially sanctioned ways to achieve that feeling of satisfaction. Organizations providing such opportunities would do well to understand how socioemotional selectivity affects when and how older adults decide to give back. Say you run a nonprofit that builds low-income housing. You might think that your product is houses, but what you're really selling is the opportunity for your volunteers to experience pride in having achieved something meaningful, which they pay for in the form of time and effort. Research suggests that older adults are more likely to make this sort of exchange if volunteering was part of their lives leading up to old age, which makes sense in the light of Carstensen's theory. When we're young, we find out what's meaningful; when we're older, we act on that information. If your organization is seeking older volunteers and philanthropists, you should of course market directly to older adults themselves. But it also makes sense to try to reach them earlier, when they're younger and still deciding what's meaningful. Later, when they're older and looking for ways to reinvest, they may well return to you.

Giving back will be just one of many possible ways for tomorrow's older adults to achieve meaning in life, however. The full extent of the business opportunity at the apex of the hierarchy of needs remains hidden, because we don't yet know exactly how or in which spheres tomorrow's older adults will chase meaning. In this respect, the future of meaningful products is just as uncertain as the future awaiting products at every other level of the hierarchy of needs. Whether your company supports life, liberty, the pursuit of happiness—or offers up happiness itself, in the form of meaning—it's hard to know what shapes demand will take in years to come.

But it's not impossible. The way to stay ahead of future demands at the highest level is the same as at the lowest: practice radical empathy, prioritize the job of the consumer, and follow the lead of the lead user.

The Legacy of a Generation

From the very start, I aligned the AgeLab with the business community for the simple reason that, like it or not, businesses play an outsized role in defining how most people live. Where you call home, what clothes you wear, what you eat—these decisions are all defined, all *constrained*, by the choices laid out by businesses, as well as by governments and nonprofit organizations. I hope it goes without saying at this point that the choices currently available in later life are distinctly lacking.

Businesses are particularly well positioned to change that. I've made a case throughout this book that the longevity economy represents a new frontier—and a chance to expand beyond the boundaries of our current, limited set of norms. That frontier is naturally filled with opportunity for businesses, but it may also prove deadly. The main problem is that we don't know what's out there. Not only is it unmapped terrain in terms of what tomorrow's consumers will want, but worse, it's as though an unknown geological magnetic anomaly is attracting everyone's compass toward a false north. The existence of a socially constructed narrative of old age has everyone convinced they know how to navigate the frontier, and so the few trailblazers brave enough to march their products confidently out into the wilderness promptly find themselves lost in an environment where there are many ways to fail. The hazards should sound familiar by now. Products that are hard for older adults to use or that violate their mental models tend not to make it far, like pioneers who immediately stumble onto an impassable river and have to turn back. Products that present an incoherent vision of life in old age, or just don't seem compelling, may take longer to fail but fail they inevitably do, like explorers who wander deeper and deeper into a swamp only to lose their boots in the muck. Products that come across as insulting to the older consumer or antithetical to her aspirations or treat her as a problem-to-be solved—these may seem to be walking perfectly sound paths for many miles, until the first malarial mosquito bites. Perhaps the most troubling mistake businesses can make is to venture onto the longevity frontier with a vision that, like traditional retirement communities, may feel compelling but may also lead to war between generations. This is like discovering a likely valley for settlement and building log cabins, only to discover that there's not enough arable land to feed everyone. Suddenly, it's everyone for him or herself in a place that only looked like a paradise.

All told, if there were one piece of advice I would give any business considering a foray onto the longevity frontier, it would be, "*Don't trust your gut.*" Your sense of direction may seem reliable, but it's actually deeply skewed by decades' worth of incorrect narrative. Far better to hire a guide of some kind, someone who understands the known terrain and can make educated assumptions about the unknown as well. There are a few ways to do this. Some major firms devote entire groups to the study of the longevity market and their place in it. The Hartford, for instance, with its Center for Mature Market Excellence, and Transamerica, with its Center for Retirement Studies, rely on teams of social scientists to test assumptions about the behavior of older insurance and financial consumers. Merrill Lynch, meanwhile, has an in-house gerontologist. If you don't at least have *someone*— within your company or an external consultant—dedicated to keeping a close, empirical eye on changes in the longevity economy, you might as well be walking around blindfolded. But focus groups and surveys produced by social scientists can only get you so far. To gain a deeper understanding, it may help to strap on your customers' shoes and take a walk. As I've discussed, an empathy aid like AGNES may go a long way. Although AGNES isn't for rent or sale, a number of similar suits now are, and I encourage organizations to pick one up. Even if they don't perfectly replicate every physiological symptom older people can develop, such measures can still impart a general sense of what it's like to be in a given space or use a given product with an older body.

But the best thing a company can do is to study lead users, who, in order to satisfy their evolving needs, find themselves modifying products or utilizing them in ways their designers never intended. Lead users are even better than guides on the unfamiliar terrain of the longevity economy: not only can they tell you what the true job of the consumer is, but they can also identify jobs of *future* consumers. Find, poll, watch, and question these people. And if they're lead-user innovators, consider hiring them or funding their projects. Don't be afraid if they don't match the stereotypical, young, male entrepreneur profile; if anything, the viewpoint of older, female lead users is more likely to be valuable than that of any other group. Their insights may allow a product intended mainly for older adults to transcend that category and find success in the broader market, like OXO's kitchenware. Or, by applying broad-market products to longevity-economy problems, they may identify valuable new use cases. Recall how Sally Lindover, who hoped to age in place, found a new use case for Airbnb and Instacart. In these sorts of instances, when wide, new swaths of users discover unforeseen uses for a product, both low-end and new-market disruption become real possibilities.

And that brings me to the final hazard posed by the longevity economy frontier: disruption cuts both ways. The only thing worse than getting lost in the woods of the longevity economy is staying home and doing nothing. If you don't go exploring, there is a very real chance you'll be left behind and fall victim to disruption—even if you don't think of aging as relevant to your company.

Especially if you don't think of aging as relevant to your company. Look around: a better, older society will alter life not just for older adults but for people of every age. From childhood on up, we may soon find ourselves operating according to a different set of basic assumptions regarding the progression of a normal life. The opportunity now facing businesses is to define that new normal. It's a chance not just to grab a piece of the longevity economy—already one of the most enormous opportunities facing industry—but also to *grow* it by empowering older people culturally, socially, and economically. By pushing the envelope of their quality of life. By making old age better.

In so doing, your business may achieve something else. It may help the baby boomers cap their many decades of outsize influence with a grand finale that will linger in memory for generations.

Whether it's in tones of eulogy or calumny, the legacy of the baby boomers and their international contemporaries will be discussed for many decades to come. Their lifetimes have "without doubt seen the most rapid transformation of the human relationship with the natural world in the history of humankind," write a team of scientists from the International Geosphere-Biosphere Programme, an interdisciplinary group devoted to the study of global change. There are innumerable reasons for why this shift—the IGBP scientists call it the Great Acceleration—occurred during the boomers' heyday, related to trends in technology, macroeconomics, and global geopolitics. But there's one lone factor that, in my opinion, supersedes all the rest: for seven decades, whenever the boomer cohort has demanded something, it has gotten built—from roads to reactors, from hulking SUVs to tiny pocket computers.

And if the boomers have fashioned, formed, and fabricated the world around them as they've seen fit, they have also destroyed whatever they've deemed unnecessary—and I'm not just talking about the natural world, either. One thing that the boomers have dismantled with extreme prejudice is the role institutions play in our lives.

Since the polling firm Gallup first began measuring such metrics in the early 1970s, confidence in organized religion has dropped by 25 percent. Similar declines have plagued the United States Supreme

Court (8%), public schools (28%), banks (33%), organized labor (7%), newspapers (19%), big business (8%), and Congress (33%). Among American institutions Gallup has tracked since the early 1970s, only the military has seen an increase in confidence—by 15 percent.

At the same time, participation in institutions of virtually all kinds has plummeted since midcentury, something the Harvard social scientist Robert Putnam describes at length in his 2000 book *Bowling Alone,* a modern classic of sociology. In the decades following the 1950s, we haven't just cut back on our participation in civic institutions such as parent-teacher associations and service organizations like the Rotary Club. We've also dialed back our religiosity and religious attendance. The two-parent nuclear family has weakened, and gatherings of extended family have waned. People visit their friends less often. The community pub, diner, or other local gathering place is now little more than a nostalgic memory. So are the single-job career and the private-sector labor union. To Putnam's list, I'd add two more institutions that boomers have done away with: the defined-benefit retirement plan—and now the very cultural institution of retirement itself.

This trend is in no way all for the bad; in fact, there's every reason to believe that the boomers' purge has destroyed more evil than good. The gains made since the 1950s against institutionalized forms of racism, sexism, and other sorts of bigotry occurred, yes, because the boomers were, as Putnam writes, "an unusually tolerant generation— more open-minded toward racial, sexual, and political minorities, less inclined to impose their own morality on others." But they also happened because the boomers, a more individualist generation than their parents, were predisposed to dismantle, outlaw, or refuse to participate in any institution they didn't like.

Although the boomers' wave of institutional demolition was virtuous in many respects, it also came at a cost—especially to older adults, whose welfare wasn't exactly at the top of youngsters' minds in the 1960s and 1970s. During the beginning and middle of the 20th century, it's no exaggeration to say that institutions were what made life in old age livable. At first, when older people were robbed of the most important institution of all in a capitalist society—one's career—they could at least count on religious, fraternal, and service organizations, veterans' groups, the extended family, and other institutions to take up some of the slack.

As institutions waned, however, two vast tears formed in the fabric of later life, which continue to grow wider with every passing year. The first concerns base-level needs like food, healthcare, and shelter. In most high-income countries, only national pension schemes stand between many older adults and destitution. In the absence of strong families and civic and religious organizations, there are few other fallback options, and it's all too possible to slip through the cracks. Meanwhile, in developing countries where older adults receive relatively little governmental support, family and multigenerational households make up the only real safety net. In Mexico, Thailand, and elsewhere, the transition away from traditional economies has caused the people who once formed multigenerational households to become geographically dispersed. When the family breaks apart in countries like these, no one pays a higher price than older adults, who can find themselves isolated, poor, sick—even homeless.

The second part of later life that's been torn out is the role institutions once played in providing older people a sense of community, identity, and purpose. From religious organizations to bowling leagues; sinecures to family dinners, a wide web of institutions once provided places for older people to simply *be* in society. Even the cultural institution of retirement cleared this low bar: although identifying as a retiree separated older adults from everyone of working age, at least that identity signified *something*.

Now there is nothing: just a worn-out narrative behind us and a stark, unpopulated frontier of unclaimed years ahead. The boomers—the generation that spent decades stripping down organizations, traditions, and expectations—face an extended stretch of life that is, ironically, in dire need of institutions.

Once again, the boomers will build as they see fit. But this time, they will erect new institutions designed to make old age more livable than ever. These will come in the form of novel, tech-enabled social institutions, like Kathie's group of friends from Stitch.net. And economic institutions, such as venture-capital organizations devoted to funding older start-up founders. And community institutions, such as Beacon Hill Village. Meanwhile, government institutions, including Social Security, Medicare, and the protections enshrined in the Older Americans Act, will take on a level of importance never before seen. And that's just scratching the surface, because in addition to foreseeable institutions, it's likely that new, unprecedented ones will form, especially wherever people and connected technologies meet.

But the most important new institution will be a cultural one: a broad, new set of narrative instructions for how to live leading up to, and in, old age. More than any other factor, this new story will be built on the testimony of longevity-economy products. It's one thing to unconvincingly state in speech or writing that older people are important, productive members of society; a resource, not a drain. It's quite another for a company to *demonstrate,* in product form, what it thinks older adults are capable of. Products that will succeed in tomorrow's longevity economy will treat older consumers not as crises to be triaged or puzzles to be solved but as full-fledged members of society with recognizable wants, needs, and ambitions. As these products win out, the connotations surrounding age will change. We will no longer need to wedge our idiosyncratic selves into a constrictive, one-size-fits-all idea of oldness. Quite the contrary: the new, bespoke narrative of old age will emerge organically from our jobs as consumers. It will fit like a tailored suit.

And, fittingly enough, the new narrative of age will solve one other problem as well. It will allow the boomers to satisfy the largest of their unfulfilled generational jobs: to leave behind a positive legacy. On an individual level, companies like Jodi Luber's will help boomers fulfill this emerging need. But the boomers as a generational whole will also want to be remembered fondly in the years to come. And if there is one surefire way they can leave behind a ledger with more black in it than red, it's by building a better old age for future generations to enjoy.

Your Legacy

Academics who study business are a pragmatic sort: we try to condense unwieldy, complex economic and behavioral systems down to manageable, actionable chunks. But sometimes those chunks become too small, too discrete, to accurately simulate reality. Take the idea of economic producers and consumers. Over the years, the notion that they are two separate groups of people has proven useful—so much so, in fact, that it's become hard to picture them otherwise. We think of producers like they're Santa's elves: hard workers who never stop to enjoy the products they make. And we imagine consumers to be like well-behaved children: always receiving, never creating. But in reality, the distinction is false. Every economic producer goes out after work or on the weekends (or furtively online at the office) and buys things. Meanwhile, almost everyone finds herself working for money at one point or another. The producer is always also a consumer, and the consumer is often a producer.

To succeed in the longevity economy, businesses will find it essential to blur these categories and think about what their consumers can create. They can produce answers, for instance: a typical consumer can tell you what job she wants solved, and a lead-user—usually, an older woman—will be able to identify the jobs that will arise tomorrow. More important, older consumers will demand products that will enable them to be productive: not just takers but also givers who can reinvest their wealth of experience and resources.

You may find it hard to think of older consumers in this way. We've all been taught, many since birth, that older people are needy, greedy vampires, incapable of producing goods, services, culture, hard work, money—even ideas.

But soon, we will rid ourselves of this tired narrative and embrace a new one. It will make the experience of old age better, and the promise of a good future will make it better to be young, too. Once this narrative shift gets started there will be no stopping it, as all-powerful older consumers elevate products that solve their true jobs and strike down those that fail to meet that standard. By that time, if your business is not part of the solution, there's a good chance it will fall victim to the ruthlessness of the free market. But early on in the process, only the most flexible minds in business will be able to penetrate the haze of the going narrative and see the real demands of the older consumer. Those who do will have the opportunity to kick-start the narrative shift and conquer the longevity frontier.

Beyond opportunity, beyond the fear of disruption, beyond even altruism, there is one more reason to make sure you and your business are part of this first wave. The overlap between consumer and producer flows both ways. Not only can older consumers act as economic producers, but, if they're lucky, all of today's economic producers will eventually become older consumers. And that means you. No matter how old you are, in the future, you will be even older—and you will still be a consumer.

The question is, what kind of old age will be available for your consumption? The world is facing a stark choice. Although I've portrayed a glowing older future as nigh inevitable, there is always the chance that the going narrative will send us down a dark path, a downward spiral filled with austerity, abandonment, and resentment between generations. No matter the size of your business, how you treat older adults is a nudge in the direction of one path or the other. And whichever we choose, the decision will stick, because the world isn't getting any younger.

Neither, for that matter, are you. It's time to enter and win the longevity economy. Doing so may haul in sales. It may position you on the right side of disruption. It may help set up a better old age for you to enjoy, where you won't have to live without liberty or happiness. Best of all, if you make the right choice now, future generations may thank you for it. In building a tomorrow where older adults can chase their dreams, have fun, contribute, achieve meaning—and yes, leave a bit of themselves behind—you won't only be helping them leave a legacy. The legacy you create may well be your own.

ACKNOWLEDGMENTS

THIS BOOK REPRESENTS a compendium of ideas drawn from widely disparate fields, from history to medicine to economics and beyond. My primary thanks goes to the researchers and thinkers on whose broad shoulders this book stands, including historians Dora L. Costa, Carolyn Thomas de la Peña, Caroll Estes, William Graebner, Bryan Greene, Carole Haber, and Robert Putnam; management experts Clayton Christensen and Eric von Hippel; tech thinkers Ruth Schwartz Cowan, Rose Eveleth, and Noam Scheiber; my academic mentor Roger W. Cobb; and my colleagues in aging research and innovation, including Age Wave's Ken and Maddie Dychtwald, Encore.org's Marc Freedman, the Milken Institute's Paul Irving, the Global Coalition on Aging's Michael Hodin, the Gerontological Society of America's Greg O'Neill, ActiveAge's Gregor Rae, and Eden Alternative's Bill Thomas. Special thanks here go to Stanford's Laura Carstensen, Atul Gawande, and AARP's CEO, Jo Ann Jenkins, for their patient insight and support.

I would also like to extend my sincere thanks to the many people who graciously agreed to be interviewed for this project, including some whose last names were omitted for the sake of privacy, and many whose interviews were influential but ultimately didn't fit into the scope of this book. These include Ken and Jackie and Craig's family, Smoke Hickman, Joan Doucette, Bill Haskell, Joanne Cooper, Kate Hoepke, and everyone else at both The Villages and the Village to Village Network; Stitch user extraordinaire Kathie; Dan Scheinman and

Danielle Barbieri; Marcie Rogo; Jonathan Gruber; David Mindell; Keith Gunura; Seth Sternberg; Jessica Beck; Tom Grape; Mike Masserman; Dina Katabi; Sanjay Sarma; Nicole Maestas; and Jodi Luber.

This book is not just my first for a wide audience, but also the first major print catalogue of the MIT AgeLab's work, ideals, and unique point of view. The many students and researchers who have passed through the MIT AgeLab since its founding have influenced the Lab's trajectory and my thinking in innumerable ways. This select group includes but is in no way limited to: Daisuke Asai, Arielle Burstein, Sarah Bush, Meredith Coley, Olivia DaDalt, Ali Davis, Jon Dobres, Angelina Gennis, Cédric Hutchings, Michal Isaacson, Daekeun Kim, Katerina Konig, Birgit Kramer, Dennis Lally, Jasmine Lau, Charles Lin, Hale McAnulty, Joachim Meyer, Dan Munger, Dick Myrick, Alex Narvaez, Michelle Pratt, Roz Puleo, and Jessica Vargas Astaíza. Distinguished AgeLab collaborators include my very good friend Michael Kafrissen; RISD's Gui Trotti and Mickey Ackerman and their talented students; as well as Paro's inventor, Takanori Shibata. My current, immediate team deserves the same degree of recognition plus extra for everything they've done to support this work, from keeping the ship upright while this book was in progress to occasional help with research. These wonderful colleagues include but again are not limited to: Dana Ellis, Adam Felts (who helped organize this book's endnotes), Chaiwoo Lee, my ever-ready assistant Adam Lovett, Jenna Ping, Marika Psyhojos, Verena Speth, Martina Raue, and Carly Ward. Worthy of special mention are lab leaders and long time friends Lisa D'Ambrosio, who heads up our social science efforts, and Bryan Reimer and Bruce Mehler, who head up the AgeLab's automotive research—whose important work in automotive human factors is supported by a large team including Hillary Abramson, Dan Brown, Lex Fridman, Tom McWilliams, Alea Mehler, and many others; my gratitude extends to them all. My thanks also goes to the thousands of volunteers and study participants who have come through our doors (and have been annoyed by our researchers online), including the courageous and tech-savvy Sally Lindover. All told, the people who have made up the AgeLab have taught me far more over the years than I ever could have taught them.

At MIT, the AgeLab and I have received considerably support from friends throughout the Institute. In addition to those mentioned above, these champions include Cindy Barnhart, Eran Ben-Joseph, Martha Gray, Hugh Herr, Hiroshi Ishii, Kent Larson, Bill Long, Dava Newman, Frank Moss, Sandy Pentland, Rosalind Picard, Christine Reif, David Rose, Nick Roy, Frederick Salvucci, Tom Sheridan, Joseph Sussman, Peter Szolovits, Olivier de Weck, Maria Yang, and Chris Zegras. Within the AgeLab's home department, the Center for Transportation and Logistics, my sincere appreciation goes to my colleagues Chris Caplice, Eric Greimann, Mary Mahoney, Nancy Martin, Karen Van Nederpelt, Jim Rice, and my longtime assistant Paula Magliozzi—many of whom have been with me at MIT from the very beginning. Speaking of which, the AgeLab owes its very existence to Yossi Sheffi, the person who brought me to MIT and placed a bet on the far-out notion of a center for a multidisciplinary, systems approach to the study of aging. Yossi has my profound and lasting thanks. Beyond the Institute, thinkers, educators, and researchers who have supported me and the AgeLab's mission include: Giuseppe Anerdi, Jon Pynoos, Richard Marottoli, and Bob Stern. One of them, the late Ken Minaker of Massachusetts General Hospital, taught me an enormous amount; he will be remembered as a geriatrics giant and I will always remember him as a true friend.

Outside the academy, individuals who were integral to the launching of the AgeLab include Bob McDonald, Horace Deets, and my dear and special friend Vicki Shepard. The Hartford, led by Chris Swift, was and remains crucial to keeping the lights on. Friends of the Lab at The Hartford's Property and Casualty Insurance group include Mary Boyd, Bev Hynes-Grace, Cindy Hellyar, Maureen Mohyde, Jodi Olshevski, Ray Sprague, and Beth Tracton-Bishop. And over at Hartford Funds, friends include John Brennan, Jim Davey, Don Diehl, Bill Doherty, Eric

Levinson, Jac McLean, Marty Swanson, and of course my indefatigable friend John Diehl. Additional thanks go to Surya Kolluri and Andy Sieg at Merrill Lynch; Ted Courtney and Adam L'Italien at Liberty Mutual; Roger Ferguson, Betsy Palmer, and Connie Weaver at TIAA; Donato Tramuto at Tivity Health; Chuck Gulash at Toyota; Klaus Bengler at the Technische Universität München; and Brian Forbes and Dave Paulsen at Transamerica.

In addition to those named above, I would like to thank my colleagues at EG&G and in the United States federal government, particularly at the Volpe National Transportation Systems Center, who first pointed me toward aging as a field of study. Important groups that have furthered that work include: Coca-Cola, CVS Health, Daimler, Denso, EDS, Fiat, Ford, Google, GlaxoSmithKline, Honda, JPMorgan Chase, Johnson & Johnson, MassMutual, MasterFoods, Monotype, New Balance, Nissan, Panasonic, PepsiCo, Procter & Gamble, The Prudential, Raymond James, Subaru, SunTrust, Toyota, Transamerica, and the USDOT.

The standout name among all these entities is AARP, which has provided significant support to the AgeLab from the very start. My sincere thanks goes to my many friends at this noble organization, including but in no way limited to: Jo Ann Jenkins, Martha Boudreau, Kevin Donnellan, Larry Flanagan, Scott Frisch, Nancy LeaMond, Cindy Lewin, Sarah Mika, Lisa Marsh Ryerson, Nancy Smith, Debra Whitman, my fellow AARP Board members, and all the other good people who have helped turn my AgeLab pipedream into a reality.

On a personal level, I'd like to express my deep appreciation for my agent Susan Rabiner, for her hard work in taking a mere notion and turning it into a tangible book and for the many profound insights she provided along the way. Perhaps chief of these was her idea to pitch this project to John Mahaney, who became my editor at PublicAffairs and whose close guidance and valuable thoughts concerning *The Longevity Economy*'s structure and arguments were essential to the final product. Most importantly concerning the production of this book, I want to once again thank my collaborator, Luke Yoquinto.

While it is the norm to thank people, not institutions, MIT deserves special thanks. MIT's community and spirit of innovation provides a uniquely rich ground for new (and often wild) ideas to grow and be rigorously tested. The chance collisions between researchers, students, and those in the "real world" enabled by this special place have made it possible for me and my team to explore life tomorrow.

Whether at MIT or beyond, there are doubtless many additional people and organizations who deserve mention in these pages: researchers, visitors, colleagues, students, friends, entities in various sectors, and more. If you are one of these and your name hasn't appeared in this section, please accept my profound apologies and thanks.

Finally, I want to thank my family: Mary and Catherine, who continue to be the greatest source of pride and joy in my life; Yiayia, who has taught me much about aging with grace and tenacity; and O'Dea, who demonstrated how caregiving, far more than mere support, is a deeply personal act of compassion for a loved one. And finally my greatest thanks goes to Emily, my best friend and loving wife who has endured my endless travel and late nights and has given me decades of support and advice. She is the person with whom I can't wait to grow old.

NOTES

Introduction: The Longevity Paradox

2   **as of 2015, life expectancy in the United States had reached 79 years:** National Center for Health Statistics, "Health, United States, 2015: With Special Feature on Racial and Ethnic Health Disparities," *NCHS*, 2016, https://www.cdc.gov/nchs/data/hus/hus15.pdf.

3   **such as South Korea, Chile, Australia, New Zealand, Canada, and Israel:** The World Bank, "Life Expectancy at Birth, Total (Years)," *World Bank*, 2014, http://data.worldbank.org/indicator/SP.DYN.LE00.IN.

3   **30-year-old woman was *12-and-a-half times* more likely to die within a year:** Year 1900 death statistics: Felicitie C. Bell and Michael L. Miller, "Life Tables for the United States Social Security Area," *Social Security Administration*, 2005, https://www.ssa.gov/oact/NOTES/pdf_studies/study120.pdf; year 2013 death statistics: "Actuarial Life Tables," *Social Security Administration*, 2013, https://www.ssa.gov/oact/STATS/table4c6.html.

3   **76 for men:** F. B. Hobbs and B. L. Damon, "65+ in the United States" (Washington, DC: US Government Printing Office, 1996), https://www.census.gov/prod/1/pop/p23-190/p23-190.pdf.

3   **85.5 and 82.9, respectively:** Elizabeth Arias, "Changes in Life Expectancy by Race and Hispanic Origin in the United States, 2013–2014," NCHS Data Brief 244 (2016): 1–8.

3   **Korean women are right behind them:** Organisation for Economic Co-operation and Development, "Life Expectancy at 65," doi:10.1787/0e9a3f00-en.

4   **hovers around 2.1 children per woman:** "Declining fertility levels have been the main propeller for population aging and rates of decline vary by region and country. Currently the total fertility rate is near or below the 2.1 replacement level in all regions except Africa." Wan He, Daniel Goodkind, and Paul Kowal, "An Aging World: 2015," *International Population Reports*, March 2016, https://www.census.gov/content/dam/Census/library/publications/2016/demo/p95-16-1.pdf.

4   **1.46 children per woman, as of 2015:** Keiko Ujikane, "Japan's Fertility Rate Inches to Highest Level Since Mid-1990s," *Bloomberg*, May 23, 2016, http://www.bloomberg.com/news/articles/2016-05-23/japan-s-fertility-rate-inches-to-highest-level-since-mid-1990s.

4   **losing large chunks of its population to emigration:** Valentina Romei, "Eastern Europe Has the Largest Population Loss in Modern History," *Financial Times*, May 27, 2016, https://www.ft.com/content/70813826-0c64-33d3-8a0c-72059ae1b5e3.

4   **much of southern and western Europe has been subreplacement for decades:** United Nations Department of Economic and Social Affairs (UN DESA), "World Population Prospects: The 2015 Revision, Key Findings and Advance Tables," Working Paper no. ESA/P/WP.241 (New York: UN DESA, Population Division, 2015), https://esa.un.org/unpd/wpp/Publications/Files/Key_Findings_WPP_2015.pdf.

4   **so would be the United States, with its fertility rate of 1.9:** The World Bank, "Fertility Rate, Total (Births per Woman)," *World Bank*, 2014, http://data.worldbank.org/indicator /SP.DYN.TFRT.IN?

4   **first-generation immigrants tend to have:** Robert A. Hummer and Mark D. Hayward, "Hispanic Older Adult Health & Longevity in the United States: Current Patterns & Concerns for the Future," *Daedalus* 144, no. 2 (2015): 20–30.

4   **the only high-income nation:** UN DESA, "World Population Prospects," 4: "During 2015–2050, half of the world's population growth is expected to be concentrated in nine countries: India, Nigeria, Pakistan, Democratic Republic of the Congo, Ethiopia, United Republic of Tanzania, United States of America, Indonesia and Uganda, listed according to the size of their contribution to the total growth."

5   **the world's old-age growth is currently coming from:** UN DESA, "World Population Ageing 2015" (New York: United Nations, 2015), http://www.un.org/en/development /desa/population/publications/pdf/ageing/WPA2015_Report.pdf.

5   **doubled from today's 8.5 percent to 16.7 percent:** He et al., "An Aging World: 2015."

5   **by immigration and relatively high birthrates:** The World Bank, "Population Ages 65 and Above (% of Total)," *World Bank*, 2015, http://data.worldbank.org/indicator/SP.POP .65UP.TO.ZS?locations=JP-US-BG-FI-DE-GR-IT-PT-SE.

5   **the United States will have joined the 20-percenters:** Jennifer M. Ortman, Victoria A. Velkoff, and Howard Hogan, "An Aging Nation: The Older Population in the United States" (Washington, DC: US Census Bureau, 2014), 25–1140.

6   **an astounding third of its population aged 65 and up:** Ibid.

7   **dance to languages to traditional flower arrangement:** Asako Sawanishi, "Karaoke Shops Offer Hobby Space to Win Back Business," *Japan Times,* November 22, 2012, http://www.japantimes.co.jp/culture/2012/11/22/music/karaoke-shops-offer-hobby -space-to-win-back-business/.

7   **more reading glasses than all other types of eyewear:** "Graying of Japan's Population Puts Older Set in Marketing Driver's Seat," *Nikkei Weekly,* November 2, 2009, 25.

7   **more adult diapers than baby diapers:** Yuki Yamaguchi, "Elderly at Record Spurs Japan Stores Chase $1.4 Trillion," *Bloomberg News,* May 9, 2012, http://www.bloomberg.com/ news/articles/2012-05-09/elderly-at-record-spurs-japan-stores-chase-1-4-trillion.

7   **taken place in the United States:** Carol Hymowitz and Lauren Coleman-Lochner, "Sales of Adult Incontinence Garments in the U.S. Could Equal Those of Baby Diapers in a Decade," *Bloomberg Businessweek,* February 11, 2016, http://www.bloomberg.com/news/ articles/2016-02-11/the-adult-diaper-market-is-about-to-take-off.

7   **spend only $29,500:** "The Grey Market," *The Economist,* April 9, 2016, http://www .economist.com/news/business/21696539-older-consumers-will-reshape-business -landscape-grey-market.

7   **worth of economic activity:** Oxford Economics and AARP, "The Longevity Economy: Generating Economic Growth and New Opportunities for Business," September 2016, http://www.aarp.org/content/dam/aarp/home-and-family/personal-technology/2016 /09/2016-Longevity-Economy-AARP.pdf.

8   **worldwide older-adult spending will reach $15 trillion:** Matthew Boyle, "Aging Boomers Stump Marketers Eyeing $15 Trillion Prize," September 17, 2013, https://www.bloomberg .com/news/articles/2013-09-17/aging-boomers-befuddle-marketers-eying-15-trillion -prize.

8   **and 86 percent of that of Germany:** J. W. Kuenen et al., "Global Aging, How Companies Can Adapt to the New Reality," *Boston Consulting Group*, 2011, https://www.bcg.com /documents/file93352.pdf.

8   **(with some going to estate taxes, charity, and estate clearing costs):** Oxford Economics and AARP, "The Longevity Economy."

8   **important to leave money to their heirs:** "2014 U.S. Trust Insights on Wealth and Worth Survey," *Bank of America Private Wealth Management,* 2014, http://www.ustrust.com /publish/content/application/pdf/GWMOL/USTp_AR4GWF53F_2015-06.pdf.

9　**business strategy focused on older adults:** "The Grey Market," *The Economist*.

9　**many marketers don't bother to cross:** David Wallis, "Selling Older Consumers Short," *AARP Bulletin*, October 2014, http://www.aarp.org/money/budgeting-saving/info-2014 /advertising-to-baby-boomers.html.

9　**cross-generational casting in commercials:** Braden Phillips, "Marketers Take Second Look at Over-50 Consumers," *New York Times*, March 4, 2016, http://www.nytimes .com/2016/03/06/business/retirementspecial/marketers-take-second-look-at-over-50 -consumers.html.

9　**more on millennials than on all other age groups combined:** Marty Swant, "Infographic: Marketers Are Spending 500% More on Millennials Than All Others: Combined Data from Turn Breaks Down Gen Y into 4 Groups," *Adweek*, November 17, 2015, http://www.adweek.com/news/technology/infographic-marketers-are-spending -500-more-millennials-all-others-combined-168176.

9　**"do not see advertising that reflects older consumers.":** "Global Consumers Highlight Opportunities for Retailers, Brand Marketers and Service Providers to Better Meet Needs of Aging Consumers," *Nielsen Press Room*, February 25, 2014, http://www.nielsen.com/gh/ en/press-room/2014/nielsen-global-consumers-highlight-opportunities-for-retailers -brand-marketers-and-service-providers-to-better-meet-needs-of-aging-consumers .html.

9　**contemporaries' portrayal unappealing and overly stereotypical:** Helen Davis, "Successful Aging: Advertising Finally Recognizing the 'Gray Dollar,'" *Los Angeles Daily News*, February 23, 2015, http://www.dailynews.com/health/20150223/successful -aging-advertising-finally-recognizing-the-gray-dollar.

10　**"people to be respected.":** "Advertising Targeting Older Adults: How the Audience Perceives the Message," *GlynnDevins*, August 2014, http://www.glynndevins.com/wp -content/uploads/2014/08/olderadults_brief.pdf.

10　**difficulties finding easy-to-open packaging:** "The Age Gap: As Global Population Skews Older, Its Needs Are Not Being Met," *Nielsen*, February 2014, http://www.nielsen .com/content/dam/nielsenglobal/kr/docs/global-report/2014/Nielsen%20Global% 20Aging%20Report%20February%202014.pdf.

11　**average consumer is nearly 50 years old:** Harley-Davidson stopped releasing its average buyer's age in 2009 when it had reached 48.

11　**popular among late-career road warriors:** "An unheralded truth about Harley-Davidson, [an industry analyst] said, is that the company is making design concessions on its more traditional products that reflect certain inevitabilities of the march of time. 'They've even begun making some adjustments on some of the bikes so that they will be more comfortable for older people, without being obvious that what they're trying to do is accommodate seniors.'" Steve Penhollow, "Harley-Davidson and the Quest for Female Customers," *Britton*, June 4, 2015, http://www.brittonmdg.com/the-britton-blog /Harley-Davidson-targeting-women-and-young-customers-in-marketing.

"Harley has worked hard on making its bikes easier to ride with controls that are more suited to manipulation by arthritic fingers, and lower seat heights that don't unduly stress worn-out knees and hips during the mounting up phase of riding." "A Harley-Davidson That's Born to Be Mild," *Stuff*, March 22, 2015, http://www.stuff.co.nz/motoring /bikes/67446988/a-harleydavidson-thats-born-to-be-mild.

"It's not just height . . . New handlebar design brings the controls two inches closer to the rider. Smaller hand grips 'reduce finger reach' to clutch and brake levers. A new 'toe tab extension' even makes it easier to reach the kickstand." Charles Fleming, "Harley-Davidson Reveals Electra Glide Ultra Classic Low, and More," *Los Angeles Times*, August 27, 2014, http://www.latimes.com/business/autos/la-fi-hy-harley-davidson-reveals-20140826-story .html.

12　**"Aging: The Next Ticking Time Bomb":** "Is the Aging of the Developed World A Ticking Time Bomb?" *International Economy* 18, no. 1 (Winter 2004): 6–19, http://www .international-economy.com/TIE_W04_Aging.pdf.

13   **will come to more than $200 trillion:** "I calculate that the 'fiscal gap'—a yardstick of total government indebtedness that I've worked on with the economists Alan J. Auerbach and Jagadeesh Gokhale—was $210 trillion last year, up from $205 trillion the previous year. Thus $5 trillion was the true deficit." Laurence J. Kotlikoff, "America's Hidden Credit Card Bill," *New York Times,* July 31, 2014, http://www.nytimes.com/2014/08/01/opinion /laurence-kotlikoff-on-fiscal-gap-accounting.html.

13   **a meaningless exercise:** Dean Baker, "Larry Kotlikoff Tells Us Why We Should Not Use Infinite Horizon Budget Accounting," *Center for Economic and Policy Research,* July 31, 2014, http://cepr.net/blogs/beat-the-press/larry-kotlikoff-tells-us-why-we-should-not-use -infinite-horizon-budget-accounting; and Paul Krugman, "Quadrillions and Quadrillions," *New York Times,* August 2, 2014, http://krugman.blogs.nytimes.com/2014/08/02 /quadrillions-and-quadrillions/.

14   **psychological well-being rises with every year of life after middle age:** Arthur A. Stone et al., "A Snapshot of the Age Distribution of Psychological Well-Being in the United States," *Proceedings of the National Academy of Sciences* 107, no. 22 (2010): 9985–9990.

14   **against older people is the norm:** "Specifically, both young and older participants have been found to associate 'pleasant' words more readily with pictures of younger adults than with pictures of older adults." Jennifer A. Richeson and J. Nicole Shelton, "A Social Psychological Perspective on the Stigmatization of Older Adults," in National Research Council (US) Committee on Aging Frontiers in Social Psychology, Personality, and Adult Developmental Psychology: *When I'm 64,* ed. L. L. Carstensen and C. R. Hartel (Washington, DC: National Academies Press, 2006), 174–208, https://www.ncbi.nlm .nih.gov/books/NBK83758/.

15   **81 percent of US deaths occur after the age of 65:** The World Bank, "Survival to Age 65, Male (% of Cohort)," *World Bank,* 2014, http://data.worldbank.org/indicator/SP.DYN .TO65.MA.ZS.

18   **rate of major dam construction has grown sixfold:** Will Steffen et al., "The Trajectory of the Anthropocene: The Great Acceleration," *Anthropocene Review* 2, no. 1 (2015): 81–98.

18   **mileage of paved roads has more than tripled:** The mileage of paved roads in the world has increased from 12 million miles in 1975 to more than 40 million in 2013. See Dale S. Rothman et al., *Building Global Infrastructure,* vol. 4 (Milton Park, Abingdon, UK: Routledge, 2015); and *The World Factbook* (Washington, DC: Central Intelligence Agency, continually updated), https://www.cia.gov/library/publications/the-world-factbook/fields/2085.html.

21   **higher-income groups generally live longer:** Raj Chetty et al., "The Association Between Income and Life Expectancy in the United States, 2001–2014," *Journal of the American Medical Association* 315, no. 16 (2016): 1750–1766.

21   **in 2014, life expectancy dropped for white women:** Kenneth D. Kochanek et al., "Deaths: Final Data for 2014," *National Vital Statistics Reports* 65, no. 4 (2016): 1; see also Anne Case and Angus Deaton, "Rising Morbidity and Mortality in Midlife Among White non -Hispanic Americans in the 21st Century," *Proceedings of the National Academy of Sciences* 112, no. 49 (2015): 15078–15083.

21   **less-educated groups are taking on major longevity losses:** National Academies of Sciences, Engineering, and Medicine, "The Growing Gap in Life Expectancy by Income: Implications for Federal Programs and Policy Responses" (Washington, DC: The National Academies Press, 2015).

21   **but enjoy better health in late life:** S. Jay Olshansky, "The Demographic Transformation of America," *Daedalus* 144, no. 2 (2015): 13–19.

Chapter 1: Vital Force

26   **the older body as fundamentally different from the young:** Older adults became "a separate class of patients requiring specific, age-related treatment." Carole Haber, *Beyond Sixty-Five* (Cambridge: Cambridge University Press, 1983), 57.

26 **biology, a term that had only been coined in 1802:** Hermione de Almeida, *Romantic Medicine and John Keats* (London: Oxford University Press), 63. [G. R. Treviranus, *Biologie: oder Philosophie der lebenden Natur,* vol. 1 (Göttingen: bey J. F. Röwer, 1802–1822).]

26 **loss of vitality created a "predisposing debility":** Esmond Ray Long, *A History of American Pathology* (Springfield, IL: Charles C. Thomas, 1962), 17, quoted in Haber, *Beyond Sixty-Five,* 5.

27 **writes historian Carole Haber:** Haber, *Beyond Sixty-Five.*

27 **more pressing question than the state of one's soul.":** Carolyn Thomas de la Peña, "Designing the Electric Body: Sexuality, Masculinity and the Electric Belt in America, 1880–1920," *Journal of Design History* 14, no. 4 (2001): 275–289, http://jdh.oxfordjournals.org/content/14/4/275.full.pdf.

28 **"extraordinary decline of corporeal powers," as one physician termed it:** John Mason Good, *The Study of Medicine* (New York: Harper & Brothers, 1835), quoted in Haber, *Beyond Sixty-Five,* 68.

28 **a doctor catalogued in 1899:** Veronica Harsh et al., "Reproductive Aging, Sex Steroids, and Mood Disorders," *Harvard Review of Psychiatry* 17, no. 2 (2009): 87–102, doi:10.1080/10673220902891877.

28 **tendency toward insanity," Haber writes:** Haber, *Beyond Sixty-Five,* 69.

29 **the same sort of insanity, differing only by degree:** Ibid., 75.

29 **and irreversible decay," Haber writes:** Ibid., 78.

29 **on the advanced age of the participants:** George M. Beard, *Legal Responsibility in Old Age* (New York: Russells' American Steam Printing House, 1874), 33, referenced in Haber, *Beyond Sixty-Five,* 77.

29 **"old people are no longer educable":** Sigmund Freud, "On Psychotherapy," in *Selected Papers on Hysteria and Other Psychoneuroses,* trans. A. A. Brill (New York: The Journal of Nervous and Mental Disease Publishing Company, 1912), http://www.bartleby.com/280/8.html.

29 **when he delivered this pronouncement:** Freud, who was born on May 6, 1856, first delivered his 1905 essay "On Psychology" in lecture form on December 12, 1904, to the Vienna Medicinisches Doktorenkollegium. See Sigmund Freud, "On Psychotherapy," in *Standard Edition of the Complete Works of Sigmund Freud,* vol. 7, trans. & ed. J. Strachey (London: Hogarth Press, 1953–1974), 257–268.

30 **"In the old man there is an organic craving for rest.":** T. S. Clouston, *Clinical Lectures on Mental Diseases* (London: J. & A. Churchill, 1892), 401–402, quoted in Haber, *Beyond Sixty-Five,* 79.

30 **writes critical gerontologist Bryan Green:** Bryan S. Green, *Gerontology and the Construction of Old Age* (New York: Aldine Transaction, 1993), 43.

31 **"population aging could be 'seen' in statistics and made a visible political problem.":** Ibid., 44.

31 **people start deciding what to do with you:** See Roger W. Cobb and Charles D. Elder, *Participation in American Politics: The Dynamics of Agenda-Building* (Boston: Allyn and Bacon, 1972), 12.

31 **"one of the great innovations in the techniques of power.":** Michel Foucault, *The History of Sexuality,* vol. 1, trans. R. Hurley (New York: Random House, 1978), quoted in Green, *Gerontology and the Construction of Old Age,* 44.

31 **and federal-level pension bill in the United States:** David Hackett Fischer, *Growing Old in America,* vol. 532 (Oxford: Oxford University Press, 1978), 157, in Greene, *Foundation of Gerontology,* 46.

31 **among adult groups claiming aid from tax revenues:** David A. Rochefort, *American Social Welfare Policy: Dynamics of Formulation and Change* (Boulder, CO: Westview, 1986), 66.

32 **a practice subsidized by local poor taxes:** Carole Haber and Brian Gratton, *Old Age and the Search for Security* (Bloomington: Indiana University Press, 1993), 118.

32 **what became known as "scientific charity":** Ibid., 70.

32   **more, on an individual basis, than outdoor relief:** Ibid., 135.

33   **Many others followed suit:** Ibid., 124.

33   **unemployment, a term first coined in 1887:** William Graebner, *A History of Retirement* (New Haven, CT: Yale University Press, 1980), 15–16.

34   **a phrase that likely descended from the Carleton poem:** The journal *American Speech* noted in 1958: "Not infrequently heard 40 or 50 years ago was the expression *over the hill to the poorhouse.* The Michigan-born Will Carleton (1845–1912) wrote a poem having that very expression as its title. Whether the title was the source of the expression or an echo of its use in common speech I do not know." In the usage examples the author provides for the term "over the hill" (sans poorhouse), early 20th-century instances use the term to mean "insolvent," but over time its meaning changes to "played out, exhausted" and finally "past the peak of one's powers." "The Hill," *American Speech* 33, no. 2 (1958): 69–72.

34   **87 percent of the money these plans paid out:** "Historical Background and Development of Social Security," *Social Security Administration,* http://www.ssa.gov/history/briefhistory3.html.

35   **how confused we are about what retirement really is:** Ruth Helman, Craig Copeland, and Jack VanDerhei, "The 2015 Retirement Confidence Survey: Having a Retirement Savings Plan a Key Factor in Americans' Retirement Confidence," Employee Benefit Research Institute Issue Brief 413 (2009), https://www.ebri.org/pdf/briefspdf/EBRI_IB_413_Apr15_RCS-2015.pdf.

35   **and the rest of the world followed suit:** Mary-Lou Weisman, "The History of Retirement," *New York Times,* March 21, 1999, http://www.nytimes.com/1999/03/21/jobs/the-history-of-retirement-from-early-man-to-aarp.html.

35   **when Bismarck was 74:** "Age 65 Retirement," *Social Security Administration,* http://www.ssa.gov/history/age65.html.

35   **18 years after his death:** "Otto von Bismarck," *Social Security Administration,* http://www.ssa.gov/history/ottob.html.

35   **immigrants and Confederate veterans weren't eligible:** Dora L. Costa, *The Evolution of Retirement: An American Economic History, 1880–1990* (Chicago, IL: The University of Chicago Press, 1998), 161.

36   **two-thirds disabled at 65, and fully disabled at 70:** Haber, *Beyond Sixty-Five,* 111–112.

36   **shall have been added to the pension list.":** "15 January 1907: Paragraph 13," in *Autobiography of Mark Twain, Volume 2,* 2013, http://www.marktwainproject.org/xtf/view?docId=works/MTDP10363.xml;style=work;brand=mtp;chunk.id=dv0089#pa002632.

36   **Union vets with pensions retired, while Confederates didn't:** Dora L. Costa, "Pensions and Retirement: Evidence from Union Army Veterans," *Quarterly Journal of Economics* 110, no. 2 (1995), 297–319, http://economics.sas.upenn.edu/~hfang/teaching/socialinsurance/readings/Costa95(6.19).pdf.

37   **chosen to work past "retirement age.":** Braedyn Kromer and David Howard, "Labor Force Participation and Work Status of People 6 Years and Older," American Community Survey Briefs (January 2013), https://www.census.gov/prod/2013pubs/acsbr11-09.pdf.

37   **the standard between 1885 and 1915:** Graebner, *A History of Retirement,* 19.

38   **"eliminates from its force inefficient men.":** Ibid., 32.

38   **"one of the best-known fallacies in economics.":** "Economics A–Z," *The Economist,* http://goo.gl/mSxBKo.

38   **tend to decrease overall economic efficiency:** Paul Krugman, "Lumps of Labor," *New York Times,* October 7, 2003, http://www.nytimes.com/2003/10/07/opinion/lumps-of-labor.html.

38   **population aging does not affect the employment of younger workers:** Nicole Maestas, Kathleen J. Mullen, and David Powell, "The Effect of Population Aging on Economic Growth, the Labor Force and Productivity," National Bureau of Economic Research No. w22452 (2016), http://www.nber.org/papers/w22452.

38   **even during the unemployment spike of the Great Recession:** Alicia H. Munnell and April Yanyuan Wu, "Are Aging Baby Boomers Squeezing Young Workers Out of Jobs?," Center for Retirement Research at Boston College Brief 12–18 (2012).

39   **younger job seekers armed with high school degrees:** Graebner, *A History of Retirement,* 18–19.

39   **dozens of firms were adding pension plans annually:** Ibid., 133.

39   **it wasn't enough to cover much of the population:** Ibid.

39   **lacked the income to support themselves:** "Historical Background and Development of Social Security," *Social Security Administration,* http://www.ssa.gov/history/briefhistory3.html.

41   **'a moral fervor that had all the earmarks of a religious revival.'":** Robert H. Nelson, *Economics as Religion: From Samuelson to Chicago and Beyond* (University Park, PA: Pennsylvania State University Press, 2002), 36.

41   **and have precedence over the older one.":** Annual Report of the Attorney General (Washington, DC: US Department of Justice, 1913), 10.

41   **would cramp overall innovation and efficiency:** Graebner, *A History of Retirement,* 124.

41   **age limits for new hires in place in the 1920s and 1930s:** Gregory Wood, "Forty Plus Clubs and White-Collar Manhood During the Great Depression," *Essays in Economic & Business History* 26, no. 1 (2008): 21–31.

41   **"We make 40 our deadline in taking on new people":** Ray Giles, "Hired After Forty," *Reader's Digest,* December 1938, 2–3, quoted in Wood, "Forty Plus Clubs," 23.

42   **ditched by employers just when they are the most capable.":** John Steven McGroarty, "Here Is an Idea to Think Over," *Old Age Revolving Pensions: A Proposed National Plan* (Long Beach, CA: Old Age Revolving Pensions, Inc., 1934), 12.

42   **stack of playing cards as high as the Empire State Building.":** Sharon Bertsch McGrayne, *Prometheans in the Lab: Chemistry and the Making of the Modern World* (New York: McGraw-Hill, 2001), 104.

43   **This one did a lot of living in a mighty little while:** Thomas Midgley IV, *From the Periodic Table to Production: The Life of Thomas Midgley, Jr., the Inventor of Ethyl Gasoline and Freon Refrigerants* (Corona, CA: Stargazer, 2001), 70.

43   **"same old dole under another name," FDR said:** Robert J. Samuelson, "Would Roosevelt Recognize Today's Social Security?," *Washington Post,* April 8, 2012, http://www.washingtonpost.com/opinions/would-roosevelt-recognize-todays-social-security/2012/04/08/gIQALChd4S_story.html.

44   **as he signed the 1935 Act into law:** Martha A. McSteen, "Fifty Years of Social Security," *Social Security Administration,* http://www.ssa.gov/history/50mm2.html.

44   **aren't a matter of economics, they're straight politics.":** Arthur M. Schlesinger Jr., *The Coming of the New Deal,* vol. 2 of *The Age of Roosevelt* (Boston, MA: Houghton Mifflin, 1988 [American Heritage Library edition]), 308–309; "Research Notes & Special Studies by the Historian's Office," *Social Security Administration,* http://www.ssa.gov/history/Gulick.html.

45   **US Office of Scientific Research and Development during World War II:** Midgley, *From the Periodic Table to Production,* 70.

47   **from hardening of the judicial arteries.":** Franklin D. Roosevelt, Fireside Chat, March 9, 1937. The American Presidency Project, University of California, Santa Barbara, http://www.presidency.ucsb.edu/ws/?pid=15381.

47   **where he was a known antagonist of the president:** Marian C. McKenna, *Franklin Roosevelt and the Great Constitutional War: The Court-Packing Crisis of 1937* (New York: Fordham University Press, 2002).

48   **could eventually get a bite at the Social Security apple:** "Chapter 6: Retirement Earnings Test," *Social Security Administration,* http://www.ssa.gov/history/pdf/80chap6.pdf.

50   **could one-up each other by offering generous pensions:** Graebner, *A History of Retirement,* 216.

50   **aimlessness on the frontier of consumption:** David Riesman, "Some Observations on Changes in Leisure Attitudes," *Antioch Review* 12, no. 4 (1952): 417–436, referenced in Graebner, *A History of Retirement,* 228.

51   **He wonders why he should have to retire at all:** Julius Hochman, "The Retirement Myth," in *Social Security: Problems, Programs, and Policies,* ed. William Haber and Wilbur J. Cohen (Homewood, IL: Richard D. Irwin, 1960), 98–109, http://archive.org/stream /socialsecurityp00habe/socialsecurityp00habe_djvu.txt.

51   **"we have to glamorize leisure as we have not.":** Graebner, *A History of Retirement,* 228.

52   **or will you miss your chance to have your dream come true?":** Hochman, "The Retirement Myth," 102.

52   **causing a traffic jam that extended far into the desert:** Andrew Blechman, *Leisureville: Adventures in a World without Children* (New York: Grove/Atlantic, 2009), 32.

54   **lead exposure likely compromised his immune health:** See Rodney R. Dietert and Michael S. Piepenbrink, "Lead and Immune Function," *Critical Reviews in Toxicology* 36, no. 4 (2006): 359–385.

54   **entwined in the ropes and pulleys attached to his bed, strangled to death:** Bill Bryson, *A Short History of Nearly Everything* (New York: Broadway Books, 2003), 152.

54   **responsible for many factory workers' deaths:** Jamie Lincoln Kitman, "The Secret History of Lead," *The Nation,* 270, no. 11 (2000), https://www.thenation.com/article /secret-history-lead/.

54   **some of the most potent greenhouse gases known:** Brett Israel, "Most Potent Greenhouse Gases Revealed," *LiveScience,* May 4, 2010, http://www.livescience.com /6416-potent-greenhouse-gases-revealed.html.

54   **"more impact on the atmosphere than any other single organism in Earth's history.":** J. R. McNeill, *Something New Under the Sun: An Environmental History of the Twentieth-Century World* (New York: Norton, 2001), 111.

Chapter 2: Myths

61   **such as the MIT's House of the Future project:** Daren Fonda, "Home Smart Home," *Boston Globe Magazine,* December 5, 1999, http://web.media.mit.edu/~kll/AA_Boston_ Globe_HomeSmartHome.pdf.

62   **and movement data to her doctor:** Tom Simonite, "Sleep Sensor Hides Beneath the Mattress," *MIT Technology Review,* November 9, 2011, http://www.technologyreview.com /news/426073/sleep-sensor-hides-beneath-the-mattress/.

63   **oldest-on-average major economy in the world after Japan:** 22.4 percent of Italy's population is over 65, according to 2015 World Bank data. The figure for Japan is 26.3 percent.

64   **"to become everything that one is capable of becoming.":** A. H. Maslow, "A Theory of Human Motivation," *Psychological Review* 50 (1943): 370–396, http://psychclassics.yorku .ca/Maslow/motivation.htm.

66   **who need hearing aids seek them out:** "Hearing Aids," *NIH Research Portfolio Online Reporting Tools,* https://report.nih.gov/nihfactsheets/viewfactsheet.aspx?csid=95.

66   **between 5 and 24 percent of hearing-aid owners:** Abby McCormack and Heather Fortnum, "Why Do People Fitted with Hearing Aids Not Wear Them?," *International Journal of Audiology* 52, no. 5 (2013): 360–368.

67   **adoption is only 14 percent higher than in the:** US Søren Hougaard and Stefan Ruf, "EuroTrak I: A Consumer Survey About Hearing Aids in Germany, France, and the UK," *Hearing Review* 18, no. 2 (2011): 12–28.

67   **Apple's own wireless earbuds, the AirPods:** Frank Swain, "This Is Why Apple Got Rid of the Headphone Jack on the iPhone 7," *New Scientist,* https://www.newscientist.com /article/2105229-this-is-why-apple-got-rid-of-the-headphone-jack-on-the-iphone-7.

69   **beef, lamb and chicken stews:** "Food for the Aged," *Time* 65, no. 24 (June 13, 1955): 94.

69   **Following World War II:** The Borden Company, "1946 Annual Report," University of Rochester Libraries, http://www.lib.rochester.edu:84/Mergent_AR_Collection /Archive/10999.pdf.

69   **milk-based nutritional supplement for older adults:** "Bulletin Board," *North Carolina Medical Journal* 8 (1947): 190, https://archive.org/stream/northcarolinamed81947medi /northcarolinamed81947medi_djvu.txt.

69   **its "pleasant, bland taste,":** "The Technical Exhibit," *Journal of the Florida Medical Association* 34, no. 4 (1947): 550, https://archive.org/stream/journalofflorida34unse /journalofflorida34unse_djvu.txt.

69   **economical because it doesn't have to be mixed with milk."):** "What Aid for the Lean Purse?," *Texas State Journal of Medicine* 44, no. 3 (1948): 30, http://texashistory.unt.edu /ark:/67531/metapth599853/m1/30/.

70   **spent nearly a decade developing Senior Foods:** "Geriatric Foods Are Tested Here," *St. Petersburg Times,* September 22, 1955, https://news.google.com/newspapers?nid=888& dat=19550922&id=kWJSAAAAIBAJ&sjid=eHoDAAAAIBAJ&pg=7287,3130346&hl=en.

70   **arranged in pinwheel fashion.":** Ibid.

70   **a classic example of brand failure:** Dina Spector, "11 Biggest Food Flops of All Time," *Business Insider,* January 12, 2012, http://www.businessinsider.com/food-failures-2012-1?op-1.

71   **"lighter, quieter, and thriftier.":** "1958 DeSoto TV Presentation with Groucho Marx," YouTube, https://www.youtube.com/watch?v=f53BJ_zZ17c.

71   **third-largest auto manufacturer in the United States:** Jerry M. Flint, "Chrysler's Beat Goes On and On and On," *New York Times,* August 10, 1968, L33.

71   **cartoonish in appearance as the 1950s drew to a close.):** Townsend's cars were "more willfully designed and better built" than any recent offerings, write Robert B. Reich and Harvard policy expert John Donahue in *New Deals: The Chrysler Revival and the American System* (London: Penguin Books, 1986), 18. In the process, Chrysler underwent an "impressive metamorphosis from a stodgy purveyor of 'practical' transportation to a full-line car company with modern designs and a refurbished image."

72   **no longer "old man's cars" took off:** Terry Parkhurst, "Lynn A. Townsend, President of Chrysler Corporation in the 1960s and 1970s," *Allpar,* http://www.allpar.com/corporate /bios/townsend.html.

72   **General Motors' rose by 9 percent:** Joel Cutcher-Gershenfeld, Dan Brooks, and Martin Mulloy, "The Decline and Resurgence of the US Auto Industry," *Economic Policy Institute,* http://www.epi.org/publication/the-decline-and-resurgence-of-the-u-s-auto-industry/.

72   **the company's net earnings increased from $11 million to $233 million:** Charles K. Hyde, *Riding the Roller Coaster: A History of the Chrysler Corporation* (Detroit, MI: Wayne State University Press, 2003), 196.

73   **only 1 percent of the 65-plus population used the technology:** Jasmine Lau, "Building a National Technology and Innovation Infrastructure for an Aging Society" (master's thesis, Technology and Public Policy Program, MIT, 2006).

74   **only 35 percent of people over 75 said they felt "old.":** "Growing Old in America: Expectations vs. Reality," *Pew Research Center,* June 29, 2009, http://www.pewsocialtrends .org/2009/06/29/growing-old-in-america-expectations-vs-reality/.

74   **devices to summon help 83 percent of the time:** B. Heinbüchner et al., "Satisfaction and Use of Personal Emergency Response Systems," *Zeitschrift für Gerontologie und Geriatrie* 43, no. 4 (2010): 219–223.

75   **77 percent of US residents aged 65 and up own cell phones:** Aaron Smith, "Older Adults and Technology Use: Adoption Is Increasing, But Many Seniors Remain Isolated from Digital Life," *Pew Research Center,* April 3, 2014, http://www.pewinternet.org/2014/04/03 /older-adults-and-technology-use/.

75   **"gigantisch," said German magazine *Focus*:** "Katharina das Große: Auf die Größe kommt es an," *Online Focus,* http://www.focus.de/digital/handy/handyvergleich/tid-11525 /senioren-handys-katharina-das-grosse-auf-die-groesse-kommt-es-an_aid_325898.html.

75 **In 2010, Fitage went out of business:** "Fitage Seniorenhandys," *Senioren-handy.info,* http://www.senioren-handy.info/seniorenhandy/fitage/.

76 **In 2000, only 14 percent of older Americans used the Internet:** Kathryn Zickuhr and Mary Madden, "Older Adults and Internet Use," *Pew Research Center,* June 6, 2012, 4, http://www.pewinternet.org/files/old-media/Files/Reports/2012/PIP_Older_adults_and _internet_use.pdf.

76 **and it continues to climb:** Aaron Smith, "Older Adults and Technology Use," *Pew Research Center,* April 3, 2014, http://www.pewinternet.org/2014/04/03/older -adults-and-technology-use/.

76 **as do 30 percent of those 65 and older:** Monica Anderson, "The Demographics of Device Ownership," *Pew Research Center,* October 29, 2015, http://www.pewinternet .org/2015/10/29/the-demographics-of-device-ownership/.

76 **more than double what they were five years earlier:** Aaron Smith, "35% of American Adults Own a Smartphone," *Pew Research Center,* July 11, 2011, http://www.pewinternet .org/files/old-media/Files/Reports/2011/PIP_Smartphones.pdf.

76 **compared with 64 percent of those in their late teens and early 20s:** Monica Anderson, "For Vast Majority of Seniors Who Own One, a Smartphone Equals Freedom," *Pew Research Center,* April 29, 2015, http://www.pewresearch.org/fact-tank/2015/04/29 /seniors-smartphones/

77 **is a normal part of aging:** "Alzheimer's News 6/19/2014," *Alzheimer's Association,* http:// www.alz.org/news_and_events_60_percent_incorrectly_believe.asp.

77 **two-thirds of people don't have dementia:** Among eight large epidemiological studies, estimates of dementia rates among the 85-plus ranged from 18 to 38 percent. See Racquel C. Gardner, Victor Valcour, and Kristine Yaffe, "Dementia in the Oldest Old: A Multi-factorial and Growing Public Health Issue," *Alzheimer's Research and Therapy* 5, no. 27 (2013), doi:10.1186/alzrt181; and "2015 Alzheimer's Disease Facts and Figures," *Alzheimer's Association,* 16, http://www.alz.org/facts/downloads/facts_figures_2015.pdf.

79 **top tech companies between 2014 and 2015:** "PayScale Compares Top Tech Companies," *Payscale.com,* http://www.payscale.com/data-packages/top-tech-companies-compared. Data were collected between January 2014 and December 2015.

79 **overall US workforce, meanwhile, is 42.3:** "Labor Force Statistics from the Current Population Survey," *Bureau of Labor Statistics,* last modified February 10, 2016, https://www .bls.gov/cps/cpsaat11b.htm.

79 **His hair pattern isn't even established," the surgeon said:** Noam Scheiber, "The Brutal Ageism of Tech."

79 **could "be tricked by anyone who looks like Mark Zuckerberg.":** Kristen V. Brown, "Inside Silicon Valley's Cult of Youth," *SFGate,* May 4, 2014, http://www.sfgate.com/news /article/Inside-Silicon-Valley-s-cult-of-youth-5451375.php.

80 **smaller than that available to younger entrepreneurs:** According to a recent survey by the Kauffman Foundation, referenced in Cheryl Connor, "Do Older or Younger Entrepreneurs Have a Greater Advantage?," *Forbes,* September 9, 2012, http://www.forbes .com/sites/cherylsnappconner/2012/09/03/do-older-or-younger-entrepreneurs-have-the -greater-advantage/#715852b83377.

80 **banned overt workplace age discrimination in 2010:** Bae Ji-sook, "Age Discrimination at Work to Be Banned," *Korea Times,* September 18, 2007, http://www.koreatimes.co.kr /www/news/nation/2007/09/113_10396.html.

80 **the practice has proven difficult to eject:** Jane Han, "Despite Ban, Age Still Matters in Hiring," *Korea Times,* April 15, 2009, http://www.koreatimes.co.kr/www/news /biz/2015/08/123_43249.html.

81 **the "pursuit of meaningful activity" for older adults:** Older Americans Act of 1965, 89th United States Congress, 1st Session, https://en.wikisource.org/wiki/Older_Americans _Act_of_1965#Sec._101._Declaration_of_Objectives_for_Older_Americans.

82 **Medicare, meanwhile, received one billion dollars:** David Rochefort, *American Social Welfare Policy: Dynamics of Formulation and Change* (Boulder, CO: Westview Press, 1986), 91.

82 **vital post of Minister for Ageing during his two years in office:** Everald Comptom, "Turnbull's Cabinet Must Include a Minister for Ageing," *ABC News Australia*, September 17, 2015, http://www.abc.net.au/news/2015-09-18/compton-turnbull's-cabinet -must-include-a-minister-for-ageing/6783774.

82 **"special policies and programs segregate and stigmatize the aged.":** Carroll L. Estes, *The Aging Enterprise* (San Francisco, CA: Jossey-Bass, 1979), 17.

Chapter 3: The Future Is Female

90 **they wield far greater sway:** Michael J. Silverstein and Kate Sayre, *Women Want More: How to Capture Your Share of the World's Largest, Fastest-Growing Market* (New York: HarperCollins, 2009), excerpted online via the Boston Consulting Group, https://www.bcgperspectives.com/content/articles/consumer_products _marketing_sales_women_want_more_excerpt/.

90 **where between $5 trillion to $15 trillion goes every year:** "US Women Control the Purse Strings," *Nielsen*, April 2, 2013, http://www.nielsen.com/us/en /insights/news/2013/u-s--women-control-the-purse-strings.html.

90 **For those 85 and over, that number drops to 60:** "Population by Age and Sex: 2012," *US Census Bureau*, http://www.census.gov/population/age/data/2012comp .html; refer to Table 1.

90 **for every 100 women in Russia over age 64 there are just 44 men:** According to 2014 data assembled by the CIA's *World Factbook*, there are an estimated 5,783,983 men and 13,105,896 women in Russia aged 65 and over. "Central Asia: Russia," *The World Factbook*, https://www.cia.gov/library/publications/the -world-factbook/geos/print/country/countrypdf_rs.pdf.

90 **solely from their family and friends:** "Women and Caregiving: Facts and Figures," *Family Caregiver Alliance*, https://www.caregiver.org/women-and-caregiv ing-facts-and-figures.

91 **more time providing care than caregiving men:** Ibid.

91 **that child is usually a daughter:** On average, this woman is 48 years old and employed; the average caregiver of the oldest-old is a 58-year-old unemployed woman. "Caregivers of Older Adults: A Focused Look at Those Caring for Someone Age 50+," *AARP Public Policy Institute and the National Alliance for Caregiving*, June 2015, p. 51, fig. 64, http://www.aarp.org/content/dam/aarp /ppi/2015/caregivers-of-older-adults-focused-look.pdf.

91 **80 percent are women:** Yoshiaki Nohara, "A Woman's Job in Japan: Watch Kids, Care for Parents, Work Late," *Japan Times*, May 11, 2015, http://www .japantimes.co.jp/news/2015/05/11/national/social-issues/womans-job-japan -watch-kids-care-parents-work-late/#.VzXjNxUrKV4.

91 **provide as much as two-thirds of all informal eldercare:** Frederique Hoffman and Ricardo Rodriguez, "Informal Carers: Who Takes Care of Them?," European Centre Policy Brief, April 2010, p. 4, fig. 3, http://www.euro.centre.org /data/1274190382_99603.pdf.

93 **tech-oriented parts of Google's workforce:** "Google Diversity," *Google*, http://www .google.com/diversity/index.html#chart.

93 **by contrast, is just 55 percent male:** Josh Harkinson, "Silicon Valley Firms Are Even Whiter Than You Thought," *Mother Jones*, May 29, 2014, http://www .motherjones.com/media/2014/05/google-diversity-labor-gender-race-gap -workers-silicon-valley.

93   **3 percent of all venture-backed tech companies have female CEOs:** Candida
     G. Brush et al., "Women Entrepreneurs 2014: Bridging the Gender Gap in Ven-
     ture Capital," *Arthur M. Blank Center for Entrepreneurship, Babson College,* Septem-
     ber   2014,   http://www.babson.edu/Academics/centers/blank-center/global-research
     /diana/Documents/diana-project-executive-summary-2014.pdf.

93   **just 11 percent of all executive positions:** David A. Bell and Shulamite Shen White, "Gen-
     der Diversity in Silicon Valley," *Fenwick and West LLP,* 2014, 13, http://www.fenwick.com
     /FenwickDocuments/Gender_Diversity_2014.pdf.

93   **but even obscure ones, like chromium intake:** Rose Eveleth, "How
     Self-Tracking Apps Exclude Women," *The Atlantic,* December 14, 2014, http://
     www.theatlantic.com/technology/archive/2014/12/how-self-tracking-apps
     -exclude-women/383673/?single_page=true.

94   **you're shit out of luck.":** Arielle Duhaime-Ross, "Apple Promised an Expansive
     Health App, So Why Can't I Track Menstruation?," *The Verge,* September 24,
     2014, http://www.theverge.com/2014/9/25/6844021/apple-promised-an-expansive-health
     -app-so-why-cant-i-track.

94   **even when the rest of the menus are alphabetical.":** Eveleth, "How Self-Tracking Apps
     Exclude Women."

94   **3 percent of creative directors at marketing firms are women:** Lydia Dishman, "Where
     Are All the Women Creative Directors?," *Fast Company,* February 26, 2013, http://www.fast-
     company.com/3006255/where-are-all-women-creative-directors.

97   **Women were *planning* to grow old:** The AgeLab conducted this research in 2014 using a
     pool of 29 participants from the Greater Boston area.

97   **and early 1990s at about 11 percent:** "Labor Force Participation of Seniors,
     1948–2007," *Bureau of Labor Statistics,* July 29, 2008, http://www.bls.gov/opub
     /ted/2008/jul/wk4/art02.htm.

97   **expects will increase to nearly 22 percent by 2024:** "Labor Force Projec-
     tions to 2024: The Labor Force Is Growing, but Slowly," *Bureau of Labor Statis-
     tics,* December 2015, http://www.bls.gov/opub/mlr/2015/article/labor-force-projec
     tions-to-2024.htm.

97   **faster than those of men for every older age segment:** Derived by comparing US Census
     data from 1990 and 2010.

98   **remain in the work force," the study's authors write:** Barry Bosworth and Kathleen
     Burke, "Changing Sources of Income among the Aged Population," Center for Retirement
     Research at Boston College Working Paper 2012-27 (2012).

98   **activities like bathing, toileting, and dressing:** "Female caregivers are more likely
     than men to help with grooming—getting dressed (36% vs. 24%) and bath-
     ing (31% vs. 17%)." See "Caregiving in the US," *National Alliance for Caregiving
     and AARP,* November 2009, http://assets.aarp.org/rgcenter/il/caregiving_09
     _es.pdf.

101 **the rate among the 50-plus doubled:** Susan L. Brown and I-Fen Lin, "The Gray
     Divorce Revolution: Rising Divorce among Middle-Aged and Older Adults,
     1990–2010," National Center for Family & Marriage Research, Working Paper
     Series WP-13-03, March 2013, https://www.bgsu.edu/content/dam/BGSU/college
     -of-arts-and-sciences/NCFMR/documents/Lin/The-Gray-Divorce.pdf.

101 **usually the woman who initiates these divorces:** Ibid., 75.

102 **has been rising steadily since 1970:** Wendy Wang and Kim Parker, "Record
     Share of Americans Have Never Married," *Pew Research Center,* September 24,
     2014, http://www.pewsocialtrends.org/2014/09/24/record-share-of-americans-have
     -never-married/.

105 **complicated 'downloading' procedures and 'human agency and choice.'":**
     Lindy West, "'Tablet for Women' Is Like a Regular Tablet, But More Fucking

Bullshitty," *Jezebel*, March 13, 2013, http://jezebel.com/5990404/tablet-for-women-is-like-a-regular-tablet-but-more-fucking-bullshitty?tag=sexism.

105 **"the sun's crone-inducing rays.":** Susan Krashinsky, "Surge in Gender-Targeted Products Creates Marketing Headaches for Companies," 2012, *The Globe and Mail*, http://www.theglobeandmail.com/report-on-business/industry-news/marketing/surge-in-gender-targeted-products-creates-marketing-headaches-for-companies/article5358521/.

105 **it spent only two years on the market:** Kat Callahan, "The Honda Fit *She's* Should Never Have Existed and It's Already Dead," *Jalopnik*, September 20, 2014, http://jalopnik.com/the-honda-fit-shes-should-never-have-existed-and-is-alr-1634318607.

106 **Faster for whom?":** Ruth Schwartz Cowan, *More Work for Mother: The Ironies of Household Technology from the Open Hearth to the Microwave* (New York: Basic Books, 1983), 12.

106 **that others were able to achieve.":** Ibid., 192.

106 **as liberating, rather than oppressive agents," she writes:** Ibid., 190–191.

109 **Christensen's 2003 book, *The Innovator's Solution*:** Clayton M. Christensen and Michael Raynor, *The Innovator's Solution: Creating and Sustaining Successful Growth* (Boston, MA: Harvard Business Review Press, 2013), 74–78.

110 **the job they were hiring the milk shake to do.":** Clayton M. Christensen, Scott Cook, and Taddy Hall, "What Customers Want from Your Products," *Harvard Business School*, January 16, 2006, http://hbswk.hbs.edu/item/what-customers-want-from-your-products.

111 **Overnight, the way people blow their noses changed—forever:** "Disposable Facial Tissues Story," *Kleenex*, http://www.cms.kimberly-clark.com/umbraco images/UmbracoFileMedia/ProductEvol_FacialTissue_umbracoFile.pdf.

112 **an article I coauthored with Luke Yoquinto for the *Washington Post*:** Luke Yoquinto and Joseph F. Coughlin, "The On-Demand Economy: Changing the Way We Live as We Age," *Washington Post*, December 14, 2015.

114 **a figure that will grow rapidly in the coming decades:** Charles Colby and Kelly Bell, "The On-Demand Economy Is Growing, and Not Just for the Young and Wealthy," *Harvard Business Review*, April 14, 2016, https://hbr.org/2016/04/the-on-demand-economy-is-growing-and-not-just-for-the-young-and-wealthy.

115 **Nearly two-thirds of these older hosts are women:** Jelisa Castrodale, "Why an Older Woman May Be Your Next Airbnb Host," *USA Today*, March 31, 2016, http://www.usatoday.com/story/travel/roadwarriorvoices/2016/03/31/airbnb-hosts-women-seniors/82462120/; and "Airbnb's Growing Community of 60+ Women Hosts," *Airbnb*, https://www.airbnbaction.com/wp-content/uploads/2016/03/Airbnb_60_Plus_Women_Report.pdf.

115 **to make money was to take on boarders in their homes:** "Between the mid-nineteenth century and 1930, older people became increasingly likely to live in homes they owned and the most likely among all age groups to own this real estate mortgage free . . . In cities they could also choose to open their homes to renters and, as keepers of boarding and lodging houses, use their property to provide for themselves." Haber and Gratton, *Old Age and the Search For Security*, 80.

116 **One-quarter of Uber's drivers are now 50 or older:** Elizabeth Olson, "Older Drivers Hit the Road for Uber and Lyft," *New York Times*, January 22, 2016, http://www.nytimes.com/2016/01/23/your-money/older-drivers-hit-the-road-for-uber-and-lyft.html?_r=0.

116 **is *absolutely essential* to millions:** "Meals on Wheels is estimated to serve just a third or so of the 25 million people over 60 who are poor or near poor." Jeanne Sahadi, "Meals on Wheels Budget Cuts: 'Slowly Developing Crisis,'" *CNN*, May 6, 2013, http://money.cnn.com/2013/05/06/news/economy/meals-on-wheels-budget-cuts/.

116   **"never having the motivation and energy to go to the store":** Farhad Manjoo, "Grocery Deliveries in Sharing Economy," *New York Times*, May 21, 2014, http://www.nytimes.com/2014/05/22/technology/personaltech/online-grocery-start-up-takes-page-from-sharing-services.html?_r=0.

118   **"until you show it to them":** Owen Linzmayer, "Steve Jobs' Best Quotes Ever," *Wired*, March 29, 2016, http://archive.wired.com/gadgets/mac/commentary/cultofmac/2006/03/70512?currentPage=all.

120   **(making them lead-user *innovators*):** This is a good resource on the lead-user concept: Joan Churchill, Eric von Hippel, and Mary Sonnack, "Lead User Project Handbook," Creative Commons license, https://evhippel.files.wordpress.com/2013/08/lead-user-project-handbook-full-version.pdf. The idea originates with Eric von Hippel, "Lead Users: A Source of Novel Product Concepts," *Management Science* 32, no. 7 (July 1986): 791–805.

120   **von Hippel's book, *Democratizing Innovation*:** Arun Sundararajan, *The Sharing Economy* (Cambridge, MA: MIT Press, 2016); see also Eric von Hippel, *Democratizing Innovation* (Cambridge, MA: MIT Press, 2005).

120   **the next thing that they would need to measure:** Eric von Hippel, "The Dominant Role of Users in the Scientific Instrument Innovation Process," *Research Policy* 5, no. 3 (July 1976): 212–239.

120   **while playing in hot, dehydrating conditions:** Churchill et al., "Lead User Project Handbook."

121   **in the coming 5–10 years:** Cal Halvorsen, "Encore Entrepreneurs: Creating Jobs, Meeting Needs," Encore.org, 2011, http://encore.org/blogs/encore-entrepreneurs-creating-jobs-meeting-needs/.

121   **highest rate of any age group of opportunity entrepreneurship:** Robert W. Fairlie et al., "The Kauffman Index: Startup Activity: National Trends," *Ewing Marion Kauffman Foundation*, 2015, http://www.kauffman.org/~/media/kauffman_org/research%20reports%20and%20covers/2015/05/kauffman_index_startup_activity_national_trends_2015.pdf.

123   **Abe's officials halved the target figure:** Kevin Rafferty, "Why Abe's 'Womenomics' Program Isn't Working," *Japan Times*, December 31, 2015, http://www.japantimes.co.jp/opinion/2015/12/31/commentary/japan-commentary/abes-womenomics-program-isnt-working/#.VzY37RUrJE6.

124   **"the mother of all undervalued opportunities":** Noam Scheiber, "The Brutal Ageism of Tech," *New Republic*, March 23, 2014, https://newrepublic.com/article/117088/silicons-valleys-brutal-ageism.

128   **First described in 1995 by Clayton Christensen:** Joseph L. Bower and Clayton M. Christensen, "Disruptive Technologies: Catching the Wave," *Harvard Business Review*, January 1995, https://hbr.org/1995/01/disruptive-technologies-catching-the-wave.

128   **a truly subcompact car until 1978:** Charles K. Hyde, *Riding the Roller Coaster: A History of the Chrysler Corporation* (Detroit, MI: Wayne State University Press, 2003), 211.

129   **Christensen has recently written:** Clayton M. Christensen, Michael E. Raynor, and Rory McDonald, "What Is Disruptive Innovation?," *Harvard Business Review*, December 2015, https://hbr.org/2015/12/what-is-disruptive-innovation.

131   **to fund their professional goals:** Leo Lewis, "Female Entrepreneurs Flock to Crowdfunding Site in Japan," *Financial Times*, January 7, 2016, https://next.ft.com/content/626d26dc-b531-11e5-8358-9a82b43f6b2f (subscription required).

Chapter 4: A Tale of Two Villages

134   **than any other one place in the world:** Kathryn Deen, "Checking In," *The Villages Magazine*, March 2016, 2.

134 **over 50,000 standalone houses:** Jennifer Brooks, "For Florida's Happy Minne-
sotans, It Takes a Village," *Star Tribune,* May 5, 2014, http://www.startribune
.com/for-florida-s-happy-minnesotans-it-takes-a-village/257818691/.

134 **totaling over 100 miles of asphalt:** Raf Sanchez, "The Strange World of Florida's Golf Cart City, The Villages," *The Telegraph,* January 11, 2015, http://www
.telegraph.co.uk/news/worldnews/northamerica/usa/11337620/The-strange
-world-of-Floridas-golf-cart-city-The-Villages.html.

135 **the golf carts, 50,000 strong:** Charles Hatcher, "How Safe Is It to Drive Golf
Carts in The Villages?," *WUFT News,* February 29, 2016, http://www.wuft.org
/news/2016/02/29/how-safe-is-it-to-drive-golf-carts-in-the-villages/.

135 *Guinness Book of World Records:* "Largest Parade of Golf Carts," *Guinness
World Records,* http://www.guinnessworldrecords.com/world-records/largest-parade
-of-golf-carts/.

135 **nearly 124,000 people live there:** Kathryn Deen, "Ken Ezell: The Men Behind the Greens,"
The Villages Magazine, March 2016, 46.

135 **for four years running:** "Maricopa County Added Over 222 People per Day in 2016, More
Than Any Other County," *US Census Bureau,* March 23, 2017, https://www.census.gov
/newsroom/press-releases/2017/cb17-44.html;
Tribune News Services, "The Villages, Florida, Is Fastest Growing Metro Area in
U.S.," *Chicago Tribune,* March 24, 2016, http://www.chicagotribune.com/news/local
/breaking/ct-census-fastest-growing-metro-area-20160324-story.html.

135 **nearly 1 percent of the nation's total:** "The President's Message—Phenomenon
of the Villages," *The Villages Homeowners' Association,* http://www.thevha.net
/?voice-articles=february-2012.

135 **sunny, Margaritaville-themed retirement communities:** Emily Sweeney, "Jimmy Buffet
to Open 'Margaritaville' Retirement Homes," *Boston Globe,* March 10, 2017, https://www.
bostonglobe.com/lifestyle/names/2017/03/10/jimmy-buffett-open-margaritaville-retire-
ment-homes/wKZmWJdCsd5vxWwost3tBO/story.html.

137 **as would 71 percent of those aged 50–64:** Rodney Harrell et al., "What Is Livable? Community Preferences of Older Adults," *AARP Public Policy Institute,* 8, http://www.aarp.
org/content/dam/aarp/research/public_policy_institute/liv_com/2014/what-is-livable-
report-AARP-ppi-liv-com.pdf.

138 **the duo had sold only 400 units:** All Villages' historical facts can be found in Andrew
Blechman, *Leisureville: Adventures in a World Without Children* (New York: Grove/Atlan-
tic, 2009).

139 **discounted greens fees to residents:** "Executive Golf," *The Villages,* https://www.thevil-
lages.com/golf/executive/executive.htm; "Championship Golf," *The Villages,* https://www
.thevillages.com/golf/championship/championship.htm.

140 **a dedicated Recreation Department:** "Enjoy Our Country Club Lifestyle," *The Villages,*
https://www.thevillages.com/images/CostofLiving.pdf.

141 **his 1952 essay on leisure and consumerism:** David Riesman, "Some Observations on
Changes in Leisure Attitudes," *Antioch Review* 12, no. 4 (1952): 417–436, referenced in
Graebner, *A History of Retirement,* 228.

142 **which spiked in the late aughts:** Marni Jameson, "Seniors' Sex Lives Are Up—
and So Are STD Cases Around the Country," *Orlando Sentinel,* May 16, 2011,
http://articles.orlandosentinel.com/2011-05-16/health/os-seniors-stds-national
-20110516_1_std-cases-syphilis-and-chlamydia-older-adults.

143 **serve as pro-Villages marketing:** Brendan Coffey, "Billionaire Morse Behind
Curtain at Villages," *Bloomberg,* June 4, 2012, http://www.bloomberg.com/news
/articles/2012-06-04/hidden-billionaire-morse-a-man-behind-curtain-at-villages.

143 **the newspaper's monthly magazine supplement:** Kathryn Deen, "25 Years of Hometown
Banking," *The Villages Magazine,* July 2016.

143 **Andrew Blechman's book *Leisureville*:** Blechman, *Leisureville.*

149   **"NO KIDS":** Meghan McRoberts, "Bhaskar Barot: Grandfather's Cars Van-
        dalized Over Having Granddaughter Visit," *WPTV News,* November 14, 2013,
        http://www.wptv.com/news/state/bhaskar-barot-grandfathers-cars-vandalized
        -over-having-granddaughter-visit; Ted White, "Vero Beach Couple Angry After
        Someone Spray-Paints 'No Kids' on Car, Minivan," *WPBF News,* November
        14, 2013, http://www.wpbf.com/news/south-florida/treasure-coast-news/vero-beach
        -couple-angry-after-someone-spraypaints-no-kids-on-car-minivan/22976138.

149   **"they take your skateboard away anyway":** Blechman, *Leisureville,* 156.

150   **housing discrimination in the United States:** According to the US Department of Hous-
        ing and Urban Development, "The 1968 Fair Housing Act . . . protects all residents from
        discrimination on the basis of race, color, national origin, religion, sex, handicap or famil-
        ial status (families with children under the age of 18 living with parents or legal guard-
        ians; pregnant women and people trying to get custody of children under 18) . . . The
        Fair Housing Act specifically exempts some senior housing facilities and communities
        from liability for familial status discrimination. Exempt senior housing facilities or com-
        munities can lawfully refuse to sell or rent dwellings to families with minor children."
        Refer to "Senior Housing: What You Should Know . . . ," *US Department of Housing and
        Urban Development,* http://portal.hud.gov/hudportal/HUD?src=/program_offices/fair
        _housing_equal_opp/seniors.

151   **immigrant families tend to have higher birth rates:** "Chapter 2: Immigration's Impact on
        Past and Future U.S. Population Change," *Pew Research Center,* September 28, 2015, http://
        www.pewhispanic.org/2015/09/28/chapter-2-immigrations-impact-on-past-and-fu-
        ture-u-s-population-change/; "2014 World Population Data Sheet," *Population Reference
        Bureau,* August 2014, http://www.prb.org/Publications/Datasheets/2014/2014-world-pop-
        ulation-data-sheet/data-sheet.aspx.
        Continental total fertility rates (TFRs) from the 2014 World Population Data Sheet:

North America
The United States and Canada have rather low TFRs: Canada at 1.6 and the United States
at 1.9. In the United States, fertility declined during the recent economic recession, a
decline that was especially sharp among Hispanics. Immigration is a significant engine of
population growth in both countries.
Europe
Europe's birth rate has plummeted to an unexpectedly low level in the past few decades.
Europe's population of 740 million is projected to decrease to 726 million by 2050, but
even that lower number depends on whether immigration helps to stall a more-rapid
decline. Today, women in Europe average only 1.6 children, compared to 2.3 in 1970. This
low fertility has created unprecedented aging. In Europe, only 16 percent of the population
is below age 15. Compare that to 41 percent in Africa and 25 percent in Asia. Europe's
population ages 65 and older is projected to rise to 27 percent by 2050.
Oceania
In Australia and New Zealand, continued growth from higher birth rates and immigration
is expected. Australia's TFR is 1.9; New Zealand's, 2.0. Australia's population of 24 million
is expected to increase to 36 million by 2050; New Zealand's population will increase from
4.3 million to 5.5 million.

151   **disappears by the second generation:** Robert A. Hummer and Mark D. Hayward, "His-
        panic Older Adult Health & Longevity in the United States: Current Patterns & Concerns
        for the Future," *Daedalus* 144, no. 2 (2015): 20–30.

151   **the school-age population is black or Latino:** "Our estimates indicate that school dis-
        tricts with increasing shares of elderly adults are more likely to cut their revenues and
        spending when the children are relatively nonwhite than they are when the school-aged

children are relatively white." David N. Figlio and Deborah Fletcher, "Suburbanization, Demographic Change and the Consequences for School Finance," *Journal of Public Economics* 96, no. 11 (2012): 1144–1153.

152   **keep Social Security, Medicare, and Medicaid afloat:** Laurence J. Kotlikoff and Scott Burns, *The Clash of Generations: Saving Ourselves, Our Kids, and Our Economy* (Cambridge, MA: MIT Press, 2014), xxi.

152   *homeless elderly people in the streets*: James H. Schulz and Robert H. Binstock, *Aging Nation: The Economics and Politics of Growing Older in America* (Westport, CT: Praeger, 2006).

153   **it feels a deep ownership:** Ibid.

156   **one of the founding members, has written:** Susan McWhinney-Morse, "Life at Beacon Hill Village," *Second Journey*, http://www.secondjourney.org/itin/12 _Sum/12Sum_McWh-Morse.htm.

158   **that failed to take notice:** Barbara Basler, "Declaration of Independents," *AARP Online Bulletin*, February 13, 2006, http://www.lancasterdowntowners.org/wp -content/uploads/2011/01/BeaconHillVillageAARP.pdf.

159   **150 more are in development:** "Is There a Village Near Me?," *Village to Village Network*, http://www.vtvnetwork.org/.

163   **rely on a largely volunteer workforce:** Andrew E. Scharlach et al., "Does the Village Model Help to Foster Age-Friendly Communities?," *Journal of Aging & Social Policy* 26, no. 1–2 (2014): 181–196.

164   **help out with minor chores:** Daniele Mariani, "Cities Face Challenge of an Age-Old Problem," *swissinfo.ch*, December 6, 2012, http://www.swissinfo.ch/eng /social-change_cities-face-challenge-of-an-age-old-problem/34118508; "WG mit Opa: 20 Stunden Arbeit für 20 Quadratmeter Zimmer," *Spiegel Online*, April 16, 2008, http://www .spiegel.de/unispiegel/studium/wg-mit-opa-20-stunden-arbeit-fuer-20-quadratmeter -zimmer-a-546934.html.

164   **exists in the United Kingdom:** Simon Murphy, "Homeshare Scheme Brings Comfort to Young and Old," *Guardian*, January 6, 2012, https://www.theguardian .com/money/2012/jan/06/homeshare-scheme-tackle-housing-crisis.

164   **monthly subsidy of up to €200 per tenant:** Sigrid Lupieri, "Aging Gracefully: Germans Grow Gray Together," *CNN*, July 19, 2013, http://www.cnn.com/2013 /06/19/world/europe/german-senior-citizens/.

Chapter 5: Radical Empathy and Transcendent Design

173   **an exercise physiologist:** The estimable Roz Puleo.

174   **that can occur with age:** Reduced peripheral sensory acuity is common in elderly populations. James W. Mold et al., "The Prevalence, Predictors, and Consequences of Peripheral Sensory Neuropathy in Older Patients," *Journal of the American Board of Family Practice* 17, no. 5 (2004): 309–318. When this occurs on the soles of the feet, it affects standing balance in particular, as opposed to walking balance. Shuqi Zhang and Li Li, "The Differential Effects of Foot Sole Sensory on Plantar Pressure Distribution Between Balance and Gait," *Gait & Posture* 37, no. 4 (2013): 532–535. Standing, as opposed to walking, balance is especially affected by age. Scott W. Shaffer and Anne L. Harrison, "Aging of the Somatosensory System: A Translational Perspective," *Physical Therapy* 87, no. 2 (February 2007): 193–207, doi:10.2522/ptj.20060083.

174   **that takes place in the fingers:** M. M. Wickremaratchi and J. G. Llewelyn, "Effects of Ageing on Touch," *Postgraduate Medical Journal* 82, no. 967 (2006): 301–304.

174   **he was mayor of Charlotte in 2013:** Then mayor Foxx was kind enough to wear AGNES at the January 2013 Conference of Mayors at the Washington Hilton in Washington, DC.

179   **disconcertingly similar to the cockpit of a Boeing 737:** Andy Enright, "BMW 7 Series (2002–2009) Review," *RAC,* November 9, 2009, http://www.rac.co.uk /drive/car-reviews/bmw/7-series/208536/.

180   **"like advanced Thai or particle theory'":** Ibid.

180   **"with the ease and clarity of James Joyce's *Ulysses*":** Tony Quiroga, "2006 BMW 7-Series First Drive Review," *Car And Driver,* June 2005, http://www .caranddriver.com/reviews/2006-bmw-7-series-first-drive-review.

180   **"iDrive, iDrive, iDrive":** "BMW 745Li (2003)," *Car Talk,* http://www.cartalk .com/test-drive-library/bmw-745li-2003.

180   **and later Reatta, model sedans:** Andrew Del-Colle, "Carchaeology: 1986 Buick Riviera Introduces the Touchscreen," *Popular Mechanics,* May 7, 2013, http://www.popularmechanics.com/cars/a8981/carchaeology-1986-buick -riviera-introduces-the-touchscreen-15437094/.

180   **in the Oldsmobile Toronado Trofeo:** Diego Rosenberg, "1980s General Motors Touchscreen a View into the Future: Video," *GM Authority,* September 24, 2016, http://gmauthority.com/blog/2014/09/1980s-general-motors-touchscreen-pre cursor-to-infotainment-units-video/.

180   **found the menu system confusing:** Jaclyne Badal, "When Design Goes Bad," *Wall Street Journal,* June 23, 2008, http://www.wsj.com/articles/SB12139046137 2989357.

183   **where we had our breakthrough:** Bryan Reimer et al., "A Methodology for Evaluating Multiple Aspects of Learnability: Testing an Early Prototype," in *Advances in Ergonomics Modeling and Usability Evaluation,* ed. Halimahtun Khalid, Alan Hedge, and Tareq Z. Ahram (Boca Raton, FL: CRC Press, 2010), 43–53.

185   **eventually the bad reviews stopped:** John R. Quain, "For iDrive 4.0, BMW Brings Back a Few Buttons," *New York Times,* October 23, 2008, http://www .nytimes.com/2008/10/26/automobiles/26DRIVE.html.

186   **especially in the kitchen:** Margalit Fox, "Sam Farber, Creator of Oxo Utensils, Dies at 88," *New York Times,* June 21, 2013, http://www.nytimes.com/2013/06/22 /business/sam-farber-creator-of-oxo-utensils-dies-at-88.html?_r=0.

186   **peeled the potato for her:** Dev Patnaik, *Wired to Care: How Companies Prosper When They Create Widespread Empathy* (Boston, MA: Pearson Education, 2009).

188   **ignored her plight or, worse, poked fun at her:** Fox, "Sam Farber."

188   **intuitive, user-oriented design across ability spectra:** Patnaik, *Wired to Care,* 168.

192   **going back to the 1960s:** For instance, in Dr. Who episodes starring Patrick Troughton. See Dave Addey, "Fontspots: Eurostyle," *Typeset in the Future,* November 29, 2014, https:// typesetinthefuture.com/2014/11/29/fontspots-eurostile/.

193   **looking away from the road:** Bryan Reimer et al., "Assessing the Impact of Typeface Design in a Text-Rich Automotive User Interface," *Ergonomics* 57, no. 11 (2014): 1643–1658.

193   **as opposed to the square grotesque:** Jonathan Dobres et al., "Utilising Psychophysical Techniques to Investigate the Effects of Age, Typeface Design, Size and Display Polarity on Glance Legibility," *Ergonomics* 59, no. 10 (2016): 1377–1391, http://dx.doi.org/10.1080/00 140139.2015.1137637.

Chapter 6: Health, Safety, and the Triumph of Magical Thinking

196   **"unless you let them hurry up and die":** Justin McCurry, "Let Elderly People 'Hurry Up and Die,' Says Japanese Minister," *Guardian,* January 22, 2013, https://www.theguardian. com/world/2013/jan/22/elderly-hurry-up-die-japanese.

196   **"who just eat and drink and make no effort?":** Justin McCurry, "Gaffe-Prone Japanese PM Offends Country's 'Doddering' Pensioners," *Guardian,* November 27, 2008, https:// www.theguardian.com/world/2008/nov/27/japan.

196   **he said in a 2014 Sapporo speech:** Agence France-Presse, "Gaffe-Prone Japan
      Deputy PM Turns Ire on Young Women," *The Daily Mail*, December 7, 2014,
      http://www.dailymail.co.uk/wires/afp/article-2864967/Gaffe-prone-Japan-deputy
      -PM-turns-ire-young-women.html.

197   **more than that of any other major economy:** "Population Ages 65 and Above (%
      of Total)," *The World Bank*, 2015, http://data.worldbank.org/indicator/SP.POP.65UP.
      TO.ZS?locations=JP-US-BG-FI-DE-GR-IT-PT-SE.

197   **well below the United States' 17 percent:** "Health Expenditure, Total (% of GDP)," *The
      World Bank*, 2014, http://data.worldbank.org/indicator/SH.XPD.TOTL.ZS.

197   **is projected to *improve* by 2032:** "Japan's dependency ratio will actually improve from
      1.03 to 0.96 dependents per worker—a figure which actually makes Japan a country with
      one of the lowest dependency ratios in the world in 2032." Clint Laurent, *Tomorrow's
      World: A Look at the Demographic and Socio-economic Structure of the World in 2032*
      (Hoboken, NJ: Wiley, 2013), 81.

197   **In a 2014 cover story for *The Atlantic*:** Ezekiel Emanuel, "Why I Hope to Die at 75,"
      The Atlantic, October 2014, https://www.theatlantic.com/magazine/archive/2014/10
      /why-i-hope-to-die-at-75/379329/.

198   **the longer your healthy life expectancy:** Jay S. Olshansky, "The Demographic Transfor-
      mation of America," *Daedalus* 144, no. 2 (2015): 13–19.

198   **appears to be decreasing, however slightly:** Walter A. Rocca et al., "Trends in the Inci-
      dence and Prevalence of Alzheimer's Disease, Dementia, and Cognitive Impairment in
      the United States," *Alzheimer's & Dementia* 7, no. 1 (2011): 80–93; Claudia L. Satizabal
      et al., "Incidence of Dementia over Three Decades in the Framingham Heart Study," *New
      England Journal of Medicine* 374, no. 6 (2016): 523–532, doi:10.1056/NEJMoa1504327.

198   **our mental processing speed slows slightly over time:** T. A. Salthouse, "Aging and Meas-
      ures of Processing Speed," *Biological Psychology* 54 (2000): 35–54.

199   **or even of physics today.":** Benjamin F. Jones and Bruce A. Weinberg, "Age Dynamics in
      Scientific Creativity," *Proceedings of the National Academy of Sciences* 108, no. 47 (2011):
      18910–18914.

199   **The mean age of Nobel-worthy discovery, meanwhile, is rising:** Benjamin
      F. Jones, "Age and Great Invention," *The Review of Economics and Statistics* 92,
      no. 1 (2010): 1–14.

199   **quiet contemplation and then death by chloroform:** Laura Davidow Hirshbein, "Wil-
      liam Osler and the Fixed Period: Conflicting Medical and Popular Ideas About Old Age,"
      Archives of Internal Medicine 161, no. 17 (2001): 2074–2078.

199   **terms coined by famed MIT economist Paul Samuelson:** Paul A. Samuelson, "Con-
      sumption Theory in Terms of Revealed Preference," *Economica* 15, no. 60 (1948): 243–253.

200   **as Emanuel and other researchers have determined:** Ezekiel J. Emanuel et al., "Man-
      aged Care, Hospice Use, Site of Death, and Medical Expenditures in the Last Year of Life,"
      Archives of Internal Medicine 162, no. 15 (2002): 1722–1728.

200   **trying to sell you "brain-training" exercises):** Monica Melby-Lervåg and Charles Hulme,
      "Is Working Memory Training Effective? A Meta-analytic Review," *Developmental Psy-
      chology* 49, no. 2 (2013): 270.

203   **extra funds to build up the caregiving sector:** Shusuke Murai, "Government Ear-
      marks Funds to Deal with Caregiver Shortage," *Japan Times*, January 21, 2015, http://
      www.japantimes.co.jp/news/2015/01/21/national/facing-severe-caregiver-shortage
      -government-dedicates-funds-to-promoting-profession/#.V7N03ZMrJE4.

203   **robots for the nursing and medicine sector:** "Japan's Robotics Industry Bullish on
      Elderly Care Market, TrendForce Reports," *TrendForce*, May 19, 2015, http://press.trend-
      force.com/press/201505191923.html#fYkeJQyQBHK6c363.99.

203   **deposit her in a wheelchair and vice versa:** Trevor Mogg, "Meet Robear, A Japanese
      Robotic Nurse with a Face of a Bear," *Digital Trends*, February 26, 2015, http://www.digi-
      taltrends.com/cool-tech/riken-robear/.

204   **data compiled by the Bureau of Labor Statistics:** Amalavoyal V. Chari et al., "The Opportunity Costs of Informal Elder-Care in the United States: New Estimates from the American Time Use Survey," *Health Services Research* 50, no. 3 (2015): 871–882.

204   **in the United States alone:** David J. Levy, "Presenteeism: A Method for Assessing the Extent of Family Caregivers in the Workplace and their Financial Impact" (Coconut Creek, FL: American Association for Caregiver Education, 2007).

204   **whether they take place in homes or in dedicated facilities:** Chari et al., "The Opportunity Costs."

204   **"make it easier for children to leave their parents?":** Sherry Turkle, *Alone Together: Why We Expect More from Technology and Less from Each Other* (New York: Basic Books, 2012), 121.

205   **"With this framing, the robots are inevitable":** Ibid., 123.

209   **return to the hospital within 30 days of discharge:** Stephen F. Jencks, Mark V. Williams, and Eric A. Coleman, "Rehospitalizations Among Patients in the Medicare Fee-for-Service Program," *New England Journal of Medicine* 360, no. 14 (2009): 1418–1428.

210   **influential venture capitalists in Silicon Valley:** These include Andreessen Horowitz (who also invested in Meebo), Thrive Capital, Syno Capital, 8VC, and Senator Bob Kerrey.

213   **technology could do for people with hearing loss":** Harry McCracken, "Doppler Labs and the Quest to Build a Computer for Your Ears," *Fast Company,* September 21, 2016, https://www.fastcoexist.com/3062996/world-changing-ideas-doppler-labs-and-the-quest-to-build-a-computer-for-your-ears.

213   **deregulated category of hearing aids:** Sarah Buhr, "Doppler Labs Is Working with Senator Elizabeth Warren to Deregulate the Hearing Aid Industry," *TechCrunch,* March 28, 2017, https://techcrunch.com/2017/03/28/doppler-labs-is-working-with-senator-elizabeth-warren-to-deregulate-the-hearing-aid-industry/.

213   **sufficient proof of the accuracy of its tests:** Warning Letter for 23andMe, Inc., "Inspections, Compliance, Enforcement, and Criminal Investigations," *US Food and Drug Administration,* November 22, 2013, http://www.fda.gov/ICECI/EnforcementActions/WarningLetters/2013/ucm376296.htm.

213   **a less comprehensive, more expensive product:** Christina Farr, "Dear Silicon Valley: There Are No Shortcuts in Health Care," *Fast Company,* February 12, 2016, http://www.fastcompany.com/3056658/startup-report/dear-silicon-valley-there-are-no-shortcuts-in-health-care; and "23andMe Launches New Customer Experience—Reports Include Carrier Status That Meet FDA Standards, Wellness, Traits, and Ancestry," *23andMe,* October 21, 2015, http://mediacenter.23andme.com/blog/new-23andme/.

213   **finally with the FDA's seal of approval:** Christina Farr, "Alphabet-Backed DNA Testing Company 23AndMe Is Back in Business," *CNBC,* April 6, 2017, http://www.cnbc.com/2017/04/06/23andme-gets-fda-approval-for-some-consumer-tests.html.

213   **refrain from owning or operating medical labs:** Andrew Pollack, "Elizabeth Homes of Theranos Is Barred from Running Lab for 2 Years," *New York Times,* July 8, 2016, http://www.nytimes.com/2016/07/09/business/theranos-elizabeth-holmes-ban.html; and "A Theranos Timeline," *New York Times,* July 8, 2016, http://www.nytimes.com/2016/07/09/business/theranos-elizabeth-holmes-timeline.html.

213   **laid off nearly half its workforce:** Madison Malone Kircher, "Theranos Closes Labs, Lays Off 40 Percent of Employees," *Select All (New York Magazine),* October 6, 2016, http://nymag.com/selectall/2016/10/elizabeth-holmes-closes-theranos-blood-testing-labs.html.

213   **helped employees bypass a required, 52-hour training course:** Claire Sudath and Eric Newcomer, "Zenefits Was the Perfect Startup. Then It Self-Disrupted," *Bloomberg,* May 9, 2016, http://www.bloomberg.com/features/2016-zenefits/.

214   **which can cause lethal oversights:** "The second patient death in four years involv-
       ing 'alarm fatigue' at UMass Memorial Medical Center has pushed the hospital to
       intensify efforts to prevent nurses from tuning out monitor warning alarms." Liz
       Kowalczyk, "'Alarm Fatigue' a Factor in 2d Death," *Boston.com,* September 21, 2011,
       http://archive.boston.com/lifestyle/health/articles/2011/09/21/umass_hospital
       _has_second_death_involving_alarm_fatigue/?camp=pm.

215   **the most effective way to cut health care costs:** Frank Moss, "Our High-Tech
       Health-Care Future," *New York Times,* November 9, 2011, http://www.nytimes
       .com/2011/11/10/opinion/our-high-tech-health-care-future.html.

215   **in search of unnecessary prophylactic surgery:** ". . . a direct-to-consumer test result may
       be used by a patient to self-manage, serious concerns are raised if test results are not ade-
       quately understood by patients or if incorrect test results are reported." From Warning
       Letter for 23andMe, Inc., "Inspections, Compliance."

216   **FDA-approved 2017 testing kit:** Farr, 2017.

216   **the results of some blood tests directly to consumers:** ". . . an Arizona law co-authored
       by Holmes' high-tech company goes into effect, allowing patients to order blood tests
       without involving a doctor. It represents a significant step towards Holmes' ultimate mis-
       sion: giving consumers control over monitoring their health via inexpensive and compar-
       atively painless tests." Marco della Cava, "Now No Doctor's Note Needed for Blood Test
       in Arizona," *USA Today,* July 2, 2015, http://www.usatoday.com/story/tech/2015/07/02/
       new-arizona-law-and-fda-approval-gives-theranos-something-to-celebrate/29634373/.

216   **its blood tests were simply inaccurate:** Christopher Weaver, "Agony, Alarm
       and Anger for People Hurt by Theranos's Botched Blood Tests," *Wall Street
       Journal,* October 20, 2016, http://www.wsj.com/articles/the-patients-hurt-by-theranos
       -1476973026.

216   **"That hallucination didn't turn out so well, did it?":** James L. Madara, "Digital Dysto-
       pia," speech given at AMA Annual Meeting, Chicago Illinois, June 11, 2016, http://www
       .ama-assn.org/ama/pub/news/speeches/2016-06-11-madara-annual-address.page.

217   **don't seem to affect overall healthcare costs:** Cinnamon S. Bloss et al., "A Prospective
       Randomized Trial Examining Health Care Utilization in Individuals Using Multiple
       Smartphone-Enabled Biosensors," *PeerJ* 4 (2016): e1554, doi:10.7717/peerj.1554.

220   **by anyone within Bluetooth range:** Kashmir Hill, "Here's What It Looks Like
       When a Smart Toilet Gets Hacked," *Forbes,* August 15, 2013, http://www.forbes
       .com/sites/kashmirhill/2013/08/15/heres-what-it-looks-like-when-a-smart-toilet
       -gets-hacked-video/#2e788a6e2b15.

221   **in the Journal of the American Medical Association:** M. Donna, M. D. Zulman, and
       C. A. Stanford, "Evolutionary Pressures on the Electronic Health Record: Caring for
       Complexity," *Journal of the American Medical Association* 316, no. 9 (2016): 923–924,
       doi:10.1001/jama.2016.9538.

224   **"what it takes to publish in this space":** Larry Hardesty, "Signal Intelligence," *MIT
       Technology Review,* October 20, 2015, https://www.technologyreview.com/s/542131
       /signal-intelligence/.

225   **less computationally unwieldy under certain conditions:** Haitham Hassanieh et al.,
       "Nearly Optimal Sparse Fourier Transform," in *Proceedings of the Forty-Fourth Annual
       ACM Symposium on Theory of Computing,* New York, May 19–22, 2012, 563–578.

225   **first such improvement since 1965:** James W. Cooley and John W. Tukey, "An Algorithm
       for the Machine Calculation of Complex Fourier Series," *Mathematics of Computation* 19,
       no. 90 (1965): 297–301.

232   **whether they'd missed their meds:** Chaiwoo Lee et al., "Integration of Medi-
       cation Monitoring and Communication Technologies in Designing a Usability
       -Enhanced Home Solution for Older Adults," in *Proceedings of the 2011 Conference on ICT
       Convergence (ICTC),* September 28–30, 2011, 390–395.

233   **Seven percent of victims lose $10,000 or more:** "The True Link Report on
      Elder Financial Abuse 2015," *True Link Financial,* January 2015, https://truelink
      -wordpress-assets.s3.amazonaws.com/wp-content/uploads/True-Link-Report
      -On-Elder-Financial-Abuse-012815.pdf.

236   **Walgreens, Walmart, Kroger, and elsewhere:** Tony Pugh, "Walk-in Clin-
      ics Bring Affordable, On-Demand Health Care to the Masses," *McClatchy DC,*
      May   7,   2015,   http://www.mcclatchydc.com/news/nation-world/national/article
      24784225.html.

236   **"not whether he's lonely":** Atul Gawande, *Being Mortal: Medicine and What Matters in the
      End* (New York: Henry Holt, 2014), 105.

236   **empty of anything [older people] care about":** Ibid., 110.

238   **it diminishes agitation:** Nina Jøranson et al., "Effects on Symptoms of Agitation and
      Depression in Persons with Dementia Participating in Robot-Assisted Activity: A Clus-
      ter-Randomized Controlled Trial," *Journal of the American Medical Directors Association*
      16, no. 10 (2015): 867–873.

239   **a de facto human right:** UN Human Rights Council, *Report of the United Nations
      High Commissioner for Human Rights on the Situation of Human Rights in Mali,* 2012,
      http://www.ohchr.org/Documents/HRBodies/HRCouncil/RegularSession/Session22
      /A-HRC-22-33_en.pdf

Chapter 7: The Pursuit of Happiness

243   **(So have men in Japan and Singapore.):** Christopher J. L. Murray et al., "Global, Regional,
      and National Disability-Adjusted Life Years (DALYs) for 306 Diseases and Injuries and
      Healthy Life Expectancy (HALE) for 188 Countries, 1990–2013: Quantifying the Epide-
      miological Transition," *The Lancet* 386, no. 10009 (2015): 2145–2191.

245   **"they are used to getting things done":** "Our Story," *Imagine Solutions,* http://www.ima-
      ginesolutionsconference.com/our-story/.

247   **smaller than those of younger people:** Susan Charles and Laura L. Carstensen, "Social
      and Emotional Aging," *Annual Review of Psychology* 61 (2010): 383.

247   **activities that we decide are less than meaningful:** Jon Hendricks and Stephen J. Cutler,
      "Volunteerism and Socioemotional Selectivity in Later Life," *Journals of Gerontology Series
      B: Psychological Sciences and Social Sciences* 59, no. 5 (2004): S251–S257; and Frieder R.
      Lang and Laura L. Carstensen, "Time Counts: Future Time Perspective, Goals, and Social
      Relationships," *Psychology and Aging* 17, no. 1 (2002): 125.

247   **recall it more easily:** Laura Carstensen and Andrew E. Reed, in *Current Research and
      Emerging Directions in Emotion-Cognition Interactions,* ed. Mara Mather, Lihong Wang,
      and Florin Dolcos (Lausanne, Switzerland: Frontiers Media SA, 2015), http://www.doa-
      books.org/doab?func=fulltext&rid=18193.

247   **more satisfied with life as they grow older:** A good review of age-related happiness
      research can be found in Susan Charles and Laura L. Carstensen, "Social and Emotional
      Aging," *Annual Review of Psychology* 61 (2010): 383.

247   **to experience and do meaningful things:** Ibid.

248   **social winnowing:** Atul Gawande, *Being Mortal: Medicine and What Matters in the End*
      (New York: Metropolitan Books, 2014). 98.

248   **during the SARS epidemic:** Carstensen and Reed , in Mather et al., *Current Research and
      Emerging Directions.*

248   **the people closest to you":** Gawande, *Being Mortal,* 97–98.

248   **when I wander out at night":** Midgley, *From the Periodic Table to Production,* 165.

249   **Chinese residents of Hong Kong:** Helene H. Fung et al., "Age-Related Positivity Enhance-
      ment Is Not Universal: Older Chinese Look Away from Positive Stimuli," *Psychology and
      Aging* 23, no. 2 (2008): 440.

251   **half what it is now:** Loraine A. West et al., "65+ in the United States: 2010" (Washington,
      DC: US Government Printing Office, 2014).

252   **more time looking for work than their juniors:** "In 2014, for example, 22.1 percent of the unemployed under age 25 had looked for work for 27 weeks or longer, compared with 44.6 percent of those 55 years and older." Karen Kosanovich and Eleni Theodossiou Sherman, "Spotlight on Statistics," *Bureau of Labor Statistics,* 2015, http://www.bls.gov /spotlight/2015/long-term-unemployment/.

252   **they had simply given up looking:** "Working Longer: The Disappearing Divide Between Work Life and Retirement," *The Associated Press-NORC Center for Public Affairs Research,* 2016, http://apnorc.org/projects/Pages/HTML%20Reports /working-longer-the-disappearing-divide-between-work-life-and-retirement -issue-brief.aspx.

252   **if the right job opened up:** Howard Schneider, "Many Who Have Left U.S. Labor Force Say They Would Like to Return," *Yahoo! News,* 2014, https://www .yahoo.com/news/many-left-u-labor-force-return-050511935.html.

252   **air traffic controllers:** Joseph Coughlin and Luke Yoquinto, "When Retirement Becomes a Crisis," *Slate,* February 2, 2016, http://www.slate.com/articles/business /moneybox/2016/02/baby_boomers_retirements_could_cripple_professions_like _air_traffic_controller.html.

254   **the fact that it will be, like, older and worse":** Ezra Klein, Matthew Yglesias, and Sarah Kliff, "Obamacare Update and Aging America," *Vox,* podcast audio, August 24, 2016, http://www.vox.com/pages/podcasts.

255   **likely far smaller than previously thought:** Robert S. Wilson et al., "Cognitive Decline in Prodromal Alzheimer Disease and Mild Cognitive Impairment," *Archives of Neurology* 68, no. 3 (2011): 351–356. For an excellent review of the implications of this work, see Sarah Raposo and Laura L. Carstensen, "Developing a Research Agenda to Combat Ageism," *Generations* 39, no. 3 (2015): 79–85.

255   **work beyond the age of retirement:** Bosworth and Burke, "Changing Sources of Income."

258   **fewer errors of the major, show-stopping variety:** Axel H. Börsch-Supan and Matthias Weiss, "Productivity and the Age Composition of Work Teams: Evidence from the Assembly Line" (December 15, 2008). MEA Discussion Paper No. 148-07, https://ssrn.com /abstract=1335390 or http://dx.doi.org/10.2139/ssrn.1335390.

258   **having children were never actually born":** Ibid. Quoted in Greg Ip, "How Demographics Rule the Global Economy," *Wall Street Journal,* November 22, 2015, http:// www.wsj.com/articles/how-demographics-rule-the-global-economy-1448203724.

258   **will increase for a number of decades":** Quoted in Jens Weidmann, "Demographic Challenges in Germany," *Deutsche Bundesbank,* November 27, 2014 (speech, Frankfurt am Main), https://www.bundesbank.de/Redaktion/EN/Reden /2014/2014_11_27_weidmann.html.

259   **similar projects in other German and Austrian plants:** Christoph Loch et al., "How BMW Is Defusing the Demographic Time Bomb," *Harvard Business Review* 88, no. 3 (2010): 99–102.

259   **represents a €20 million investment:** J. W. Kuenen et al., "Global Aging: How Companies Can Adapt to the New Reality," *The Boston Consulting Group,* 2011, https://www.bcg.com/ documents/file93352.pdf.

259   **has begun experimenting with such devices:** "At an office-building construction site in the center of Japan's capital, 67-year-old Kenichi Saito effortlessly stacks 44-pound boards with the ease of a man half his age. His secret: a bendable exoskeleton hugging his waist and thighs, with sensors attached to his skin. The sensors detect when Mr. Saito's muscles start to move and direct the machine to support his motion, cutting his load's effective weight by 18 pounds. 'I can carry as much as I did 10 years ago,' says the hard-hatted Mr. Saito." Jacob M. Schlesinger and Alexander Martin, "Graying Japan Tries to Embrace the Golden Years," *Wall Street Journal,* November 29, 2015, http://www.wsj.com /articles/graying-japan-tries-to-embrace-the-golden-years-1448808028.

262   **prices in the mid-to-high tens of thousands of dollars:** Signe Brewster, "This $40,000 Robotic Exoskeleton Lets the Paralyzed Walk," *MIT Technology*

Review, February 1, 2016, https://www.technologyreview.com/s/546276/this-40000 -robotic-exoskeleton-lets-the-paralyzed-walk/.

262   **nonpowered upper-body exoskeleton as well:** The "Ekso Vest," developed by Ekso Bionics of Richmond, California, is in use in BMW's Spartanburg, South Carolina, plant. Rudolph Bell, "Greer Plant a Showcase of BMW's Latest Technologies," *Greenville News,* June 15, 2016, http://www.greenvilleonline.com /story/money/business/2016/06/15/journalists-tour-bmw-plant-ahead-mexican -groundbreaking/85842558/.

263   **within a company and without:** "Annual Study of Intangible Asset Market Value from Ocean Tomo, LLC," *Ocean Tomo Intellectual Capital Equity,* March 4, 2015, http://www. oceantomo.com/2015/03/04/2015-intangible-asset-market-value-study/.

264   **reported the Government Accountability Office in 2014:** "Report to the Ranking Member, Committee on the Budget, U.S. Senate," *US Government Accountability Office,* January 2014, http://www.gao.gov/products/GAO-14-215.

265   **experts are former P&G execs:** Barrett J. Brunsman, "Exiting P&Gers Targeted by Wealth Managers, Consultants," *Cincinnati Business Courier,* April 24, 2015, http://www. bizjournals.com/cincinnati/news/2015/04/24/wealth-managers-consultants-target-exit-ing-p-gers.html; and Alexander Coolidge, "As P&G Slims Down, YourEncore Ramps Up," *Cincinnati.com,* December 27, 2015, http://www.cincinnati.com/story/money/2015/12/27 /pg-slims-down-yourencore-ramps-up/77780186/.

266   **run at least twice as fast as that!":** Lewis Carroll, *Through the Looking-Glass* (New York: Bantam Classics, 2006, orig. pub. 1865), 135.

267   **a new job every two-and-a-half years:** "Number of Jobs Held, Labor Market Activity, and Earnings Growth Among the Youngest Baby Boomers: Results from a Longitudinal Survey," *Bureau of Labor Statistics,* March 31, 2015, http://www.bls.gov/news.release/pdf/ nlsoy.pdf.

269   **positive spin on it—is utilitarian:** Author interview with Sanjay Sarma at MIT.

269   **and aerial drone components:** Jacob Bunge, "Farmers Reap New Tools from Their Own High-Tech Tinkering," *Wall Street Journal,* May 2, 2016, http:// www.wsj.com/articles/farmers-reap-new-tools-from-high-tech-tinkering-146 1004688.

276   **already booming in Japan:** Michiko Toyama, "Postcard: Tokyo," *Time* 172, no. 1 (2008): 4.

276   **from 5.8 percent of income in 2013 to 7.5 in 2016:** "America's Retirement Score: In Fair Shape—But Fixable," *Fidelity Investments,* 2016, https://www .fidelity.com/bin-public/060_www_fidelity_com/documents/18608-02-Exec Sum.pdf.

277   **report saving consistently:** Jen Mishory, "Millennials, Savings, & Retirement Security," *Young Invincibles,* February 2016, http://younginvincibles.org /wp-content/uploads/2016/02/WorkAndSaveMemo_2016.pdf.

277   **spend more on dining out than any other generation:** Khushbu Shah, "Millennials Spend More Money Dining Out Than Non-Millennials," *Eater,* June 5, 2015, http://www.eater.com/2015/6/5/8737197/millennials-spend-more-money-dining -out-than-non-millennials.

Chapter 8: Meaning and Legacy in the Longevity Economy

282   **everything that one is capable of becoming:** Abraham Maslow, "A Theory of Human Motivation," *Psychological Review* 50, no. 4 (1943): 370.

282   **slogan that ad agency N. W. Ayer created for the US Army:** Tom Evans, "All We Could Be: How an Advertising Campaign Helped Remake the Army," *On Point: The Journal of Army History* 12, no. 1 (2015), https://armyhistory.org/all-we-could -be-how-an-advertising-campaign-helped-remake-the-army/

282   **perhaps as few as one in a thousand:** Francis Heylighen, "A Cognitive-Systemic Recon-
       struction of Maslow's Theory of Self-Actualization," *Behavioral Science* 37, no. 1 (1992):
       39–58.

282   **none younger than middle age:** "In addition, in a first research with young people, three
       thousand college students were screened, but yielded only one immediately usable subject
       and a dozen or two possible future subjects ('growing well'). I had to conclude that self-ac-
       tualization of the sort I had found in my older subjects perhaps was not possible in our
       society for young, developing people." Maslow, "A Theory of Human Motivation," 370.

282   **and sometimes behave so":** Abraham Maslow, Robert Frager, and Ruth Cox, *Motivation
       and Personality,* ed. James Fadiman and Cynthia McReynolds, vol. 2 (New York: Harper &
       Row, 1970).

284   **having never gone to medical school":** Jodi Luber, "Grandma's Sweet and Sour
       Meatballs," *The Jewish Kitchen with Jodi Luber,* http://jewishlivingmedia.com
       /thejewishkitchen/recipe/grandmas-sweet-sour-meatballs/.

287   **are said to be older adults:** Lisa Fernandez, "More Retirees Are Self-Publishing
       Their Memoirs as a Family Legacy," *The Mercury News,* August 13, 2016, http://
       www.mercurynews.com/2011/10/04/more-retirees-are-self-publishing-their
       -memoirs-as-a-family-legacy/.

287   **largest self-publishing house in the United States:** Diane C. Lade, "Senior Wordsmiths
       Find Voice in Self-publishing," *The Portland Press Herald,* January 6, 2013, http://www.press-
       herald.com/2013/01/06/senior-wordsmiths-find-voice-in-self-publishing_2013-01-06/.

288   **part of their lives leading up to old age:** Jon Hendricks and Stephen J. Cutler, "Volun-
       teerism and Socioemotional Selectivity in Later Life," *The Journals of Gerontology Series B:
       Psychological Sciences and Social Sciences* 59, no. 5 (2004): S251–S257.

292   **group devoted to the study of global change:** Will Steffen et al., *Global Change and the
       Earth System: A Planet Under Pressure.* Global Change—The IGBP Series (New York:
       Springer, 2004).

293   **an increase in confidence—by 15 percent:** Data derived by comparing "Confi-
       dence in Institutions," *Gallup,* June 1–5, 2016, http://www.gallup.com/poll/1597
       /confidence-institutions.aspx; with Jeff Jones and Lydia Saad, "Gallup Poll Social
       Series: Consumption—Final Topline," *Gallup,* July 8–11, 2010, http://www.gallup
       .com/file/poll/141515/Confidence_Institutions_July_22_2010.pdf.

293   **the very cultural institution of retirement itself:** Robert D. Putnam, *Bowling Alone* (New
       York: Simon & Schuster, 2000).

294   **become geographically dispersed:** For a description of the decline of the multigenera-
       tional household, see Mason M. Bradbury, Nils Peterson, and Jianguo Liu, "Long-Term
       Dynamics of Household Size and Their Environmental Implications," *Population and
       Environment* 36, no. 1 (2014): 73–84. For a useful framework to understand countries'
       readiness for an older population, whether they support that population through gov-
       ernmental channels or through families, see Richard Jackson, Neil Howe, and Keisuke
       Nakashima, *The Global Aging Preparedness Index* (Washington, DC: Center for Strategic
       and International Studies, 2010).

INDEX

Joseph F. Coughlin, PhD, is the founder and director of the Massachusetts Institute of Technology AgeLab, a multidisciplinary research program created to understand the behavior of the 50-plus population, the role of technology and design in their lives, and the opportunity for innovation to improve quality of life for older adults and their families. He teaches in the Department of Urban Studies & Planning and the Sloan School of Management's Advanced Management Program. Coughlin is a Behavioral Sciences Fellow of the Gerontological Society of America and recipient of one the Society's highest awards, the Maxwell A. Pollack Award for Productive Aging, in recognition of his innovative work in translating research into practice. Named by the *Wall Street Journal* as "one of 12 people shaping the future of retirement" and recognized by *Fast Company* as "one of the 100 most creative in business," Coughlin is a member of the Board of Directors of AARP. He speaks to and advises major companies, nonprofits, and governments worldwide.